The Future Perfect: Images of the Time to Come in Philosophy, Politics, and Cultural Studies

Series Editors:
Michael Marder, IKERBASQUE Research Professor of Philosophy, University of the Basque Country, Spain
Patricia Vieira, Associate Professor, Spanish and Portuguese, Georgetown University, USA

The Future Perfect series stands at the intersection of critical historiography, philosophy, political science, heterodox economic theory, and environmental thought, as well as utopian and cultural studies. It encourages an interdisciplinary reassessment of the idea of futurity that not only holds a promising interpretative potential but may also serve as an effective tool for practical interventions in the fields of human activity that affect entire countries, regions, and the planet as a whole.

Titles in the Series

The Future of Europe: Democracy, Legitimacy, and Justice After the Euro Crisis, edited by Serge Champeau, Carlos Closa, Daniel Innerarity and Miguel Poiares Maduro
Taming an Uncertain Future: Temporality, Sovereignty, and the Politics of Anticipatory Governance, by Liam P. D. Stockdale
The Politics of Virtue: Post-Liberalism and the Human Future, by John Milbank and Adrian Pabst
The Future of Meat without Animals, edited by Brianne Donaldson and Christopher Carter
The End of the World: Contemporary Philosophy and Art, edited by Marcia Sa Cavalcante Schuback and Susanna Lindberg
Manifestos for World Thought, edited by Lucian Stone and Jason Bahbak Mohaghegh
The Task of Philosophy in the Anthropocene: Axial Echoes in Global Space, edited by Richard Polt and Jon Wittrock
Futures of Life Death on Earth: Derrida's General Ecology, by Philippe Lynes
The Future of Humanity: Revisioning the Human in the Posthuman Age, edited by Pavlina Radia, Sarah Fiona Winters, and Laurie Kruk

The Future of Humanity

Revisioning the Human in the Posthuman Age

Edited by Pavlina Radia, Sarah Fiona Winters, and Laurie Kruk

London • New York

Published by Rowman & Littlefield International, Ltd.
6 Tinworth Street, London SE11 5AL
www.rowmaninternational.com

Rowman & Littlefield International, Ltd. is an affiliate of
Rowman & Littlefield
4501 Forbes Boulevard, Suite 200, Lanham, Maryland 20706, USA
With additional offices in Boulder, New York, Toronto (Canada), and London (UK)
www.rowman.com

Copyright © 2019 by Pavlina Radia, Sarah Fiona Winters, and Laurie Kruk

All rights reserved. No part of this book may be reproduced in any form or by any electronic or mechanical means, including information storage and retrieval systems, without written permission from the publisher, except by a reviewer who may quote passages in a review.

British Library Cataloguing in Publication Information
A catalogue record for this book is available from the British Library

ISBN: HB 978-1-78660-956-4

Library of Congress Cataloging-in-Publication Data

Names: Radia, Pavlina, editor.
Title: The future of humanity : revisioning the human in the posthuman age / edited by Pavlina Radia, Sarah Fiona Winters, Laurie Kruk.
Description: Lanham, MD : Rowman & Littlefield Publishing Group, Inc., 2019. | Series: Future perfect : images of the time to come in philosophy, politics, and cultural studies | Includes bibliographical references and index.
Identifiers: LCCN 2019014420 (print) | LCCN 2019980618 (ebook) | ISBN 9781786609564 (cloth) ISBN 9781786609571 (ebook) | ISBN 9781538147962 (pbk)
Subjects: LCSH: Humanism. | Humanism—History—21st century. | Humanism—Forecasting. | Philosophical anthropology.
Classification: LCC B821 .F88 2019 (print) | LCC B821 (ebook) | DDC 128—dc23
LC record available at https://lccn.loc.gov/2019014420
LC ebook record available at https://lccn.loc.gov/2019980618

Contents

Introduction: Reflections on the (Post)Human Future   1
   Pavlina Radia

I: Humanity, Big History, and Politics of Progress   11

1. Humanity Has a Choice: Our Common Future from a Big History Perspective   15
   Fred Spier

2. Investing in Disaster: Technical Progress and the Taboo of Diminishing Returns   29
   David Witzling

3. Gender, Religions, and the SDGs: A Reflection on Empowering Buddhist Nuns   49
   Manuel Litalien

II: Genocidal Fractures: The Eternal Return of the Past   65

4. The Pilgrimage to Auschwitz: Making Meaning in Late Modernity   69
   Gillian McCann

5. From Gas Chambers to 9/11: The Future of Postmemory and Contemporary America's Commodity Grief Culture   83
   Pavlina Radia

6. Art, Trauma, and History: A Survivor's Story   101
   Aaron Weiss

III: Doctrines Revisited: Rewriting the Margins   117

7. The Shock Doctrine in Apocalyptic Fiction   121
   Christine Bolus-Reichert

8 Guy Vanderhaeghe and the Future of the Marginalized Canadian
    Male   133
    Laurie Kruk

Part IV: Posthuman Futures   **147**

 9 Human versus Cyborg Life   151
    Catherine Jenkins
10 "Not Born in a Garden": Donna Haraway, Cyborgs, and
    Posthuman Contemporary Art   165
    Eric Weichel

V: Humanity in the Digital Era   **181**

11 Radical Post-Cartesianism: Or the Posthuman Potentials of
    Artificial Neural Networks in Our Hyperconnected Age   187
    Christopher Vitale
12 Actual Fantasy, Modulation Chains, and Swarms of Thought-
    Controlled Babel Drones: Art and Digital Ontology in the
    Posthuman Era   205
    Adam Nash

Index   223

About the Editors   235

About the Contributors   237

Introduction

Reflections on the (Post)Human Future

Pavlina Radia

In a world where the human, on the one hand, has become the ultimate force of nature and where, on the other hand, the progress of new technologies continues to challenge the very notion of humanity; as we are persistently confronted by the challenges of climate change, economic inequities, ideological extremism, and an ever-increasing global population; no topic is more urgent for humans to debate through the lenses of their different disciplines than the future of humanity. What is the future of the human species? What does it mean to be "human"? Or, as Richard Grusin (2015) suggests in *The Nonhuman Turn*, are we experiencing a different kind of "humanity" in the twenty-first century? Are humans mere "climatological and geological forces on the planet that operate just as nonhumans would, independent of human will, belief, or desire"[1] as Grusin suggests? What role do humanities and sciences play in shaping our future? In what ways are disciplinary statements "events" and "performances" unto themselves? If the future is in crisis, then what does it mean to *live*? Is life itself "a subjective category" as Alain Badiou (2009) proposes in *The Theory of the Subject*, or is it an "open-ended, inter-relational, multisexed and trans-species flow," as Rosi Braidotti[2] has argued?

For the last century or so, scholars have debated the various (re)conceptualizations of humanity, challenging humanism's biological essentialism, arguing for a more inclusive and diversified view of humanity as a robust and open ecology. Recent studies by Rosi Braidotti (2013), Jane Bennett (2010), Anna Tsing (2015), and Donna Haraway (2016) have called for inter-, multi-, and transdisciplinary methodologies that address some of the larger questions that inform human and nonhuman life. As Haraway

(2016) writes, "making kin" or "working with" rather than *working on* contemporary issues is crucial to fostering new ways of thinking about and understanding the complex ecologies and environments that surround us.[3] Haraway urges us to "change the story" because, as she eloquently puts it, "with good questions, even or especially mistakes and misunderstandings can become interesting."[4]

Echoing Haraway's suggestion, this edited collection of essays does not shy away from asking difficult questions or from changing the story. The collection constitutes an interdisciplinary conversation about several possible futures for the human species and its ways of knowing about itself. It is as daring as it is innovative in its approach. The chapters in this collection span a variety of disciplines, offering various disciplinary entry points to ponder some of the challenges and potentially hopeful developments humanity will face in the future. The collection is organised around five thematic parts: Part I: "Humanity, Big History, and Politics of Progress"; Part II: "Genocidal Fractures: The Eternal Return of the Past"; Part III: "Doctrines Revisited: Rewriting the Margins"; Part IV: "Posthuman Futures"; and Part V: "Humanity in the Digital Era." The chapters range from the future of humanity's existence on the planet to the future of humanity's relationship with technology, the future of humanity's relationship with the human body, the future of humanity's relationship with the arts, the future of humanity's ways of learning about the past, and indeed the future of humanity's ways of thinking about the future. The unifying theme linking the chapters is the notion of the human as a complex ecology rather than a humanist subject, defined (or limited) by the Cartesian mind–matter binary. In fact, all chapters in this book reframe the human to align with what Rosi Braidotti (2013) refers to as "the posthuman condition," a condition that not only requires a "qualitative shift in our thinking about what exactly is the basic unit of common reference for our species,"[5] but also what it means to think beyond biogenetic paradigms. The chapters in this book highlight the intricate interconnections between history and memory, technology and ethics, economy and sustainability, art and progress.

Initiating this interdisciplinary trouble is Part I: "Humanity, Big History, and Politics of Progress." This opening section explores "big" planetary implications of human progress. Chapters by Fred Spier, David Witzling, and Manuel Litalien examine the ways in which global capitalism harnessed to the powers of the Internet and social media has not only expanded humanity's planetary ambitions, but also precipitated some of the more dangerous aspects of our (post)humanity: power asymmetries among and within diverse countries; challenges to sustainable development and social welfare; and spiritual well-being. Sarah Fiona Winters's introduction to the section raises important concerns about the ever-increasing embrace of science and technology at the expense of philosophical thinking, spirituality, and ethics. The chapters in Part I echo concerns raised by science scholars like Martin Rees. According to Rees (2018), twenty-first-century technological advances allow for some positive solutions to climate change, world hunger, and sustainability. He writes:

> Without technology the world can't provide food, and sustainable energy, for an expanding and more demanding population. But we need it to be wisely directed. Renewable energy systems, medical advances, and high-tech food production (artificial meat, and so forth) are wise goals; geoengineering techniques probably are not. However, scientific and technical breakthroughs can happen so fast and unpredictably that we may not properly cope with them; it will be a challenge to harness their benefits while avoiding their downsides.[6]

Indeed, how to harness the positive aspects of technology while restraining its negative effects has been and will continue to be humanity's ultimate challenge. For centuries, humanity has wrestled with the notion of the machine taking over the man, with anxieties about the power of steam that precipitated the Industrial Revolution, the invention of the automobile that expanded humanity's mobility, and the invention of the airplane that shifted and reduced our concept of time and space dramatically, not to mention the rise of the Internet and the ever-expanding power of the computer-machine whose learning capabilities are increasingly on a par with the human brain and its networking abilities.

Part I of this book does not attempt to provide answers, but rather contemplates what it means to deploy technology and science in a positive and sustainable manner. It also highlights the importance of understanding humanity in its relation to other species, objects, and environments. In their emphasis on ethical progress, the chapters of Part I evoke what Jane Bennett (2010) has recently called an "ecological sensibility,"[7] an understanding of complex forces and materialities "circulating around and within human bodies" and their environments.[8] Such a sensibility requires a new approach not only to humanity as an ontology, but also to science and its many developments. It invites an opportunity to challenge global capitalist agendas, but it also opens a much-needed discussion about an ethical engagement with our planet as outlined in Spier's chapter on "Big History." It encourages a reconsideration of how our policies and politics depend on drumming up "disaster" politics, as acutely discussed in Witzling's chapter on diminishing returns. But it also advocates for an ethical engagement with diverse cultures and their traditions, as highlighted by Litalien's chapter on the transnational role of the Sakyadhita and the Alliance for Bhikkhunis. As the chapters of Part I reveal, political agendas are inevitably tied to cultural history and the ways in which history, politics, and economic needs are not only represented, but also addressed through various forms of narrativization.

Part II: "Genocidal Fractures: The Eternal Return of the Past" emphasizes that historical narratives, including *who* tells them and *how* they are told, will continue to matter. One of the side effects of "progress" is the perpetuation of violence in the name of ideology, religion, or politics. In her work on the posthuman paradigm, Braidotti raises the issue of "the brutality of the new wars, in a globalised world run by the governance of fear."[9] The politics of fear and anxiety continue to rely on the humanist agenda of pitting the human against the nonhuman other. Humanity does not have a good track record when it comes to embracing Bennett's "ecological sensibility," nor has it done away with the penchant for nativist paranoia and xenophobia that marginalise those who do not fit the normative prescription of national(ist), cultural, ethnic, racial, or religious belonging. The chapters by Gillian McCann, Pavlina Radia, and Aaron Weiss in Part II of this book advise us to heed history when it comes to political agendas and ideologies that depend on the us-versus-them binary.

As Laurie Kruk emphasizes in her introduction to Part II, to learn from history means to bear witness to diverse stories and viewpoints. In their chapters, McCann and Radia both ponder what it means to bear witness to atrocities and genocidal events *after the fact*, generations removed from the violent event, specifically through retrospective retelling that underpins the very tenets of what has been referred to as *dark* or *death tourism*. Whereas McCann considers death tourism in the context of atonement and a secular pilgrimage, Radia explores the consumer and commodifying lenses of death tourism and the ways in which art can provide an alternative, subversive reading of memory that challenges commodification. An important through line of Part II is Aaron Weiss's chapter on the influence of transgenerational trauma on the family of a Holocaust survivor. Highlighting the important role that art has played in history, specifically as an essential platform of expression, Weiss invites scholars to consider the diverse roles that art plays and has played in bearing witness to atrocities and genocidal violence. As Marianne Hirsch (2012) has noted, we live in the age of postmemory when some generations are far removed from the context of traumatic history. Hence, how we shape and frame memory and historical events will continue to remain an important ethical question for posterity. Whether we agree with Braidotti that "art is . . . cosmic in its resonance and hence posthuman by structure, as it carries us to the limits of what our embodied selves can do or endure,"[10] or whether we concur with Hirsch that art can prompt retrospective witnessing, the imperative to *remember* is essential not only to art, but also to the very future of (post)humanity.

Part III: "Doctrines Revisited: Rewriting the Margins" furthers the conversation about the significant role that art and literature play not only in shaping our understanding of history, but also in bearing witness to the various cultural phenomena that inform our present, past, and future. As

Sarah Fiona Winters notes, the chapters by Christine Bolus-Reichert and Laurie Kruk explore the effects of humanity's progress—be it scientific, cultural, or economic—on gender and power relations. Both chapters comment on the dystopian vision of the kind of necrotechnological progress critiqued by Braidotti, Rees, or Harraway, for example. Drawing on the literary works by P. D. James and Nalo Hopkinson, Bolus-Reichert's chapter strikes a hopeful note in spite of the dystopian nature of the narratives she examines. As Bolus-Reichert writes, "telling different stories about the future, telling stories in which humans are part of something larger than themselves" can be an important vehicle for "identify[ing] ideologies that we ought to be resisting." Similarly, Laurie Kruk in her chapter on Guy Vanderhaeghe's collection of stories explores the influence of progress on hegemonic masculinity. Examining what she calls the characters' "mourning [of] the loss of hegemonic masculinity," she emphasizes Vanderhaeghe's strategic use of "double voicing" to comment on the complexities of the increasingly shifting paradigm of masculinity in postmillennial Canada.

With ever-evolving scientific progress and new digital technologies, humanity is not only changing, but it is also realizing its globally networked and, to an extent, cosmic potential. The rise of biomedicine and biotechnologies, including in vitro fertilization, prosthetics, and synthetic transplants, has inevitably exploded traditional concepts of human corporeality by pushing human bodies into a more adaptive and integrated realm where the physical body is not only in contact with the machine, but also becomes one with it. Part IV: "Posthuman Futures" tackles the anxious subject of posthuman embodiment. How have our bodies changed? Attached to various devices, but also subjected to medical scanning and biotech inventions, the very notion of the physical body has been radically reframed. In her chapter, Catherine Jenkins ponders the necropolitics of the highly digitised, Western medical industry and its increasing reliance on cyborgs and robots. As Jenkins emphasizes, the incessant push for better technologies in medical science is tied closely to humanity's quest for eternal life. A desire as old as humankind itself, immortality is the Holy Grail that has evaded generations.

In the twenty-first century, however, we might be close to its realization, as scholars like Yuval Noah Harari (2015) have noted. Recent developments of artificial intelligence (AI) technologies have launched the possibility of using virtual "doctors" to read magnetic resonance imaging (MRI) scans with an uncanny precision. In her recent CNN interview with Fareed Zakaria, the AI researcher Daphne Koller spoke about the potential benefits of using AI to expedite a medical diagnosis of a serious illness like cancer or Alzheimer's disease. Although acknowledging some of the benefits of biotechnologies, biogenetics, and the use of AI, Jenkins leaves open the question as to whether the quest for immortality is privileging quantity over quality. She asks: "The ultimate question becomes, is the quality of life suffering because of our fixation on the quantity of life?" (Koller 2019).

On the other hand, in its embrace of the posthuman as humanity's reality or, to put it differently, *virtuality*, Eric Weichel's chapter on the postfeminist cyborg and contemporary media art offers a more subversive and open-ended vision of the posthuman. Invoking Donna Haraway's (1984) "Cyborg Manifesto," Weichel showcases how contemporary media artists like Bharti Kher, Andrea Crespo, Sally McKay, Patricia Piccinini, and Burton Nitta engage with the posthuman cyborg in the ways that challenge some of the necrotechnological "perverse form[s] of the posthuman,"[11] to use Braidotti's words. From a critique of reproductive technologies and racist representations of women to the fetishization of the female and the cyborg body, the artists discussed in Weichel's chapter provide a subversive counternarrative to the anxious cyborgean. But they also reject the hegemonic and hypersexualized version of the cyborg permeating the capitalist imaginary of contemporary mass media, online games, and the military, to name a few. Aligning the human body with functional MRI, for example, Sally McKay's work pays homage to the complex posthuman assemblages that humans have become. In Weichel's terms, "McKay allows for valuable insights into what needs a future humanity might have." These needs, as Weichel emphasizes, will have to involve "innovative solutions" to the diverse problems that humanity has already been facing in the wake of global warming, depleted natural resources, and shrinking biodiversity. For Weichel, the bigger question concerning cyborgs is not so much whether they are posthuman, but rather how to align the already *posthuman* human with a cyborgean vision that is emancipatory and sustainable. In its open-ended exploration of the posthuman as the future that is, rather than a future that is yet to come, Part IV paves the way to the final section of this book.

Part V: "Humanity in the Digital Era" expands the posthuman debate outlined by Jenkins and Weichel by examining the posthuman in relation to the digital. Concluding the debate over the future of humanity in this collection are the two final chapters by Chris Vitale and Adam Nash. Bringing together art, philosophy, and major ethical questions about humanity's past, present, and future with new digital technologies like artificial neural networks, machine learning, and AI, Vitale and Nash offer a virtuoso ending to our conversation about the future of humanity, an ending that is also a new beginning. In their erudite and creative integration of philosophy and technology, art and artificial intelligence, both Vitale and Nash argue that humanity has never been anything but a complex assemblage of Deleuzian becomings. And yet the digital era has taken this notion to a whole new level. As Nash argues, "the digital era is the era of media as environment." Similarly, exploring the potentialities of the artificial neural networks (ANNs) like Siri, Vitale cautions against imperialist abuses of these ANNs for military or commercial purposes. Exploring the neuralisation of computers, Vitale suggests that the spread of ANNs is shaking us out of our humanist slumber, asking us to acknowledge that just as computers are becoming organic, so our bodies are machine-like. Rather than fearing the posthuman, Vitale calls for a "posthuman worldview" that acknowledges the human–nonhuman relationship as a complex networked environment, or what he calls a "networkology." Vitale's concept echoes Braidotti's (2013) concept of the posthuman as hybrid, nomadic, creolized, multipurpose, open-ended, and postanthropocentric.

Aligning with Vitale's postanthropocentric philosophical stance, Nash's chapter embraces the posthuman as a co-located environment that not only lives *with* us, but is also an inevitable part of us as we are an inevitable part of *it*. As a media artist, Nash explores the chains of signification produced by linking the (post)human (mind) to the latest technologies like AI, robotics, and machine learning to ignite a new, philosophico-artistic way of thinking in which the cyborg, posthuman, or robot are no longer *othered* but rather *mothered* by the sensible ecologies of the human–nonhuman connection. Through his interactive installations, Nash brings us into a realm of virtual reality that is sensible and sensitive. His most recent *Child in the Wild* project, with John McCormick, transforms the discourse of the cyborg-threat into a cyborg-friend, an affective topology that invites us to rethink the notion of the robot as an object-thing. Instead, it asks us to embrace what Donna Haraway (2016) calls "sympoiesis—making with" rather than understanding the world as a foreclosed, *made* environment.[12]

Nash, like Vitale, argues that to see the posthuman in all its complexities, we need to be open to a new narrative. As Haraway says, "simply, we *must* change the story; the story *must* change."[13] To change the story, however, we need to "think with."[14] In her words, "to think with is to stay with the naturalcultural [and we should add "virtual"] multispecies trouble on earth."[15] To think with, however, also means acknowledging that there is no final conclusion or ontology to make us feel better, to save us from all the trouble. Similarly, this collection remains open-ended: there are many subjects and areas that we did not cover. Yet the chapters in this collection provide multiple entry points, a palimpsestic maze of stories viewed from diverse perspectives. We have not finished this conversation. We have merely started. Taking the cue from Donna Haraway, we have taken the risk of "staying with the trouble," of "making kin" with philosophies, ideologies, networkologies, robots, and cyborgs, animals, humans and objects.[16]

Consequently, this collection engages with only some of the issues that trouble our very understanding of what it means to be human in the twenty-first century. Expanding on the recent scholarly discussions about the posthuman and nonhuman turn while simultaneously contributing to the increasing push towards inter-, multi-, and cross-disciplinary thinking, the chapters in this collection speak to the multifaceted ecologies and counter-ecologies of humanity, addressing its possible futures. Some of these include ecological issues generated by centuries of neglecting our environment(s); power asymmetries stemming from economic and cultural globalization; violence and its affective politics informed by cultural, ethnic, and racial genocides; religious disputes; social inequities produced by consumerism; gender normativity; issues of identity and agency; and, last but not least, the increasing influence of digital and AI technology on not only the very concept of the human, but also historical, sociopolitical, and ethical relations the implications of which are not minor, but planetary. Since the future is yet to come, perhaps this book trailblazes a pathway to new, alternative ways of seeing it as an ever-unfolding becoming-(post)human.

BIBLIOGRAPHY

Bennett, Jane. *Vibrant Matter: A Political Ecology*. Durham, NC: Duke University Press, 2010.
Braidotti, Rosi. *The Posthuman*. Cambridge: Polity Press, 2013.
Grusin, Richard. *The Nonhuman Turn*. Minneapolis: University of Minnesota Press, 2015.
Harari, Yuval Noah. *Homo Deus: A Brief History of Tomorrow*. New York: Signal Books, 2015.
Haraway, Donna. *Staying with the Trouble: Making Kin in the Chthulucene*. Durham, NC: Duke University Press, 2016.
Hirsch, Marianne. *The Generation of Postmemory: Writing and the Visual Culture after the Holocaust*. New York: Columbia University Press, 2012.
Koller, Daphne. Interview with Fareed Zakaria on AI and Health Care. CNN, 18 February 2019. https://www.cnn.com/videos/tv/2019/02/18/exp-gps-0217-daphne-koller-interview-ai.cnn
Rees, Martin. *On the Future: Prospects for Humanity*. Princeton, NJ: Princeton University Press, 2018.
Tsing, Anna. *Friction: An Ethnography of Global Connection*. Princeton, NJ: Princeton University Press, 2005.

NOTES

1. Richard Grusin, *The Nonhuman Turn* (Minneapolis: University of Minnesota Press, 2015), vii.
2. Rosi Braidotti, *The Posthuman* (Cambridge: Polity Press, 2013), 89.
3. Donna Haraway, *Staying with the Trouble: Making Kin in the Chthulucene* (Durham, NC: Duke University Press, 2016), 88.
4. Harraway, *Staying with the Trouble*, 127.
5. Braidotti, *The Posthuman*, 2.
6. Martin Rees, *On the Future: Prospects for Humanity* (Princeton: Princeton University Press, 2018), 60.
7. Jane Bennett, *Vibrant Matter: A Political Ecology* (Durham, NC: Duke University Press, 2010), xi.
8. Bennett, *Vibrant Matter*, ix.
9. Braidotti, *The Posthuman*, 9.
10. Braidotti, *The Posthuman*, 107.
11. Braidotti, *The Posthuman*, 7.
12. Haraway, *Staying with the Trouble*, 5.

13. Haraway, *Staying with the Trouble*, 41.
14. Haraway, *Staying with the Trouble*, 40.
15. Haraway, *Staying with the Trouble*, 40.
16. Haraway, *Staying with the Trouble*, 1.

I

Humanity, Big History, and Politics of Progress

Sarah Fiona Winters

In 1944, C. S. Lewis outlined his view of the future in *The Abolition of Man*. In that philosophical work, he draws a distinction between past-oriented people operating within the attitudes and knowledge of what we would call the humanities and future-oriented people working in the field of applied science: "For the wise men of old the cardinal problem had been how to conform the soul to reality, and the solution had been knowledge, self-discipline, and virtue. For . . . applied science . . . the problem is how to subdue reality to the wishes of men: the solution is a technique."[1] Lewis was writing from a conservative position, but the dichotomy he draws here reappears in *Homo Deus: A Brief History of Tomorrow* (2015) by Yuval Noah Harari, in particular in his sections on the applied science of biochemical treatments of mood:

> If science is right and our happiness is determined by our bio-chemical system, then the only way to ensure lasting contentment is by rigging this system. Forget economic growth, social reforms and political revolutions: in order to raise global happiness levels, we need to manipulate human biochemistry.[2]

> The biochemical solution is to develop products and treatments that will provide humans with an unending stream of pleasant sensations, so we will never be without them. The Buddha's suggestion was to reduce our craving for pleasant sensations, and not allow them to control our lives. . . . At present, humankind has far greater interest in the biochemical solution.[3]

Both Lewis and Harari believe that the future of humanity will be one in which the technique is preferred to knowledge, self-discipline, and virtue. Both point out that humans of the past and of their own presents (the 1940s and the 2010s) are torn on this future, some welcoming it and others resisting it. The three chapters in this section seem to fall on the side of virtue rather than technique, for each considers the options humans have to solve the problems of the present in order to bring about a better future or avert a worse one, and each suggests that knowledge, self-discipline, and virtue, the solution of the "wise men of old," is the right approach to take.

Fred Spier's chapter begins with some of humanity's most impressive techniques, or technologies, for the subduing of reality: the technologies of rockets and cameras for the subduing of time and space. But the focus of the chapter is on the human response to the truths, both facts and ideas, conveyed by these technologies: Spier analyses the history of his own imaginative and emotional response to the "moonrise" photograph of 1968 and its role in his work in developing "Big History" courses. He proposes that the future for humanity depends not on developing further techniques to subdue the realities of time and space to human desires, but on adjusting human desires, through education and conversation, to the limits that time and especially space impose upon us. He argues that "humanity must consider trying to live in as much harmony as possible with both our natural environment and each other" and that one way to make this attempt is by bringing together the sciences, social sciences, and the humanities.

Narrowing the focus from the Big History of humanity on earth and in space to the smaller history of Western, mostly American, humans in the twentieth century, David Witzling's chapter also criticises the human tendency to try to subdue reality through technology rather than submit and adjust to problems through wisdom, or, in his frame of reference, policy. Witzling summons an impressive range of statistics concerning food production, medicine, and the software industry to support his thesis that "[m]any of the problems human societies face at this juncture in history are better resolved through policy measures, and the West's emphasis on technological solutions marginalises effective investments in simpler strategies," a pragmatic and social-science variation on the idealistic, humanities-oriented argument of Lewis.

Whereas Witzling's chapter provides a North American focus on the questions raised by Lewis and Harari, Manuel Litalien's chapter provides an Asian perspective. Litalien's chapter on the United Nations and Buddhist nuns reveals that Western solutions to human problems must not be viewed as the default human solutions. Litalien argues that "the future of humanity rests in part on how development organizations can negotiate the rights of women in the religious sphere by providing support to women who ground their social work and activism in a religious framework," a position that emphasizes the different humans (e.g., the western, male, secular human vs. the eastern, female, religious human) who coexist and must negotiate with each other under the umbrella term *humanity*. Witzling's argument that policy, not technology, should be the primary instrument of problem-solving for humanity is therefore given more nuance by Litalien's argument that policy must always be contextualised in culture.

Both Lewis, pessimistically, and Harari, more neutrally, conclude that the years ahead will involve humans choosing technique over "knowledge, self-discipline, and virtue," technology over "economic growth, social reforms and political revolutions." Spier, Witzling, and Litalien represent aspects of resistance to that vision of the future.

BIBLIOGRAPHY

Harari, Yuval Noah. *Homo Deus: A Brief History of Tomorrow*. London: Signal, 2015.
Lewis, C. S. *The Abolition of Man*. New York: HarperCollins, (1944) 2001.

NOTES

1. C. S. Lewis, *The Abolition of Man* (New York: HarperCollins, [1944] 2001), 77.
2. Yuval Noah Harari, *Homo Deus: A Brief History of Tomorrow* (London: Signal, 2015), 45.
3. Harari, *Homo Deus*, 49.

Chapter One

Humanity Has a Choice

Our Common Future from a Big History Perspective

Fred Spier

"For all its upheavals and frustrations, the year [1968] would be remembered to the end of time for the dazzling skills and Promethean daring that sent mortals around the moon. It would be celebrated as the year in which men saw at first hand their little earth entire, a remote, blue-brown sphere hovering like a migrant bird in the hostile night of space. The year's transcendent legacy may well be that in Christmas week 1968, the human race glimpsed not a new continent or a new colony, but a new age, one that will inevitably reshape man's view of himself and his destiny. For what must surely rank as one of the greatest physical adventures in history was, unlike the immortal explorations of the past, infinitely more than a reconnaissance of geography or unknown elements. It was a journey into man's future, a hopeful but urgent summons, in Poet Archibald MacLeish's words, 'to see ourselves as riders on the earth together, brothers on that bright loveliness in the eternal cold—brothers who know now they are truly brothers.'" —*Time Magazine,* January 3, 1969, "Men of the Year" [the astronauts of Apollo 8], 9.

"The biggest philosophy, foundation-shaking impression was seeing the smallness of the Earth. . . . Even the pictures don't do it justice, because they always have this frame around them. But when you . . . put your eyeball to the window of the spacecraft, you can see essentially half of the universe. . . . That's a lot more black and a lot more universe than ever comes through a *framed* picture. . . . It's not how small the Earth was, it's just how big everything else was." —Apollo 8 astronaut William Anders in Chaikin and Kohl (2009), 158.

December 24, 2018 CE, was the fiftieth anniversary of the day that the first manned spacecraft to go to the moon, Apollo 8, entered lunar orbit and circled our celestial companion ten times before returning to Earth. I was sixteen years old in 1968 and followed these great adventures intensively in the Netherlands, collecting pictures and making a scrapbook that I still have.

My father and I watched the black-and-white live television broadcasts of the launch; of the flight to the moon, during which the first images of Earth at a distance were shown, images of a big white blob, the result of overexposure of the Apollo TV camera; of the most impressive and moving transmission from lunar orbit on Christmas Eve, when, unseen by earthly viewers, the astronauts Bill Anders, Jim Lovell, and Frank Borman read the first lines from the Book of Genesis while showing the approaching sunset on the lunar surface through the spacecraft's window; and of the astronauts' helicopter landing on the flight deck of the aircraft carrier Yorktown, and them exiting it, after their successful splashdown on December 27 right before dawn in the still-dark Pacific Ocean.

Using my Asahi Pentax S1 35-mm camera mounted on a tripod, I took a number of photos of those television broadcasts. I did so because I was not sure whether these images would be preserved for posterity. (All of this was happening before there were home video recorders.) Later during the flight, when my father also became interested in recording it, we decided to mount his Elmo 8-SS double-eight movie camera on the tripod, while I took the rest of my pictures by hand (which did not make any great difference in quality, as we saw after I developed the film). I still have the negatives and my father's short movie. Both of them may actually have conserved a unique record of what was shown of the Apollo 8 mission at that time on Dutch television.

What I did not know—in all likelihood only the astronauts themselves knew it at the time—was that right before the Christmas Eve television broadcast something had happened in the cabin of the spacecraft that would have a considerable effect on human history. During the third lunar orbit the spacecraft rotated while flying behind the moon, as seen from Earth, and was thus out of radio contact. As a result, the cabin windows were now facing forward.

As soon as the spacecraft began flying over the side of the moon that is visible from Earth, the astronauts saw for the first time the little blue-and-white Earth rising above the forbidding grey lunar landscape, surrounded by a black and mostly empty universe. This view impressed them greatly, and they quickly took a few pictures with their specially adapted Hasselblad 500 EL photo camera. Furthermore, a record of what was said during those exciting moments was preserved on tape inside the cabin, which was later "dumped" to Earth and subsequently transcribed in Mission Control and record in the *Apollo 8 Onboard Voice Transcription*, as were all taped conversations that took place while the spacecraft was out of radio contact with Earth.

What was that conversation like? To understand this transcription, some explanation is required. First, the conversation was dated in terms of *Mission Elapsed Time*: the time that had passed since launch. For instance, the numbers 03 03 47 30 refer to 3 days, 3 hours, 47 minutes and 30 seconds after lift off.

In addition, the following abbreviations were used:

CDR = Commander: Frank Borman

CMP = Command Module Pilot: James Lovell

LMP = Lunar Module Pilot: William Anders (Apollo 8 did not carry a Lunar Module, which was a major reason why Anders was in charge of photography.)

In the middle of page 113 of the *Apollo 8 Onboard Voice Transcription* the conversation begins as follows (113–14):

03 03 47 30 CDR: Oh, my God! Look at that picture over there! Here's the earth coming up. Wow, is that pretty!

03 03 47 37 LMP: Hey, don't take that, it's not scheduled.

03 03 47 39 CDR: (Laughter) You got a color film, Jim?

03 03 47 46 LMP: Hand me that roll of color film quick, will you—

03 03 47 48 CMP: Oh, man, that's great!

03 03 47 50 LMP: —Hurry. Quick.

03 03 47 54 CDR: Gee.

03 03 47 55 CMP: It's down here?

03 03 47 56 LMP: Just grab me a color. That color exterior.

03 03 48 00 CMP: . . .

03 03 48 01 LMP: Hurry up!

03 03 48 06 LMP: Got one?

03 03 48 08 CMP: Yes, I'm looking for one. C 368.

03 03 48 11 LMP: Anything, quick.

03 03 48 13 CMP: Here.

03 03 48 17 LMP: Well, I think we missed it.

03 03 48 31 CMP: Hey, I got it right here!

03 03 48 33 LMP: Let . . . let me get it out of this window. It's a lot clearer.

03 03 48 37 CMP: Bill, I got it framed; it's very clear right here. You got it?

03 03 48 41 LMP: Yes.

03 03 48 42 CDR: Well, take several of them.

03 03 48 43 CMP: Take several of them! Here, give it to me.

03 03 48 44 LMP: Wait a minute, let's get the right setting, here now; just calm down.

03 03 48 47 CDR: Calm down, Lovell.

03 03 48 49 CMP: Well, I got it ri— Oh, that's a beautiful shot.

03 03 48 54 CMP: 250 at f:11. [1/250 seconds film exposure, at lens aperture f/11; all of this was done manually.]

03 03 49 07 LMP: Okay.

03 03 49 08 CMP: Now vary the . . . vary the exposure a little bit.

03 03 49 09 LMP: I did. I took two of them.

03 03 49 11 CMP: You sure we got it now?

03 03 49 12 LMP: Yes, we'll get . . . we'll . . . It'll come up again, I think.

03 03 49 17 CMP: Just take another one, Bill.

Here the recorded conversation ends. The next words mentioned in the *Onboard Voice Transcription* were spoken about 1.5 hours later. This should not surprise us. Only thirteen seconds after the last sentence mentioned above was spoken, radio contact with Mission Control in Houston was reestablished. During the rather technical exchange that immediately followed, as recorded in the *Apollo 8 Technical Air-to-Ground Voice Transcription*, no reference at all was made to the excitement the astronauts had just experienced while witnessing the first Earthrise ever seen by humankind.[1]

After the films had been developed and printed by NASA in Houston, the photos deemed most impressive were immediately made available to the news media through the Associated Press. All of that happened within twenty-four hours. Thanks to the fact that my parents had a subscription to *Time* magazine, I saw the astronauts' "lunar album" in the 10 January 1968, issue (Atlantic edition). On page 29 the picture series opens with a large colour photo of the Earth rising above the lunar landscape, with the caption, "The Awesome Views from Apollo 8." The text below the photo describes it as "the first 'earthrise' that any man has ever seen." This may well have been the first time that this photo was called *Earthrise*, as it became known later.

As described in the Preface of my book *Big History and the Future of Humanity* (2010, 2015, xii–xiii), while looking at this picture, I experienced a shock that I had never felt before and never have experienced since. Within a second my perspective of Earth was changed beyond recognition. While no one else in my family seemed to be that interested in those photos, I tore them out carefully before the issue was discarded, stuck the Earthrise picture and others onto the wall of my room, and looked at them for a long time. I still have all these pictures and treasure them greatly.

None of my education had prepared me for this new look at Earth. At school, I had received a classical Dutch, perhaps West European, education, which included Latin and ancient Greek; modern languages such as English, French, and German; mathematics, physics, chemistry, geography, and history. Yet all these portions of discrete knowledge were never related to one another or presented from one single perspective. This left me totally unprepared for the extraordinary sight of our blue-and-white planet surrounded by dark space, rising above that forbidding grey lunar landscape. These pictures showed for the first time how different Earth was from its cosmic surroundings, as witnessed by human eyes. It also made people around the globe, including me, wonder what we were doing to our home in space. This led to an unprecedented upsurge of environmental awareness, including the establishment of the first Earth Day in 1970 CE, as outlined, for instance, in Robert Poole's excellent book titled *Earthrise: How Man First Saw the Earth* (2008).

The most influential environmental publication at the time was a study commissioned in 1970 CE by an independent group of intellectuals who called themselves the Club of Rome, because they had started their meetings in this ancient city. Executed at the Massachusetts Institute of Technology under the leadership of Dennis Meadows and financed by the Volkswagen Foundation, the final report was called *The Limits to Growth: A Report for the Club of Rome Project on the Predicament of Mankind*. It was published in many languages, including Dutch.

Great attention was paid to five variables deemed important: population growth, food production, industrial production, the limited supplies of natural resources, and pollution. The conclusion was that all of these factors in whatever combination would act as a brake on human well-being in the near future. Especially in the Netherlands, this study received a great deal of attention and sold well. According to Frits Böttcher, a Dutch member of the Club of Rome, this would have been the case because the Netherlands had the highest income per hectare in the world and, as a result, was already experiencing many of the highlighted problems on a daily basis.[2]

While this was going on, none of the people I was surrounded by, including my teachers at secondary school and later at university, ever mentioned the profound change in perspective that the pictures of Earth from space had produced. Given this situation, I kept most of my thoughts and feelings to myself. Yet I began to feel what I would now describe as a most distressing disconnect. Not only was I increasingly worried about environmental problems, but I also wanted to know how humanity had gotten itself into this situation.

This curiosity about human history was fuelled by a paragraph in the Dutch introduction to *The Limits to Growth*, which stated that we would only be able to effectively change our current situation for the better if we understood how the current situation differed from those earlier periods of history that had shaped humans in a biological and cultural sense. At that time, academic environmental history did not yet exist, nor was I aware of any world history accounts that could help me in this respect. As a result, I began a long intellectual search for a better understanding of human history, which reached its culmination when I became familiar with big history.

Big history is the attempt to tell a coherent story of all of history, starting with the beginning of the universe, now thought to have happened 13.8 billion years ago, and ending with life on Earth here and now. The term *big history* was coined by the Australian historian David Christian at Macquarie University, Sydney, Australia, where in 1989 CE he had started a multidisciplinary course in which specialists from all the academic fields involved—astronomy, geology, biology, palaeontology, anthropology, prehistory, classical history, and modern history—all told their part of the story. This turned out to be a successful course model.

At the University of Amsterdam, the sociologist Johan Goudsblom and I copied the approach while adapting it to our own possibilities and limitations. We started our first course by the end of 1994 CE as an elective module. Thanks to continued enthusiastic student interest, this course has been running ever since. Later, our tiny group, most notably including my younger colleague Esther Quaedackers, started organizing other big history courses at a number of institutions of higher learning in the Netherlands.

As shown by the participants' reactions, our courses have been a considerable success among the thousands of students that have taken them. The reason for this success is, I think, because big history offers a coherent academic account of how everything that we witness today has become the way it is, for all of us living on this tiny but very special globe swinging through a huge and inhospitable universe. As a result, big history places all of us in time and space like no other approach to human history has done before, while providing the best possible coherent viewpoint of what the future may bring. In this contribution, big history will not be summarised any further. Readers who want to know more about big history may want to visit my website at www.bighistory.info.

While organizing the course and discussing a great many aspects of it with all the lecturers involved for about twenty years, step-by-step I realised that there were regularities visible in big history that could only be observed while looking big. This insight led to my first book *The Structure of Big History* (1996) and later to *Big History and the Future of Humanity* (2010, 2015), which provides an explanatory framework for all of history. All of this represents only a first beginning, or so I think, of understanding all of history. I suspect that in the future many more regularities will be found that will help us to understand big history better.

While exploring a great many aspects of big history, including its history, very much aided by the emergence of the Internet, I discovered that David Christian and I were not the first to look at history this way. A considerable number of pioneers had, in fact, preceded us, perhaps most notably the US astrophysicist Eric Chaisson—to whom we also owe a great deal in a theoretical sense—and the US cosmologist Carl Sagan, who popularised the big view in the 1980s CE in his famous *Cosmos* book and television series, many episodes of which can now be watched on YouTube.

A more detailed overview of the history of big history can be found in chapter one of *Big History and the Future of Humanity*. What matters here is that most, if not all, of these pioneers were influenced by the Earthrise photo, which urgently stimulated their efforts to do something about these apparently serious global environmental problems. Scholars influenced by the Earthrise photo include the US astrophysicists Eric Chaisson, Carl Sagan, and Siegfried Kutter; US geologist Preston Cloud; French-Canadian astrophysicist Hubert Reeves; British scientist James Lovelock; and US educator and historian Cynthia Stokes Brown.

Of these, Carl Sagan is perhaps the most widely known through his *Cosmos* TV series, in which he openly expressed his worries, then also in terms of a possible nuclear holocaust as a result of the Cold War. Today, such nuclear concerns have resurfaced as a result of the current global political situation. And this is how US geologist Preston Cloud expressed it in his book *Cosmos, Earth, and Man: A Short History of the Universe* (1980):

> Our reach toward the stars has given us a new vision of Earth. We have looked through the camera's eye from space and seen the whole planet in one field of view—floating against the empty blackness beyond like a multicolored oriental lantern. Some lantern! Some view! Mother Earth will never seem the same again. No more can thinking people take this little planet, bounteous and beautiful though it be, as an infinite theater of action and provider of resources for man, yielding new largesse to every demand without limit. Born from the wreckage of stars, compressed to a solid state by the force of its own gravity and radioactivity, clothed in its filmy garments of air and water by the hot breath of volcanoes, shaped and mineralized by four and a half billion years of crustal evolution, warmed and peopled by the sun, this resilient but finite globe is all our species has to sustain it forever. (Cloud 1978, 285)

While over the past fifty years many advances have been made in our academic understanding of our "predicament" which will not be summarised here, many of those who have watched human history unfold after the Earthrise picture feel that much more could have been done, and that much more still needs to be done, if we want to guarantee a reasonably sustainable and secure life to as many earth dwellers as possible for the longest foreseeable future.

Most, if not all, observers think that our main problems are twofold: social and ecological. They consist of (1) our continued, often unsustainable exploitation of finite planetary resources, and (2) the growing differences in wealth and poverty within and among many countries. The average economic standards of life in many countries have risen, as exemplified by their growing middle classes, while in many countries that were among the first to industrialise the middle classes are in decline. This global situation will not be elaborated further here. What matters here is to address the question: given this situation, what more could humanity do to ensure a sustainable future, if anything, other than what it is already doing?

Seen from an historical point of view, perhaps the most remarkable aspect of human reality today is that so many of us all around the globe are so tightly interconnected and can, as a result, communicate with each other almost instantaneously, while having unprecedented access to unprecedented amounts of information. Right now, there are, for instance, eight billion mobile phone connections (more than the entire world population), many with Internet access, while Facebook has about two billion users today.

Of course, billions of poor people may not yet have Internet access. Some estimates indicate that only about 40 percent of the world population may be privileged in this way. But if the rest do not yet have such access themselves, it seems likely that most of them will soon be living close to places where Internet access is available or will be connected to people who do have such access. In such materially less well-endowed places, human social contacts tend to be more intensive and interwoven, which would make it possible for

Internet access to be sporadically made available to virtually all people through such basic forms of human cooperation and sharing.

This situation makes it possible, in principle, to initiate a global discussion among all citizens of planet Earth about where we want to go as humankind. It may be extraordinarily challenging to organise such a discussion in a way that will allow all these views to be heard, while trying to find common ground and act accordingly, without seeking to manipulate those views. This may or may not be feasible, but we will only know for sure whether this can be done after having tried it.

Given the large differences in living situations today, such discussions will inevitably involve both social and ecological issues, in the sense that humanity must consider trying to live in as much harmony as possible with both our natural environment and with each other. If this goal cannot be achieved, the future of most of humanity may look bleak, and we may fail as a planetary civilization as a result. This is the choice that humanity faces today, or so it seems to me and to many other likeminded scholars as well. But at least humanity has a collective choice today, which it has never had before.

I do not know how to organise such discussions in great detail. Such a mammoth effort could only be done by large numbers of volunteers worldwide who seek to elicit as many views as possible from as many people as possible, with as much respect for each other's views as possible, while trying not to manipulate those views but instead to organise the most honest and open possible global discussion.

In doing so, we may not always be able to count on goodwill and good intentions, however important these will be. Organizing such discussions will therefore probably require certain social control mechanisms. The most important aspect of such a control mechanism may be to inform all the inhabitants of planet Earth that their views and actions, or the lack of them, will be preserved for posterity. This will make it possible for all the participants, as well as for those who will live after us, to assess the content and make corresponding moral judgments about who said what in terms of the general goals.

To organise such a discussion, we need good knowledge. First, participants need to understand that we are living on the surface of one single globe of finite dimensions, and that we may be running out of vital resources while our numbers are greater than ever before. And not only that. We need to make clear that we are inextricably linked to the rest of the universe, and our position in it, for our well-being. We also need to make clear that geography is not just a two-dimensional affair, as so many people still appear to think intuitively; rather, we live on the surface of a globe of limited dimensions. The biosphere, the area fit for human habitation and effective production of foodstuffs, is a tiny zone; depending on latitude, the biosphere is no more than five kilometres thick at most.

We can travel, for instance, ten thousand kilometres or more along the Earth's surface without finding ourselves in serious trouble. But if we go down only a few hundred metres, unprotected human life will soon become impossible; the deepest that humans have drilled into the Earth is only ten kilometres. And if we go up only five kilometres or more, unprotected human life will become impossible, too. So we are inextricably bound to that very thin layer of the biosphere covering the surface of our planet, which is of course part of that biosphere.

In my opinion, we need far more unitary knowledge about the state of our planet than we have today, including the current efforts to teach and further develop big history. Humanity has lost precious time since the great Prussian scholar and traveller Alexander von Humboldt (1769–1859 CE) outlined such a program in the 1840s and 1850s CE in his *Kosmos* book series, then widely read and translated into many languages. Instead of building on his magnificent work, and as a result fostering and developing a unitary view of ourselves and our planet within the universe, von Humboldt's pioneering studies have mostly been cast aside, to the extent that today only a few scholars may even know about them, while even fewer may have read any of them. This situation emerged in the second half of the nineteenth century, when the sciences and the humanities specialised more and more, without making any systematic academic attempts to place all of that new knowledge into a larger, newer, and better, whole.

In big history, such an attempt is being made today. Even though considerable progress has been made during the past fifty years, that effort is still marginal today in terms of academic presence. Much more could have been done through a sustained academic effort, as a result providing the best possible information on the situation in which we find ourselves today.

How could we change this situation? My proposal is that we dedicate 10 percent of our academic budgets, and 10 percent of our school time, worldwide, to further investigate and teach the academic science of the whole cosmos, in terms of an integrated combination of the natural sciences, the social sciences, and the humanities. This will hopefully make clear not only our position in space and time, but also, far more importantly in my view, make clear what our main problems are, and what could be done about them. Such a program should be formulated as part of one single worldwide academic umbrella program, tentatively called "The State of Our Home Planet," in which not only big history but also many other academic approaches could play a role.

Certainly this proposal raises all sorts of questions about the effectiveness and ethics of such a mechanism, such as the following:

How is this different from what we have now, where nothing really disappears from the Internet? My answer is that there is currently no place on the Internet that systematically registers what all earthlings think about their ecological and social situation; what to do about it, if anything; and can save all of this information for posterity in a systematic and accessible fashion.

How will anonymity feature into this control mechanism? As I see it, anonymity would not be allowed. But ensuring that people participate only with their true identities, while not distorting the comments of others, may be a very difficult issue to resolve.

How will our descendants read literally billions of comments and judge any of us individually for them? They can search for specific names and comments and go from there.

I am sure that a great many more serious issues will need to be confronted, if this proposal is to be turned into reality. But if this plan were not to work as a result of a lack of sincerity and involvement of the human species, it would mean that humankind is not up to the task of using this opportunity to turn itself into a more sustainable planetary civilization by peaceful means.

I will refrain from further trying to outline the great many problems that might be encountered along the way, but rather focus on the positive gains that may come as a result. I realise full well that such global discussions may take many years, and that any results may be difficult to turn into effective action. But whatever may happen, such a grassroots, Internet-based discussion may focus the attention of the entire world population on realizing what is at stake, and that the moment may have come to act as one single global family under threat; all participants may realise that we all are temporary visitors living on this extraordinary planet swinging through mostly empty space. As Apollo 8 astronaut William Anders, who took the Earthrise picture, observed in a 1997 BBC documentary produced by Ella Bahaire, "All of the views of the Earth from the moon have led the human race, and its political leaders, and its environmental leaders, and its citizenry, to realize that we're all jammed together on one really kind of dinky little planet, and we'd better treat it, and ourselves, better, or we're not gonna be here very long."

BIBLIOGRAPHY

"The Awesome Views from Apollo 8," *Time Magazine* (Atlantic edition), 10 January 1969, 29.

Bahaire, Ella [producer]. *Decisive Moments: The Photographs That Made History. How Photography Became a Force to Be Reckoned with in the 1960s.* BBC 2 television documentary, 1997.

Chaikin, Andrew, and Victoria Kohl. *Voices from the Moon: Apollo Astronauts Describe Their Lunar Experiences.* New York: Viking Studio, 2009.

Chaisson, Eric J. "The Broadest View of the Biggest Picture: An Essay on Radiation, Matter, Life," *Harvard Magazine*, January–February (21–25), 1982.

Chaisson, Eric J. *Cosmic Dawn: The Origins of Matter and Life.* New York: W. W. Norton, 1981.

Chaisson, Eric J. "The Cosmic Environment for the Growth of Complexity." *Biosystems* 46(13–19), 1998.
Chaisson, Eric J. *Cosmic Evolution: The Rise of Complexity in Nature*. Cambridge, MA: Harvard University Press, 2001.
Chaisson, Eric J. *The Life Era: Cosmic Selection and Conscious Evolution*. New York: Atlantic Monthly Press, 1987.
Chaisson, Eric J. "The Scenario of Cosmic Evolution." *Harvard Magazine*, November–December (21–33), 1977.
Chaisson, Eric J. *Universe: An Evolutionary Approach to Astronomy*. Englewood Cliffs, NJ: Prentice Hall, 1988.
Christian, David. "The Case for 'Big History.'" *Journal of World History* 2, no. 2 (1991): 223–28.
Christian, David. *Maps of Time: An Introduction to Big History*. Berkeley: University of California Press, 2004.
Christian, David, Cynthia Stokes Brown, and Craig Benjamin. *Big History: Between Nothing and Everything*. New York: McGraw-Hill, 2013.
Cloud, Preston. *Cosmos, Earth and Man: A Short History of the Universe*. New Haven, CT: Yale University Press, 1978.
Meadows, Dennis L. *Rapport van de Club van Rome: De grenzen aan de groei*. Utrecht: Het Spectrum, Aula 500, 1972.
Meadows, Donella H., Dennis L. Meadows, Jørgen Randers, and William W. Behrens III. *The Limits to Growth: A Report for the Club of Rome Project on the Predicament of Mankind*. New York: Potomac Associates, 1972.
National Aeronautics and Space Administration. *Apollo 8: Christmas at the Moon*, 19 December 2014. https://www.nasa.gov/topics/history/features/apollo_8.html.
National Aeronautics and Space Administration. *Apollo 8 Onboard Voice Transcription, as recorded on the spacecraft onboard recorder (data storage equipment)*, January 1969. Houston: Manned Spacecraft Center, 1969.
National Aeronautics and Space Administration. *Apollo 8 Technical Air-to-Ground Voice Transcription (Goss Net 1)*, December 1968. Houston: Manned Spacecraft Center, 1968.
National Public Radio. "On Anniversary of Apollo 8, How the 'Earthrise' Photo Was Made," 23 December 2013. https://www.npr.org/sections/thetwo-way/2013/12/23/256605845/on-anniversary-of-apollo-8-how-the-earthrise-photo-was-made?t=1532414548855
Poole, Robert. *Earthrise: How Man First Saw the Earth*. New Haven, CT: Yale University Press, 2008.
Sagan, Carl. *Cosmos*. New York: Random House, 1980.
Spier, Fred. *The Structure of Big History: From the Big Bang until Today*. Amsterdam: Amsterdam University Press, 1996.
Spier, Fred. *Big History and the Future of Humanity*. Oxford: Wiley Blackwell, 2010.
Spier, Fred. *Big History and the Future of Humanity*, 2nd ed. Oxford: Wiley Blackwell, 2015.
Spier, Fred. *The Structure of Big History: From the Big Bang until Today*. Amsterdam: Amsterdam University Press, 1996.
Von Humboldt, Alexander. *Kosmos: Entwurf einer physischen Weltbeschreibung*. Stuttgart and Augsburg, J. G. Cotta'scher: Verlag, 1845–1862.
Woods, David, and Frank O'Brien. *The Apollo 8 Flight Journal*, version 10, April 2017, https://history.nasa.gov/afj/ap08fj/index.html.

NOTES

1. Some later representations of this conversation contain discrepancies concerning who said what. This is mostly the result of the voices of Frank Borman and Bill Anders sounding rather similar. The version used here is the one found in the *Apollo 8 Onboard Voice Transcription* from January 1969, the most authoritative source. See also Woods and O'Brien 2017. For a visualization of those moments plus the original audio recording, see National Public Radio 2013.

2. Dennis Meadows, *Rapport van de Club van Rome: De grenzen aan de groei* (Utrecht & Antwerpen: Het Spectrum, Aula 500, 1972), 7.

Chapter Two

Investing in Disaster

Technical Progress and the Taboo of Diminishing Returns

David Witzling

"An affluent society, that is also both compassionate and rational, would, no doubt, secure to all who needed it the minimum income essential for decency and comfort." —John Kenneth Galbraith

In some ways, in the West, science now resembles a religion, commanding an uncritical faith that new technologies will solve all manner of social, environmental, and economic problems. Although rational science has certainly improved humanity's lot in life, organised science is no longer strictly rational, and needs new criteria for "progress." The catechism teaches the following: Humans are tool-making technologists. Rational science is the pinnacle of human achievement. Methodological inquiry can uncover and control all secrets of nature. Science and technology always improve. Every new technological development supersedes whatever came before. Increased investments in organised science repeatedly improve our lives with new innovations. If only our barbarous ancestors had discovered science sooner, their hellish lives wouldn't have been so "solitary, poor, nasty, brutish and short."[1]

As with many belief systems, the dogmas of organised science interfere with critical inquiry. "Revolutionary" new gadgets appear daily, but technology journalists never write: "If you're most concerned with a long, healthy life, this new product is just so-so compared to what is already available, but hey, so is more or less *everything invented since 1950!*" Whatever any "upgrade" may purport to "revolutionise" on behalf of consumers, reporters routinely celebrate gadgets, but are rarely historians, economists, or computer scientists. The idea that Western societies might be better off with *less* technology is rarely discussed. Instead, "faith" in science as the infallible engine of technology tends to preclude the idea that global challenges like hunger and climate change might be best resolved without technical innovation. Yet it is more important now than ever before to examine the role of technology in Western society, and to evaluate the role of diminishing returns in our social relationships with technology.

THE SOCIAL CONSEQUENCES OF DIMINISHING RETURNS

Diminishing returns predicts that repeated investments yield proportionally fewer benefits. The idea is straightforward: if somebody eats five ice cream cones in a row, the first may be delicious, but the fifth may cause a stomach ache. Because organised science is a social enterprise bound up with organised industry and structured finance, the economic law of diminishing returns implies limits on the efficiency of technology research. In economics, diminishing returns is a scientific law, which means it is descriptive rather than explanatory. While in casual speech, *theory* implies "conjecture" whereas *law* implies "certainty," within scientific disciplines, laws are not categorically superior to theories, but assert a different kind of knowledge. Newton's laws of gravity do not explain why gravity is invisible, or why bodies attract, but this law describes and predicts gravitational interactions quite precisely; Darwin's theory of evolution explains the differentiation of species in terms of natural selection, but cannot be used to calculate what the biosphere will look like in ten thousand years.

Consider an analogy: the laws of physics may describe the trajectory of a football, but cannot explain why the football makes some spectators cheer while others groan. The practice of explaining involves crafting a description of some phenomenon that captures relevant generalities, and which connects observations to relevant laws.[2]

In this chapter, I explore diminishing returns where organised science meets industrial food production, modern medicine, and the computer industry. I also discuss why organised science—under its current techno-centric ideology—is improperly equipped to address the problems humanity faces in the next century. Many of the problems human societies face at this juncture in history are better resolved through policy measures, and the West's emphasis on technological solutions marginalises effective investments in simpler strategies.

A CLOSER LOOK AT THE PROBLEM

In a 2017 appeal for financial contributions, Susan Hockfield, president of the American Association for the Advancement of Science (AAAS), wrote to her members:

> With the world population predicted to grow to more than 9 billion by 2050, we face daunting challenges, including the need for improved access to sufficient food, clean water, sustainable energy and health care. These needs will only be met through fundamental scientific and engineering research, accompanied by the translation of that research into market-ready applications.[3]

With government officials, industrialists, and academics among its ranks, the AAAS speaks for organised science in the United States. Their advocacy, however, furthers the needs of industry more than the search for scientific truth. While the AAAS's appeal for more "scientific and engineering research" may sound straightforward, on closer inspection, many of the challenges described may have effective nontechnical solutions.

As I discuss in this chapter, a relatively small number of policy changes could provide for many people. The major impediments are not technical, but entrenched Western cultural habits and organised industry's control over those habits. Westerners need a way to think clearly about options rarely discussed in the commercial speech of organised industry—or in its echoes on commercial social media.

In the United States, Americans face rational and moral choices about how to best use available resources, but many important choices are not on the AAAS's advocacy agenda. Americans could feed and clothe millions by sharing surplus production with the developing world (even though sharing is un-American). The default approach—in the name of "progress"—addresses humanitarian problems by investing in uncertain new technologies like CRISPR gene editing, atmospheric reengineering, and vat-grown meat, despite unresolved ecological, consumer safety, and ethical concerns. While Western science as "the search for truth" has a long history, winding through medieval monasteries, Moorish Spain, and Pythagorean mystery cults, "progress" is a relatively recent idea, and "making progress in the name of science" is a largely untested basis for social organization. For millennia, Westerners viewed the future sceptically and the remote past idealistically. In Antiquity, Greeks and Romans considered humanity to have degraded since a lost Golden Age; Abrahamic peoples bewail a lost Eden; the Renaissance venerated Antiquity; and then, somewhere between the European Enlightenment and Modernity, the past suddenly began to look exceedingly barbaric, and the future seemed increasingly tractable through rational control.

To frame a big-picture view: the human genus is roughly 2.5 million years old, behaviourally modern humans appeared perhaps fifty thousand years ago, and agriculture appeared with civilization about ten thousand years ago.[4] Human societies changed little until about two hundred and fifty years ago, after the West rediscovered Roman knowledge and started burning coal because of deforestation. These and related developments, often called "progress," have brought the planet to the brink of ecological catastrophe in an evolutionary split second. Given that the average mammal lasts about one million years,[5] our modern, civilised, tool-making brains may yet be a failed evolutionary experiment, more a liability than a survival advantage. If we are to think about the future and work for better outcomes, another approach is needed. Increasing investments in technical "progress" are unlikely to be effective or efficient, and, in what follows, I discuss why.

THE RISE OF INDUSTRIAL FOOD PRODUCTION

Throughout the twentieth century, organised science, allied with organised industry, promised food security through technical innovation. Thomas Malthus's 1798 *Essay on Population* influenced modern concerns about food security on a growing planet; in line with these concerns, technical innovations in early twentieth-century agriculture, including industrial fertilizer, mechanized farm equipment, and rural electrification, increased crop yields dramatically.

Yet, remarkably, fears of global food shortage persist into the twenty-first century, even though most of the basic problems of production were solved in Charlie Chaplin's time. Harvard economist John Kenneth Galbraith considered it a "modern paradox" that "as production has increased in modern times concern for production seems also to have increased."[6] Paradoxically, dramatic increases in industrial output helped precipitate the Great Depression, which involved a price collapse alongside the famous stock market collapse (figure 2.1). Given how indelibly cultural memories of the Great Depression linger in the American psyche, it is also remarkable to note that the hungriest years of the Depression were years of unprecedented agricultural abundance.[7] Technically, the 1929 market failure was a failure of distribution, not production: the market-based price system failed to get food to the hungry.

Many factors contributed to the 1929 economic disaster, including geopolitical strife, unregulated economic forces, organised industry expanding into agricultural markets, and a price bubble. The cultural movement known as *Modernism* also exerted influence on both sides of the Atlantic, fetishizing the miracles of industry along with anything new in art or society. These factors converged on the US economy during World War I. Because the war

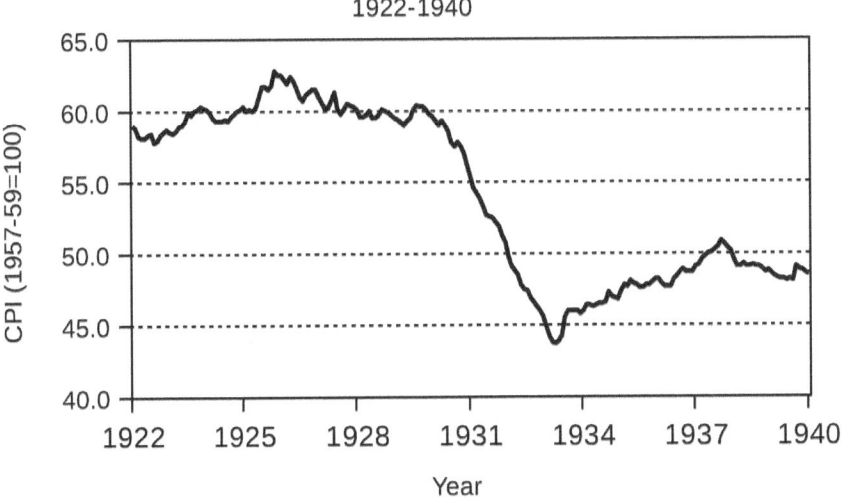

Figure 2.1. US Consumer Price Index (CPI), 1922–1940. Widespread overproduction during the "Roaring '20s" contributed to a price collapse. *Source data from National Bureau of Economic Research series M04128USM350NNBR and Federal Reserve Bank of St. Louis*

ravaged European farmlands, US grain exports increased: wheat exports peaked twice, once at 37.3 percent of production in 1914, and again at 37.1 percent in 1920.[8] Throughout World War I, annual US wheat production averaged 812,932,000 bushels. With an average 27.36 percent dedicated to exports, annual domestic supply averaged 590,118,000 bushels.[9] As Europe recovered, wheat exports fell to 16.6 percent of production in 1928; by 1933, exports stood at just 4.6 percent.[10] Wheat prices peaked in 1925 and hit bottom in 1932; over this period, production averaged 837,329,000 bushels annually and exports averaged 15.3 percent, with domestic supply averaging 709,217,000 bushels. Although peacetime output was comparable to the boom years, exports declined.

Since farmers never slowed production as exports declined, domestic supply increased considerably, contributing to a price collapse. Furthermore, farmers held mortgages they suddenly couldn't afford; hence, other areas of the economy were threatened, causing panic to spread. After the 1929 price collapse, wheat farmers increased production through 1931, before realizing that it is impossible to out-produce the problems of overproduction. When Congress finally acted in 1933, total wheat stocks stood at 377,942,000 bushels—nearly four times the 108,401,000 bushels in stocks when prices peaked in 1925.[11] But the market failed to deliver this unprecedented abundance to those in need, families lost their land, and millions went hungry.

AGRICULTURAL PRODUCTIVITY AND THE GREAT DEPRESSION

Alongside dramatic increases in the quantity of basic goods manufactured, organised industry also increased its *productivity*, a term used by economists to measure labour efficiency. As agriculture underwent a wave of industrialization between 1920 and the 1929 crash, the US population increased by roughly fifty million, from 105,711,000 to 120,694,000; in this same time, however, farm populations *dropped* by roughly one million, from 31,614,000 to 30,220,0000.[12] Amidst all the starvation and declining farm populations, where was the over-abundance coming from?

Some clues can be found in the Agricultural Adjustment Act of 1933. Attempting to rein in the collapse, Congress sought to stabilise farm prices, regulate aggregate demand, and protect the financial system connecting agriculture to industry. In the 1933 Act's "Declaration of Policy," Congress established a standard for agricultural prices, excepting tobacco, calculated from prebubble "base period" data between 1909 and 1913.[13] Congress recognised that "the present state of acute economic emergency" was "in part the consequence of a severe and increasing disparity between the prices of agricultural and other commodities, which . . . has largely destroyed the purchasing power of farmers for industrial products," and "broken down the orderly exchange of commodities." Consequently, the economic downturn "seriously impaired the agricultural assets supporting the national credit structure."[14]

Understanding the role of diminishing returns in the 1929 disaster requires critically appraising agricultural industrialization and mechanization. In discussing his policy objectives for agriculture in 1916, President Woodrow Wilson advocated a "generous provision for the improvement of farm production."[15] Additionally, some three years after the Federal Reserve System was created, President Wilson took "particular note of the special needs of the farmer by making larger provisions for loans through national banks on farm mortgages."[16] As policy wove together agriculture, finance, and industry, war came and went. Wheat exports declined between the First and Second World Wars, while policy encouraged increased output. In 1927, exports declined to 21.7 percent, and to 15.6 percent in 1928. Purchases of industrial farm equipment, however, increased.[17] Between 1922 (just after the war boom) and 1927 (just before exports fell off sharply), farmers purchased an annual average of $126,729,000 in motorised tractors, combines, power hay pressers, and the like.[18] Farmers purchased $183,862,000 worth of powered farm equipment in 1928, and, in 1929, purchases increased to $223,308,000.[19]

In agriculture and across industry, much of the increase in output during the first half of the twentieth century "can reasonably be imputed to technological improvement in capital and parallel improvement in the people who devise the better capital equipment and operate it."[20] The result of unbridled "progress" in farm technology, however, struck a point of diminishing returns, where repeated investments yielded proportionally fewer benefits. The market price of agriculture's output could no longer support repeated investments in industrial technology. As Congress observed in the Agricultural Adjustment Act, the result was a decline in the "purchasing power of farmers for industrial products" which threatened "the national credit structure." Too much technology proved disastrous, creating second-order problems requiring their own increasingly complex and costly solutions.[21]

ISSUES IN CONTEMPORARY AGRICULTURAL PRODUCTIVITY

Diminishing marginal utility is not unique to technical "progress." In the US dairy industry between 1850 and 1910, labour productivity declined by 17.5 percent due to the inherent "costliness of animal husbandry" combined with other demands of bureaucratic modernity: new sanitation requirements, adapting dairy farming to winter months, and changes in industrial feeding practices.[22] Organised industry amplifies diminishing returns, however, because industry is complex and costly. Industrial agriculture costs more than subsistence farming in part because it is more resource-intensive.[23] According to archaeologist Joseph Tainter, whenever it "becomes necessary to use less economical resources marginal returns automatically decline."[24] The industrialization of agriculture was characterised by diminished marginal returns because expenditures on industrial farm equipment, fertilizer, and energy increased, as did the cost of infrastructure and management.

Rationally, it seems unlikely, as Hockfield and the AAAS advocate, that additional investments in "fundamental scientific and engineering research, accompanied by the translation of that research into market-ready applications" will be the most efficient way to address "access to sufficient food" for a "world population predicted to grow to more than 9 billion by 2050." The West does not need to tolerate hunger anywhere now or in the foreseeable future. Developed nations waste somewhere between 30% and 50% of annual food production.[25] Industrial food waste, by tonnage, is nearly identical to the projected need of sub-Saharan Africa,[26] where UN statistics place most population growth in the next half century.[27] The means to end hunger have existed for a long time and the cost of doing so is marginal, but it simply isn't a serious policy objective in the West.

Since 2005, when the US Congress required ethanol blended into gasoline, fuel now accounts for roughly 40% of US domestic corn production, the artificial demand for which increases the price of a key food staple in "developing" nations.[28] Roughly 70% more calories could be made available for direct human consumption if diverted from current use for biofuels and animal feed, potentially yielding enough calories to provide a subsistence for approximately four billion people.[29] On average, livestock are fed six kilograms of plant protein to produce one kilogram of meat, and the fossil fuel energy inputs for producing animal protein are roughly eleven times greater than grain.[30] Given that industrial agriculture accounts for 17% of US fossil fuel use,[31] a simple and cost-effective measure available to typical Americans who want to reduce their carbon footprints and fight global hunger may simply be to reduce meat consumption and rely less on industrial agriculture. Unfortunately, existing policy encourages the current state of affairs.

PROGRESS IN MODERN MEDICINE

The requirements for bringing effective medicine to the world's poorest residents are quite modest in terms of technological needs, though made formidable thanks to Western preferences for solutions that are organizationally complex, technologically sophisticated, costly to administer, and therefore profitable to supply and finance. As with other areas of socioeconomic activity, repeated investments in modern medicine exhibit diminishing marginal returns. Magnetic resonance imaging scans, Viagra, and electronic record-keeping all have their place, but many of modern medicine's most potent innovations, from surgery to preventive medicine, largely depend on a few basic innovations: hygiene, anaesthetics, antibiotics, and immunization.

After the polio vaccine became widespread in 1955, modern medicine's productivity declined precipitously (figure 2.2).[32] This happened partially because easier problems get solved first; in the words of physicist Max Planck: "with every advance the difficulty of the task is increased."[33] As the law of diminishing returns predicts, solving more difficult technical problems costs more because it requires specialised training and higher-paid executives to finance and administer it all.[34] Accordingly, many disciplines today are dominated by highly trained specialists concerned with extremely esoteric problems, resulting in an increasing cost per solution.[35] This is why increasing investments in medical technology do not continue to yield proportionally greater increases in life expectancy (figure 2.3).

In modern medicine, the germ theory's success explaining disease gave credence to the outlandish views of Ignaz Semmelweis, a nineteenth-century obstetrician who, after observing better outcomes among certain physicians

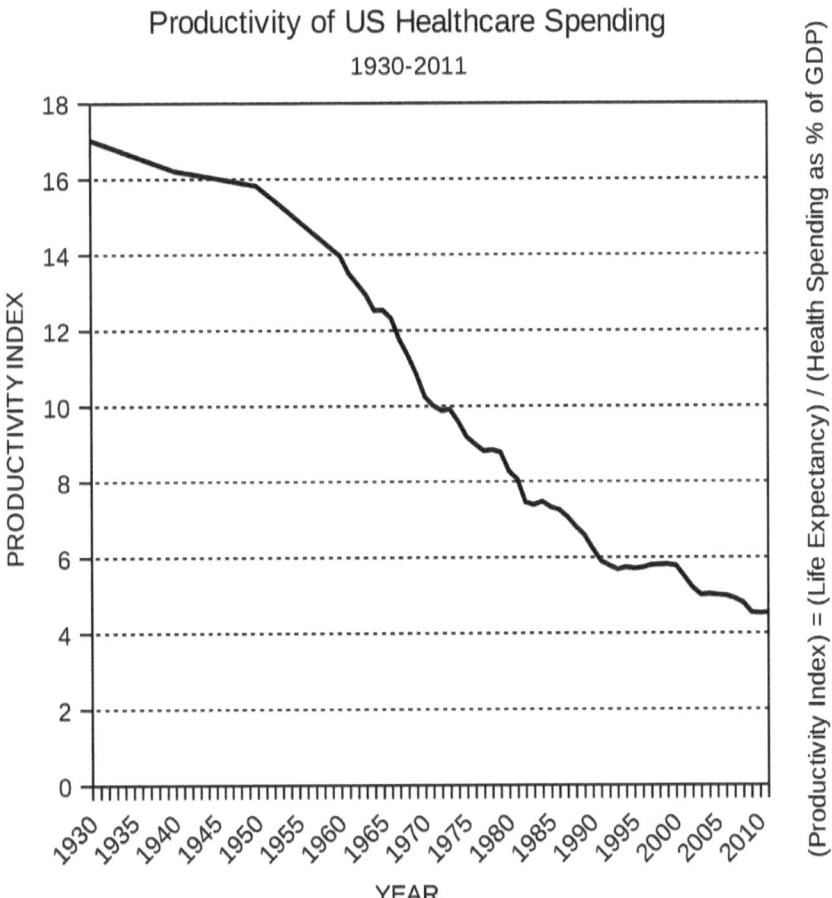

Figure 2.2. Productivity of the US health care system, 1930–2011. *After Joseph Tainter, The Collapse of Complex Societies (1988), ch. 4, fig. 11. Life expectancy data acquired from from Clio Infra (EU), compiled by Richard Zijdeman and Filipa Ribeiro da Silva (IISH Dataverse). Healthcare expenditure and GDP data from US Census Bureau and World Scientific Handbook of Global Health Economics and Public Policy (ed. Richard M. Scheffler, 2016), 198, Table 5: "Decennial employment and expenditures 1850–2010."*

at Vienna General Hospital, perversely advocated that doctors wash their hands. Thanks to various types of painkillers and anaesthetics, few patients now die of neurogenic shock watching a limb get hacked off. The few tens of thousands of dollars spent developing penicillin in the 1930s has benefited every Westerner who has ever had surgery or chlamydia, or who has been

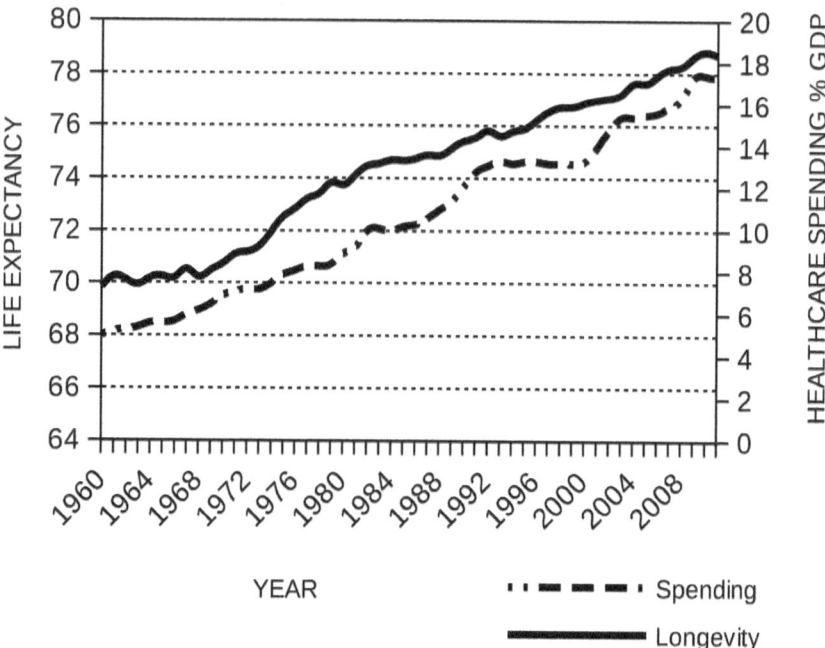

Figure 2.3. US longevity vs. healthcare spending. While life expectancy increased 12% in the second half of the 20th century, healthcare spending by GDP more than doubled. *Life-expectancy data from US Census Bureau and Clio Infra (IISH Dataverse). Pre-1960 spending figures from World Scientific Handbook of Global Health Economics and Public Policy, Table 5: Decennial employment and expenditures 1850–2010 (ed. Richard Scheffler, 2016).*

bitten by a deer tick. Very few medical developments can claim so many beneficiaries for so few dollars.

Since immunization became common in the 1950s, modern medicine's focus has shifted increasingly to niche problems like X-linked hypophosphatemia and autosomal dominant polycystic kidney disease, and to addressing the adverse health effects of industrial civilization itself on environmental toxicity, poor diet, sedentary lifestyle, and infectious disease among high population densities. By gross domestic product, the United States spends two to three times more on healthcare than other developed nations (figure 2.4), but, as diminishing returns predicts, American life expectancy is not proportionally greater than that of citizens of analogous European heritages in, say, Luxembourg or Germany (figure 2.5). US life expectancy in the twentieth century increased dramatically, from just under fifty to just over seventy-five by the year 2000. Modern longevity is not, however, unique to medical "progress." A detailed study that set out "to assess the mortality profiles of all extant hunter-gatherers for which sufficient high-quality demographic data exist"[36] found that "conditional upon surviving to age 15, for our composite categories of hunter-gatherers, forager-horticulturalists, and acculturated hunter-gatherers . . . the sample of premodern populations shows an average modal adult life span of about 72 years, with a range of 68–78 years." After two hundred and fifty years of "progress," we in the West are for the most part just living for as long as our bodies evolved to survive (figure 2.4).

If life extension can be considered a frontier of medical science, there is a lesson here for those who dream of popping youth pills while snacking on potato chips and watching television. When Faust asked Mephistopheles to cure him of his age, the devil retorted that neither magic nor physicians were required: "Just go into the fields and see what fun it is to dig and hoe; live simply and keep all your thoughts on a few simple objects glued; restrict yourself and eat the plainest food . . . that is the surest remedy: at eighty you would still be young."[37] Modern medicine is largely devoted to solving problems caused by civilization, and many improvements during the late twentieth century may reasonably be attributed to simpler developments from the early twentieth century. Given that sanitation, anaesthetics, antibiotics, and immunization can address many risks and complications of childbirth, infancy, and childhood at little cost, an evidence-based approach might argue that, from the perspective of longevity and overall health, "progress" in medical science largely ended in the mid-1950s.

DIMINISHING RETURNS FOR FUN AND PROFIT

Perhaps few modern industries are as wholly characterised by "progress" as the computer industry, which aggressively markets a constant stream of hardware and software upgrades at consumers to induce eager anticipation for new conveniences and sensory pleasures on screens of all sizes.

The upgrade model is a key source of revenue for the software industry, a source of constant change and a driver of diminishing returns. Many businesses invested in computer technology following the release of Windows 95 because the graphic user interface offered clear usability and productivity advantages over the command line interface used in the earlier DOS operating system. Later Windows releases like Vista were heavily criticised,[38] however, for the frustration and lost productivity due to bugs, incompatibilities, new hardware requirements, and unexpected changes to the user inter-

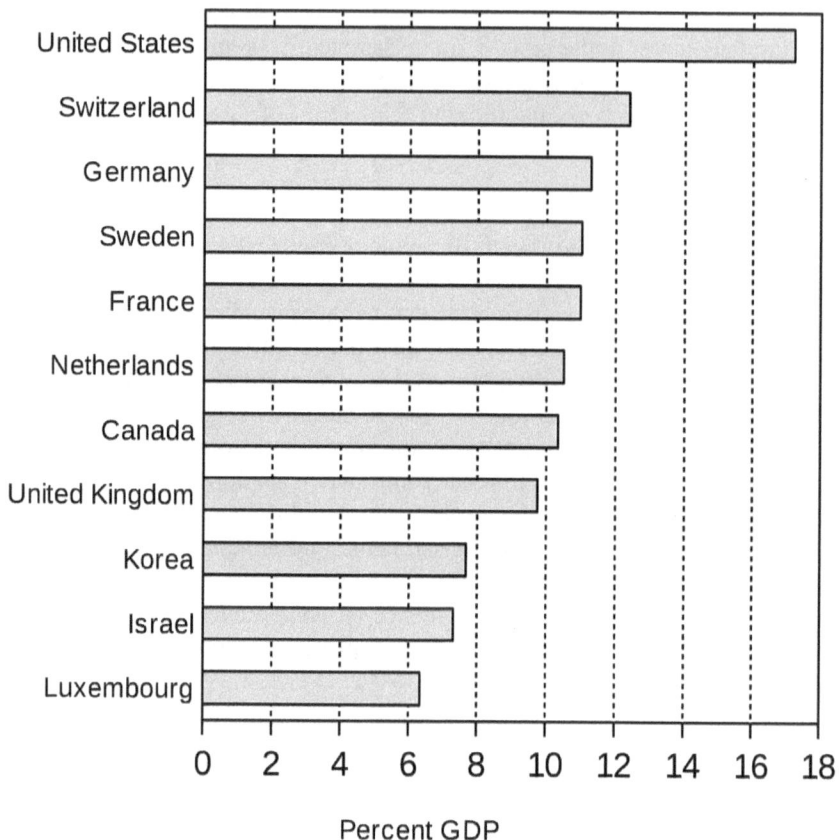

Figure 2.4. 2016 National healthcare expenditures as a percentage of GDP. *Source: Organization for Economic Cooperation and Development "Health expenditure and financing" data set*

face.[39] Commercial software upgrades like Vista offer computer users diminishing marginal utility for their existing computer investments.

Roughly one third of all computer users still ran Windows XP in 2013, just before Microsoft stopped issuing updates[40] (figure 2.6). Many computer users do not care to upgrade because, perhaps even indirectly, they recognise the trend towards diminishing returns. Although many users might prefer or require the stability of a familiar platform over some upgrade's new features,

20th Century Longevity Data Compared

Year	United States	France	Sweden	Luxembourg	Cuba	Argentina	Brazil
1905	49.3	48.3	54.5	46.2	34.2	39.7	
1910	51.8	51.3	57.8	49.7	36.0	44.2	31.0
1920	55.4	51.5	58.8	54.6	39.0	48.7	32.0
1930	59.6	56.8	63.2	56.8	42.0	52.6	34.0
1940	63.2	49.6	66.7	61.9	45.0	56.5	37.0
1950	68.1	66.4	71.1	66.0	59.4	62.5	51.0
1960	69.8	70.4	73.0	69.0	65.3	65.3	55.9
1970	70.7	72.1	74.7	69.6	71.0	67.2	59.8
1980	73.7	74.2	75.7	72.6	74.2	70.2	63.5
1990	75.4	76.8	77.6	75.4	74.8	72.1	67.5
2000	76.9	79.1	79.7	77.7	77.2	74.3	71.0

Figure 2.5. 20th-century longevity data compared. Note Ignaz Semmelwiss advocated handwashing around 1850, and surgeons often operated without masks until the 1890s. Despite a trade embargo restricting available funds to invest in modern medicine, Cuba managed to increase longevity because most of modern medicine is derived from a very few basic innovations. *Life-expectancy data from Max Roser, "Our World in Data" (Oxford).*

upgrades are routinely made compulsory. The installed base of commercialised Linux code on web servers, browsers, mobile devices, embedded devices, point of sale systems, and video arcade equipment[41] provides evidence outside of sales figures that many users and developers want a familiar, stable computing platform. Nonproprietary and cost-free software play an important role in the modern software "ecosystem," and the growth dynamics of commercial software must be understood in terms of "the market" simultaneously failing to provide for this need.

Microsoft maintains monopoly power through a variety of anticompetitive business practices,[42] with European legal fines around $3.4 billion in one decade[43] just representing a routine expense on the road to market domination. One such technique for compelling upgrades, called "vendor lock-in," leverages proprietary file formats to keep customers attached to specific

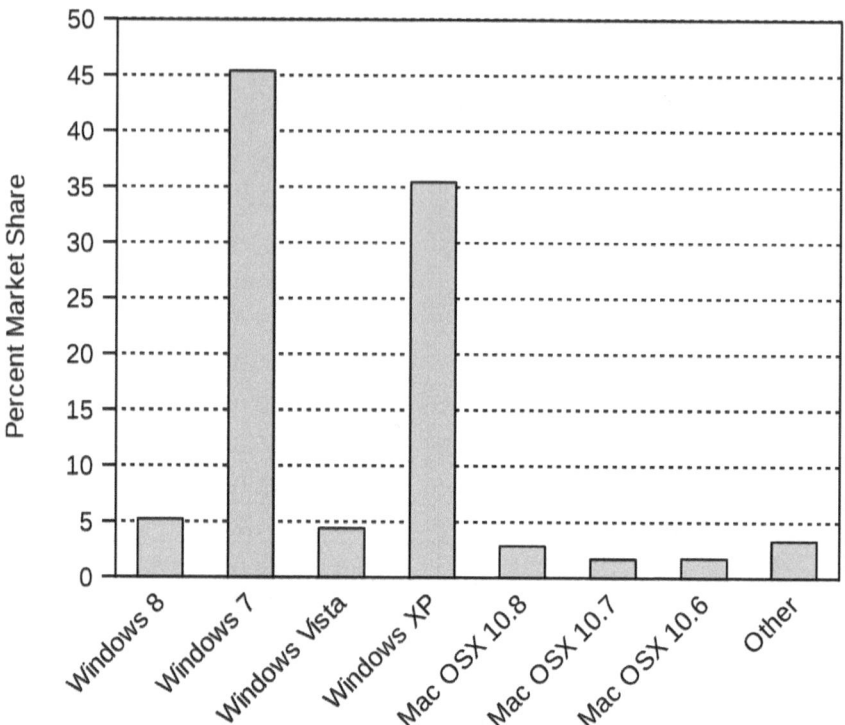

Figure 2.6. Operating system market share. Values are averaged across the year 2013, just before Microsoft stopped issuing security updates to Windows XP, then a 12-year-old operating system. *Data from Net Applications*

software packages, so that if the file format is changed, customers must upgrade to retain access to their data. A patent in the Microsoft Office file format prompted the Commonwealth of Massachusetts to establish an open standards policy in 2004.[44] Speaking at the time, Secretary of Administration and Finance Eric Kriss observed, "It should be reasonably obvious for a lay person who looks at the concept of Public Documents that we've got to keep them independent and free forever, because it is an overriding imperative of the American democratic system that we cannot have our public documents locked up in some kind of proprietary format or locked up in a format that you need to get a proprietary system to use some time in the future." For Massachusetts, the advantages of electronic record-keeping were as evident as certain disadvantages to perpetual commercial upgrades, and Microsoft eventually capitulated, opening their file formats.[45]

Many car owners would consider it absurd if gasoline were reformulated to require an entirely new engine every three years, although this is the routine cost of doing business in the computer world. Schools that train students for specialised industry-standard software get caught in the upgrade cycle along with students, and the compounded social impact of diminishing returns in software investments will only increase as more computing devices are put into use. In 2002, the US National Institute of Standards and Technology estimated that, shared between consumers and producers, the cost of bugs and incompatibilities stood around $59 billion,[46] even though total software sales only amounted to $180 billion.[47]

Many cost-free and open-source software components exist, awaiting only organised labour to put them to use. As an alternative to subsidizing industry, some business owners might consider financing or developing custom software solutions built around open standards. University administrators with a tight budget and ongoing software needs might consider developing similar grant-funded open-source solutions to provide practical coding and visual design experience for students. Open-source collaborations and casual "piracy" may both continue to be common ways of acquiring high-quality software in virtue of an informal recognition that the cost of doing business in the computer world is not always worth it, and probably exploitative. Growth trends in the software industry may not accurately reflect the whole range of consumer preferences, however, due to the coercive business practices built around the upgrade cycle. Indirect costs like lost productivity and security holes subsidise a growth industry built around poorly made products. In the words of Dan Geer, Chief Information Security Officer at the CIA's venture capital firm In-Q-Tel, "the only two products not covered by product liability today are religion and software, and software should not escape for much longer."[48]

CONCLUSION

As with agriculture in the 1920s, disaster may well loom on the horizon today, where computerization and artificial intelligence are poised to displace portions of the traditional white collar workforce, much as mechanization and automation displaced blue collar workers in the twentieth century (figure 2.7).

Large swaths of the world live with disaster daily, and if Westerners want to talk seriously about need in the twenty-first century, we need to talk about how problems like global hunger are the result of policy, not an opportunity for high-tech, market-based solutions. It is for policy reasons that Americans burn excess grain production instead of feeding the hungry. The dynamics of diminishing returns make it unlikely that solving the social problems of the

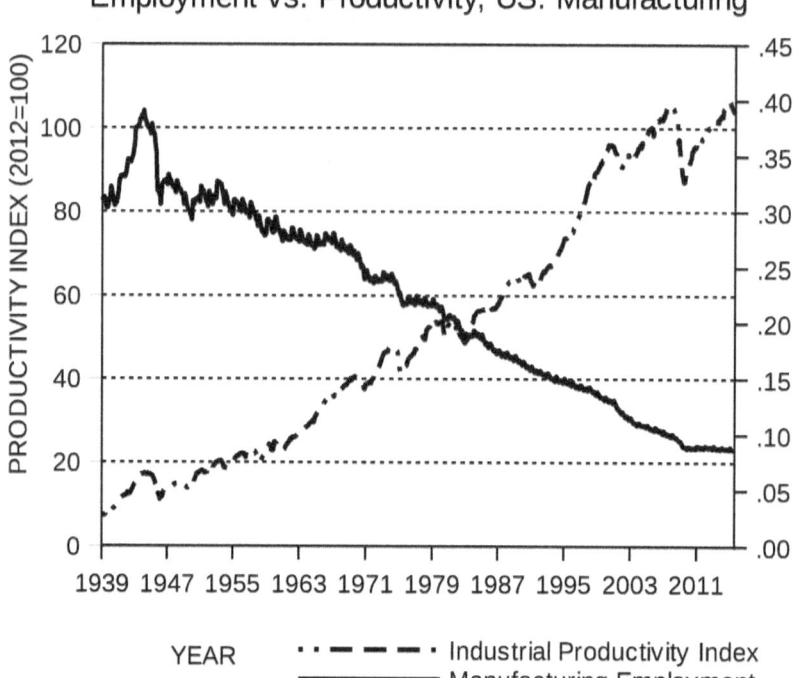

Figure 2.7. Employment vs. productivity, US manufacturing, 1939–2015. Gains in productivity due to automation and mechanization have translated directly into job losses. *Data from St. Louis Federal Reserve, INDPRO and MANEMP/PAYNSA data series*

modern world require "fundamental scientific and engineering research, accompanied by the translation of that research into market-ready applications." Historically and at present, the industrial system exists for the owners of capital, not for ordinary individuals. If industry existed for individuals and their needs, historic increases in productivity would have translated into employers asking employees if they would prefer more pay, a shorter workweek, or, perhaps, more say in management practices. Instead, major employers locked in the forty-hour workweek as a cultural norm, shed jobs, and enjoyed their increasingly financialised wealth.

The basic problems of production and public health were solved nearly a century ago. Effective solutions to the "daunting challenges" we will face on a planet of "more than 9 billion" will most likely need to be policy solutions, not technical solutions. Moral arguments in favour of market-based solutions to human need must address the implication that all need today is prima facie evidence of markets failing to solve these problems. As presently constituted, markets are unlikely to solve these problems in the future. When one looks at how the dynamics of diminishing returns weave through different areas of industrial commerce, a systems approach to policy solutions begins to take shape. For example, global climate change conferences are elaborate, opulent, expensive, high-security affairs—and unlikely to accomplish much, especially if attendees insist on complex "market-based" approaches like "cap and trade" management of industrial carbon dioxide. An alternate approach might target energy use with an "industrial remediation tax" that would invest tax revenues in conservation measures known to be effective, returning wealth captured through misguided policies to those who produced the wealth both in the West and abroad.

If policy made energy more expensive, energy use would decrease. Decreased energy use would reduce carbon dioxide emissions without burning fossil fuels to make expensive wind turbines or solar panels. Because industrial meat production is so energy-intensive, the cost of meat would increase and consumers would consume less. Beyond the emissions and animal welfare issues that can be addressed by dramatically reducing meat consumption, changes in industrial meat production can also address ecological issues associated with agricultural runoff from fertilizer and manure. Ruminant animals evolved while eating grasses. Since industrial meat production typically feeds these animals a grain diet, their slow stomachs breed harmful bacteria like *salmonella* and *E. coli*. Because livestock typically live in crowded, stressful, unhygienic conditions, as much as 80% of the antibiotics used in the United States are administered to livestock prophylactically.[49]

If these bacteria develop immunity to antibiotics, medicine will become more expensive because an old problem will need a new and difficult solution. The mass production of cheap hamburgers in America is a threat to one of modern medicine's most crucial tools; this can and should be addressed through agricultural policy. Policies that have the result of encouraging healthier diets may also have beneficial effects on quality of life and longevity without requiring new technologies or increasing investments in medical science. Yet it is an odd symptom of our new world order that typical Americans may be able to do more about the weather through dieting than about policy through the ballot box.

BIBLIOGRAPHY

Berlind, David. "Microsoft: We Were Railroaded in Massachusetts on ODF." *ZDNET*, 17 October 2005. http://www.zdnet.com/article/microsoft-we-were-railroaded-in-massachusetts-on-odf.

Durham, Jr., Joel. "Quick Fixes for Five Nasty Vista Problems." *PC Magazine*, 14 March 2007. https://www.pcmag.com/article2/0,2817,2104022,00.asp.

Finley, Klint. "Linux Took over the Web, Now It's Taking over the World." *Wired*, 25 August 2016. https://www.wired.com/2016/08/linux-took-web-now-taking-world.

Galbraith, John Kenneth. *The Affluent Society*. Boston: Houghton Mifflin, 1964.

Geer, Dan. "Cybersecurity as Realpolitic." Keynote, Black Hat Conference, Las Vegas, 6 August 2014. http://geer.tinho.net/geer.blackhat.6viii14.txt.

Goethe. *Faust*. Translated by Walter Kaufmann. New York: Doubleday, 1961.

Gurven, Michael, and Hillard Kaplan. "Longevity Among Hunter-Gatherers." *Population and Development Review* 33, no. 2 (June 2017): 321–65.

Hobbes, Thomas. *Leviathan*. In *Modern Political Thought*, edited by David Wooten, 122–302. Indianapolis: Hackett Publishing Company, 1996.

Jones, Chuck. "Bring Back Apple's Mac vs. PC Ads since Windows XP Isn't Supported." *Forbes*, 14 April 2014. https://www.forbes.com/sites/chuckjones/2014/04/14/bring-back-apples-mac-vs-pc-ads-since-windows-xp-isnt-supported.

Jones, Pamela. "The Jan. 14th Eric Kriss Speech on Open Formats." Groklaw, 18 January 2005. https://web.archive.org/web/20150906123901/http://www.groklaw.net/articlebasic.php?story=2005011807275883.

Jones, Pamela. "Microsoft Litigation Resource Page." Groklaw, 7 January 2005. https://web.archive.org/web/20170703231435/http://www.groklaw.net/articlebasic.php?story=20041228040645419.

Kanter, James. "European Regulators Fine Microsoft, Then Promise to Do Better." *New York Times*, 6 March 2013. http://www.nytimes.com/2013/03/07/technology/eu-fines-microsoft-over-browser.html.

McKenna, Maryn. "Update: Farm Animals Get 80 Percent of Antibiotics Sold in U.S." *Wired*, 24 December 2010. https://www.wired.com/2010/12/news-update-farm-animals-get-80-of-antibiotics-sold-in-us.

PBS. "The Current Mass Extinction." Evolution. http://www.pbs.org/wgbh/evolution/library/03/2/l_032_04.html.

Pickerell, John. "Timeline: Human Evolution." *New Scientist*, 4 September 2006. https://www.newscientist.com/article/dn9989-timeline-human-evolution.

Pimentel, David, and Marcia Pimentel. "Sustainability of Meat-Based and Plant-Based Diets and the Environment." *The American Journal of Clinical Nutrition* 78, suppl. (2003): 660S–63S.

Pylyshyn, Zenon. *Computation and Cognition*. Cambridge, MA: MIT Press, 1984.

Rice, Tim. "Biofuels Are Driving Food Prices Higher." *Guardian*, 1 June 2011. https://www.theguardian.com/global-development/poverty-matters/2011/jun/01/biofuels-driving-food-prices-higher.

RTI. *Planning Report 02-03: The Economic Impacts of Inadequate Infrastructure for Software Testing*. Gaithersburg, MD: National Institute of Standards and Technology, 2002.

Tainter, Joseph. *The Collapse of Complex Societies*. Cambridge: Cambridge University Press, 1988.

United Nations, Department of Economic and Social Affairs, Population Division. *World Population Prospects: The 2015 Revision, Key Findings and Advance Tables*. New York: United Nations, 2015.

United States Congress. *Agricultural Adjustment Act of 1933*. In Vol. II, *Documents of American History*, edited by Henry Steele Commager, 4th ed., 422–26. New York: Appleton-Century-Crofts, 1948.

United States Department of Agriculture. *Agricultural Statistics 1939*. Washington, DC: United States Government Printing Office, 1939.

Vaughan-Nichols, Steven J. "The 10 Worst Operating Systems of All Time." *PC World*, 9 April 2009. https://www.pcworld.com/article/162866/worst_operating_system.html.

West, Paul C., James S. Gerber, Peder M. Engstom, Nathaniel. D. Mueller, Kate A. Brauman, Kimberly M. Carlson, Emily S. Cassidy, et al. "Leverage Points for Improving Global Food Security and the Environment." *Science* 345, no. 6194 (18 July 2014): 325–28.

NOTES

1. Thomas Hobbes, *Leviathan*, in *Modern Political Thought*, ed. David Wootton (Hackett Publishing Company, 1996), 171.
2. Zenon Pylyshyn, *Computation and Cognition* (MIT Press, 1984), 1–21.
3. AAAS member correspondence via post; similar wording can be found on AAAS webpage. Archived at https://web.archive.org/web/*/https://www.aaas.org/news/new-aaas-president-emphasizes-making-case-science.
4. John Pickerell, "Timeline: Human Evolution," *New Scientist*, 4 September 2006, https://www.newscientist.com/article/dn9989-timeline-human-evolution.
5. PBS Evolution Library, "The Current Mass Extinction," http://www.pbs.org/wgbh/evolution/library/03/2/l_032_04.html.
6. John Kenneth Galbraith, *The Affluent Society* (Houghton Mifflin, 1964), 99.
7. Galbraith, *Affluent Society*, 222.
8. USDA, *Agricultural Statistics 1939* (US Government Printing Office, 1939), 9–10.
9. USDA, *Agricultural Statistics 1939*, 9–10.
10. USDA, *Agricultural Statistics 1939*, 9–10.
11. USDA, *Agricultural Statistics 1939*, 23.
12. USDA, *Agricultural Statistics 1939*, 484.
13. US Congress, *Agricultural Adjustment Act of 1933*, in *Documents of American History*, ed. Henry Steele Commager (Appleton-Century-Crofts, 1948), vol. II, 423.
14. Congress, *Agricultural Adjustment Act*, 423.
15. President Wilson, letter to A. F. Lever dated 11 August 1916, in Commager, *Documents*, vol. II, 294.
16. Wilson, letter to A. F. Lever, 296.
17. USDA, *Agricultural Statistics 1939*, 489.
18. USDA, *Agricultural Statistics 1939*, 489.
19. USDA, *Agricultural Statistics 1939*, 489.
20. Galbraith, *Affluent Society*, 104.
21. Joseph Tainter, *The Collapse of Complex Societies* (Cambridge University Press, 1988), 116.
22. Tainter, *Collapse*, 95.
23. Tainter, *Collapse*, 91.
24. Tainter, *Collapse*, 95.
25. Paul C. West, James S. Gerber, Peder M. Engstrom, et al., "Leverage Points for Improving Global Food Security and the Environment," *Science* (18 July 2014), issue 6194: 327.
26. Jenny Gustavsson, Cristel Cederberg, Ulf Sonesson, et al., *Global Food Losses and Food Waste—Extent, Causes and Prevention*, (Food and Agriculture Organization of the United Nations, 2011), 5.
27. United Nations, *World Population Prospects: The 2015 Revision, Key Findings and Advance Tables* (Department of Economic and Social Affairs, 2015), Working Paper No. ESA/P/WP.241, 3.
28. Tim Rice, "Biofuels are driving food prices higher," *Guardian* (1 June 2011), https://www.theguardian.com/global-development/poverty-matters/2011/jun/01/biofuels-driving-food-prices-higher.
29. West, Gerber, Engstrom, et al., "Leverage Points," 326.
30. David Pimentel and Marcia Pimentel, "Sustainability of meat-based and plant-based diets and the environment," *The American Journal of Clinical Nutrition* (2003), 78(suppl): 661S–62S.
31. Pimentel and Pimentel, "Sustainability," 660S.
32. Tainter, *Collapse*, 103.
33. Tainter, *Collapse*, 114.
34. Tainter, *Collapse*, 99–105.
35. Tainter, *Collapse*, 99–102.
36. Michael Gurven and Hillard Kaplan, "Longevity among Hunter-Gatherers," *Population and Development Review* (June 2017), 33(2): 334.

37. Goethe, *Faust*, trans. Walter Kaufmann (Doubleday Anchor Books, 1961), 235.

38. Steven J. Vaughan-Nichols, "The 10 Worst Operating Systems of All Time," *PC World* (April 9, 2009), https://www.pcworld.com/article/162866/worst_operating_system.html?page=3.

39. Joel Durham, Jr., "Quick Fixes for Five Nasty Vista Problems," *PC Magazine* (March 14, 2007), https://www.pcmag.com/article2/0,2817,2104022,00.asp.

40. Chuck Jones, "Bring Back Apple's Mac vs. PC Ads since Windows XP Isn't Supported," *Forbes* (14 April 2014), https://www.forbes.com/sites/chuckjones/2014/04/14/bring-back-apples-mac-vs-pc-ads-since-windows-xp-isnt-supported.

41. Klint Finley, "Linux took over the web, now it's taking over the world." *Wired* (25 August 2016), https://www.wired.com/2016/08/linux-took-web-now-taking-world.

42. Pamela Jones, "Microsoft Litigation Resource Page," *Groklaw*, https://web.archive.org/web/20170703231435/http://www.groklaw.net/articlebasic.php?story=20041228040645419.

43. James Kanter, "European Regulators Fine Microsoft, Then Promise to Do Better." *New York Times* (6 March 2013), http://www.nytimes.com/2013/03/07/technology/eu-fines-microsoft-over-browser.html.

44. Pamela Jones, "The Jan. 14th Eric Kriss Speech on Open Formats," *Groklaw*, https://web.archive.org/web/20150906123901/http://www.groklaw.net/articlebasic.php?story=2005011807275883.

45. David Berlind, "Microsoft: We were railroaded in Massachusetts on ODF." *ZDNET* (17 October 2005), http://www.zdnet.com/article/microsoft-we-were-railroaded-in-massachusetts-on-odf.

46. RTI, *The Economic Impacts of Inadequate Infrastructure for Software Testing* (US National Institute of Standards and Technology, May 2002), Planning Report 02-3, 8-1.

47. RTI, *Economic Impacts*, ES1.

48. Dan Geer, "Cybersecurity as Realpolitic," Keynote, Black Hat Conference (Las Vegas, 6 August 2014), http://geer.tinho.net/geer.blackhat.6viii14.txt.

49. Maryn McKenna, "Update: Farm Animals Get 80 Percent of Antibiotics Sold in U.S.," *Wired* (24 December 2010), https://www.wired.com/2010/12/news-update-farm-animals-get-80-of-antibiotics-sold-in-us.

Chapter Three

Gender, Religions, and the SDGs

A Reflection on Empowering Buddhist Nuns

Manuel Litalien

In her recent book on religions and development, Emma Tomalin asks the following questions: "Is religion negative for women's development and the pursuit of gender equality? Is there a gender consequence that results from engagement with religion?[1] In an attempt to answer these questions, this chapter examines whether the United Nations Sustainable Development Goals (SDGs) can empower a group of marginalised Buddhist women, support them against existing power relations, and achieve integration over sources of power. Its premise is that the future of humanity rests on how development organizations can negotiate the rights of women in the religious sphere by providing support to women who ground their social work and activism in a religious framework. It suggests that in order to move forward with many new SDGs, including the elimination of poverty, as well as ensuring inclusive health and promoting well-being, quality education, gender equality and empowering women, reduced inequalities, peace, justice, and strong institutions,"[2] it is imperative to consider the many facets of religious contexts and the increased politicization of culture. The chapter argues for the importance of religious women in social development, a neglected area in development studies.

In their current form, SDGs confirm the commitment of the United Nations to work with state actors, community leaders, and religious authorities to transform gender stereotypes. The importance of this inclusive, multifaceted, and integrated approach to development is welcome, but remains problematic in some sectors. To understand the challenges that lie ahead in implementing the SDGs, the gender politics of religious institutions are explained in the context of Buddhism, one of the major religions in Southeast Asia.

Religion gives meaning to the existence of large numbers of men and women in the region, and is understood as an indissociable part of their identity and their social development. Building on this reality, women in the region have relied on their religious traditions to provide a means of fighting existing conservative patriarchal institutions. Therefore, this chapter supports the view that gender equality should be based on a "culturally nuanced and a contextual approach" for successful implementation of the SDGs.[3]

The struggle for Buddhist women is not just religious in nature: it is intertwined with political, economic, educational, and cultural factors. This is why the links between the various targets and actors proposed by the SDGs are promising, but implementation strategies remain vague considering the scale of the steps necessary to empower women in traditional institutions. As stipulated by the SDGs, to "Leave no one behind" might prove to be overtly ambitious with persistent high gender gaps[4] in developed and developing nations across the globe.[5] Consequently, Jane Parpart reminds us that women's empowerment is not limited to the place they hold in the workplace, to motherhood, or their access to higher education: empowerment must happen at the institutional, material, and discursive framework levels. Parpart presents empowerment as both a process and an outcome, but sometimes the process is the outcome.[6] In other words, empowerment can fail due to strong patriarchal cultural practices and structures. In sum, this chapter argues that the current proposition in the United Nations 2030 Agenda to engage with religious authorities is far from providing a proper venue to all the "unheard" voices of marginalised religious groups.

ASIA AND THE PACIFIC, GENDER EQUALITY AND RELIGION

The Asia-Pacific region is home to some of the world's most powerful economies, but it also hosts two-thirds of the world's poorest, according to UN Women (2016).[7] Additionally, according to the Pew Research Centre (2012), the Asia-Pacific region is also the place where the highest concentrated percentage of religious groups in the world is found.[8] These statistics do not bode well for proponents of gender equality, since a recent study suggests that a positive correlation exists between the number of nonreligious people, and a country's "material gender equality."[9] The research avoids essentialist conclusions, including the notion that gender equality is impossible in profound religious settings. Nevertheless, the research underlines how equality progresses well in countries with high number of nonreligious people. Given these reasons, this chapter argues that, because religious practices and values are present in every aspect of life in Asia Pacific, they should at least be at the forefront of any strategies to fight discrimination and poverty in the region. In spite of the growing literature on the importance of religion in development, it is barely mentioned in the United Nations' new 2030 Agenda.[10] In other words, the future vision of development and humanity by the United Nations only timidly involves religion.

The idea behind the empowerment of women is not to simply add the "gender" component to development approaches, but to create conditions under which women can empower themselves.[11] Any exclusionary attitudes by leading religious institutions do provide a contrast with the 2030 Agenda, and because the SDGs lack specific implementation strategies, one wonders how the guidelines will make a difference from previous approaches to gender and development initially focusing on welfare, equity, antipoverty, or efficiency. The Agenda should recognise and include the importance of religion on gender empowerment, or in our case, Buddhist nuns in the Asia-Pacific.

GENDER INDEXES, ASEAN, RELIGION AND DEVELOPMENT

In August 2017, the Chair of the Association of Southeast Asian Nations (ASEAN) called on member states to overcome gender inequality. The aim is to fight discrimination so women in the region can have equal access to trade opportunities, but also find equality beyond the economic sphere and in their own communities for the benefit of everyone.[12] This echoes the ASEAN HeForShe campaign launch from December 2017 to promote a general culture of respect for women.[13] The areas of effort were named as employment, education, health, politics, and identities. Empowering women is here perceived by the United Nations and the ASEAN as a means to bring forward the development of gender equality. However, this requires proper tools of measurement to evaluate progress. Unfortunately, neither the Global Gender Gap Index (GGGI) (World Economic Forum, 2016) nor the Gender Development Index (GDI) (United Nations Development Program 2018)[14] account for the religious variable to determine the progress of gender equality in the religious sphere. According to Hastings (2013), there is a "shortage of indicators" to measure gender equality subnationally and internationally, even when taking into account the Human Security Index, or the World Bank's GenderStats. Schnabel (2016) addresses this, and takes a different route in trying to determine whether religions around the world hinder or help gender equality. He notably points to the famous studies done by Inglehart and Norris (2003) and their World Values Survey (WVS). They established predictable and systematic differences between the level of human development and cultural viewpoints on gender equality according to generation, education, and marital status.[15] The problem noted in the development studies literature is that, generally, religion has been a neglected variable.[16] Again, by failing to firmly engage with religion and development, the SDGs risk missing some of their goals, namely Goal 5, to "Achieve Gender Equality and Empower All Women and Girls." Drawing a parallel between the former millennium development goals (MDGs), the current SDGs, and the social status of Buddhist nuns is therefore key to moving toward meeting development goals. Despite some success stories, nuns in the Theravada tradition generally have limited financial resources in contrast with the monks; it is not uncommon to see some of them relying on monks for survival or given a subordinate status in the Buddhist clergies.[17] Fighting disparities means providing equal access to resources and opportunities for Buddhist nuns across the region. These women should benefit from the same institutional, social, and financial recognition as the monks in Asia and the Pacific. However, the local and the national contexts are complex and situated at the intersection of broader forces that are working against the empowerment of Buddhist nuns. The new objectives of the SDGs on paper are, in essence, empowering, as they advocate for a sustainable development Agenda "of the people," "by the people," and "for the people."[18] It appears, however, that this universalistic understanding of development is problematic, despite the important recognition of adopting a mixed approach to development, bottom-up and top-down. The resolution, as it stands, assumes that leaders across nations are supportive and capable of changing patterns of oppression related to poverty, and to inequality in less than fourteen years, an overly optimistic position, if one recalls the politically volatile environment of Southeast Asia, which is subject to frequent military interventions in politics, has long-standing authoritarian regimes, and has a poor human rights records; ASEAN's influence is also limited due in part to its noninterference principles.[19] These factors point to possible long-term "hiccups" to human development, gender empowerment, and social stability, also affecting the religious sphere. Political leaders still see economic development or a business-as-usual growth model as a natural provider of social development, rather than investing in human capital, free civil society, and protection of marginalised groups or equal opportunity to minority rights. Women are no exception to social discrimination, regardless of progress accomplished in the last three decades in countries with the largest Buddhist majority in the region, or by the portrayal of Buddhism as a religion based on equality.[20]

SDGS, HUMAN RIGHTS, DIVERSITY, AND WOMEN IN RELIGION

The broad, good intentions—such as the recognition that all cultures and civilisations can contribute to sustainable development—behind the SDGs are commendable.[21] However, Southeast Asian observers can recall the Asian Values (AV) debates of the 1990s, in which culture was seen as playing a key role in development, which the World Bank defined as the East

Asian Economic Miracle. Championing the view that human rights were incompatible with "Asian 'Confucian' Values" was Singapore's Lee Kuan Yew, contrasting human rights to the familialistic[22] and paternalistic welfare approach he assumed to be defining social elements for most countries in East and Southeast Asia.[23] Eventually, the debate was accused of being purely scholarly, as Taiwan and South Korea maintained strong democratic systems in the region, along with Indonesia, and ailing democratic Thailand.[24]

The economic crisis of 1997 was a rude awakening to the advocacy of the Asian Values "culturalist" approach to development. The task for the SDGs is daunting, especially when it rests on the adoption of an Agenda demanding strong commitment from world, national, and community leaders.[25] It also emphasises a democratic approach to development, as it wishes to include "all people" in the success of the SDGs. In sum, the task assumes "full commitment to equality, sustainable development, and ecological protection from developed countries and large corporations."[26] It also takes for granted that developed countries will agree to give up some form of their autonomy (political or cultural) and leadership. In the words of Gupta and Vegelin (2015), the negotiation between different social and community perspectives seems inevitable: "Bringing up the 'bottom' will 'inevitably' require lowering the 'top.'" Here, the authors argue that business as usual can no longer continue, thus hinting at the problematic nature of current social class divisions. One then speculates about how the Buddhist nuns' view of development will be acknowledged and included in traditional institutions maintaining the importance of protecting paternalistic religious and community values in the region.

In an environment where democratic values are a work in progress, where freedom of speech is tightly monitored, electoral politics are tied to vote buying, and civil society is perceived as dubious by the power in place, one further wonders if the "plan of action for the people, the planet and prosperity" is overly optimistic.[27] For there to be current advocates of "collaborative partnership" to end poverty, all stakeholders must have a recognised voice in the decision-making process to end inequality. However, rarely do minority groups, migrants, or refugees occupy positions of high status and authority in the region.[28] Women in religious traditions in Southeast Asia provide no exception to this lack of social mobility.[29] Successful SDGs are confronted with centuries-old institutionalised and systemic gender hierarchies. More doubts can be raised, as other venues to empower women are already in place, such as the Sakyadhita and the Alliance for Bhikkhunis, which are in line with the SDGs. Both associations predate the SDGs and the MDGs by more than a decade, yet they have yielded modest results. In light of the social context enumerated previously, the United Nations' resolution appears like another commitment from selected members of the international community to pursue equality for all through specific channels of political and religious leadership, guidance, and recommendations.

SDGS, WOMEN IN RELIGION, AND PARTICIPATION

In this context, how does the United Nations' post-2015 development agenda complement other institutions focusing on the promotion of women? To correct its poor commitments to put the guidelines into effect, and its weak capacity to enhance "relational inclusive"[30] development, the United Nations General Assembly (UNGA) can join forces with potential partners that do provide tools to pressure political powers for institutional accountability, such as the Sakyadhita and the Alliance for Bhikkhunis. The latter wishes to fight the marginalization of women in Buddhism both internationally and nationally. Overall, can the SDGs' guidelines operate as an alternative to current ones available through different established (or new) religious organizations? Can nongovernmental organizations (NGOs) provide inclusive development to women? How can marginalised women in Buddhism be included in the elaboration of empowerment strategies when they lack recognition by leading religious institutions?

SDGS, SOCIAL CONTEXTS, AND LEGAL CHALLENGES

Target 5.2 on Gender Equality and Empowerment underlines the importance of attempting to eliminate all forms of violence in the public and the private spheres. If gender equality is encouraged, in some cases, in the public sphere, it might face different sets of challenges in the private sector. The thirty-five-page document itself underlines the importance of recognising "cultural" diversity, intercultural understanding, tolerance, and mutual respect.[31] It rests, however, on the assumption that gender equality is a universally accepted value, and that "all cultures and civilizations can contribute to, and are crucial enablers of, sustainable development."[32] Gender equality and empowerment also depends on reaching Target 16, whereby sustainable development requires equal access to a fair justice system, an inclusive society or communities, and accountable and inclusive institutions.[33] The "inclusive element" is traced to participation in the decision-making process regionally, nationally, and internationally at all levels.[34] Here, the resolution presents important points: the access to equal opportunities must be located in education, economic resources, and political spheres for all women. Despite arguing that sustainable development will be impossible if half of humanity is denied "full human rights and opportunities," the document fails to engage in institutionalised religious forms of oppression toward women, and their lack of opportunities in that sphere of society. Instead of engaging with the topic of inequality in the religious sector, the General Assembly avoided it. A clear example of legalised discrimination against Buddhist women who seek full ordination is Thailand's Sangha Act of 1928, whereby Thai monks are forbidden to grant full ordination to nuns in the Kingdom. Groups of nuns have previously mobilised to challenge the Act. A renewed attempt to be recognised under Thai law came in the form of a petition to Thailand's National Human Rights Commission in 2017.[35] In another example of discrimination, in 2017 the Bhikkhunis (nuns) were denied entrance to the Grand Palace to pay their respects to the late King Bhumibol unless they dressed differently and entered through a different gate than that of the monks.[36]

What happens when the distinction between the public and the private spheres is blurred? When the low status of women in religion is correlated with the inferior status of women in society? In an environment where religious and political institutions are inseparable, nationwide development progress often depends on the patronage of male religious leaders. Despite the importance of the SDGs, their strengths are also their weaknesses: specifically, the interdependence of all seventeen goals of development. Much of the latter rests on the presence of inclusive societies (Goal 16). This requires the agreement, mobilisation, and commitment of a multitude of social actors, whose interests are often in opposition to the notion of gender equality and different types of empowerment promoted by the United Nations' new resolution. It holds the potential to be perceived as being rooted in Western or "foreign" values when the goals clash with more conservative sections of society. A recent study on the SDGs concludes "that while the text on the SDGs fares quite well on social inclusiveness, it fares less well in respect to ecological and relational inclusiveness."[37] The merit of the SDGs is also in its promotion of taxing the rich and reforming global institutions, but "relational" politics do receive less attention in the overall Resolution.[38] Here Gupta and Vegelin advance that inequalities may at times be rooted in ideological and normative practices (2015). This is why the United Nations cannot omit studying gender, religion, and development together, lest it risk missing out on its target of gender empowerment.

SDGS AND ENTRENCHED PATRIARCHAL VALUES

When patriarchal values are persistent and deeply entrenched in culture and institutions, education and employment do not empower women.[39] Kim argues that in settings of persistent gender inequality, changes need to be made to "legal, institutional, and cultural barriers."[40] In the case of Buddhist religious biases specifically pertaining to gender, the empowerment of women through these suggestions might prove to be a ground for a clash between religious and "secular" authorities. The SDGs, by omitting to engage with religion and development, are at risk of being perceived as a set of secular guidelines. How, then, can they facilitate reforms without creating mass mobilisation and destabilisation to the social, economic, and political systems in place? How to ameliorate gender equality in religion is not clearly specified in the 2030 Agenda. Actors on the ground already know this will require efforts from the government and the groups concerned. Clear implementation strategies are needed.

The following list seeks to illustrate the prevalence of discrimination in relation to the ordination of Buddhist nuns.

Buddhist Nuns and Laywomen in the World (2004)

*Societies **with** a Tradition of Fully Ordained Nuns*	*Nuns and Laywomen in Societies **without** a Tradition of Full Ordination**
China	Bangladesh
Taiwan	Bhutan
Korea	Cambodia
Vietnam	Laos
	Mongolia
	Myanmar
	Nepal
	Sri Lanka
	Thailand
	Tibet

*Women have lesser status; a subordinated role in religious establishments affects attitudes of women and attitudes toward women as whole in society.[41]

BUDDHIST NUNS (BHIKKUNIS): PAST, PRESENT, AND FUTURE

Initiatives that precede the SDGs are numerous; here, the Sakyadhita and the Alliance for Bhikkhunis can be named. They are tools to empower Buddhist women from the bottom up, as they are working from the grassroots level. Both associations seek to transform prevalent patriarchal views in Buddhist conservative institutions. They claim Buddhist nuns lack education opportunities, and are often delegated to memorise Buddhist chanting or recite scriptures. In 2010, according to the Pew Research Center, four out of five Buddhist nuns were blocked in their practices by their monastic order in 2004.[42]

This is, however, changing rapidly,[43] with initiatives to recognise the contributions of Buddhist women, such as the Outstanding Women in Buddhism Award. This ceremony has been held since 2002, and at present, approximately two hundred women from twenty different countries have been recipients of the award. The award was initiated in Thailand by two Buddhist nuns, Thai Bhikkhuni Rattanavali and American Bhikkhuni Dr. Lee.

CONCLUSION

It is not uncommon to hear from leading conservative Buddhist institutions that women can only access enlightenment if they are reborn as male or that they have reached an institutional impasse regarding interpretation of the Buddhist scriptures. This attitude limits women's development; it disempowers them. In this context, by seeking gender equality, the SDGs are taking a controversial position, whereby they literally take a liberal secular stance that conflicts with conservative religious elements of society. This chapter argues that by focusing on the universality of its message, the UN fails to recognise that its message could be perceived as indirectly prescribing what it means to be a Buddhist, to be a Buddhist woman, and to be a Buddhist nun to leading religious institutions. There is a risk of a clash between religious ideology and the "secular" stance promoted by the UN, in the name of gender equality. For instance, the revival of the Bhikkhuni ordination already rests on transnational as well as local initiatives. It remains unclear how the UN's new Resolution will be successful in empowering Buddhist women already involved in development, without being perceived as either the promotion of a liberal feminist agenda or a push for a new form of "development colonialism" by leading conservative religious institutions. Additionally, past fieldwork has indicated that funding and daily needs for survival of nuns' communities depend essentially on local and national support. Moreover, the revival of the female order (Bhikkhunis) depends on collaboration with monks, as well as transnational and national networks of Buddhist nuns.[44] In sum, gender empowerment in the Theravada and Vajrayana traditions requires much more than a set of guidelines. One main critique already present in the literature is that the SDGs provide "little emphasis on how power differentials that lie at the heart of inequality can be addressed."[45] This chapter confirms this observation in the case of how to proceed with the empowerment of Buddhist nuns in their own religious traditions.

To promote gender empowerment in the future of humanity, a new religious narrative needs to take place: one in which female spirituality is of equal value to that of male spirituality and transcends gender-based spiritual hierarchies. Some elements of religious culture can be oppressive, and conflict with the SDGs' current, somewhat secular, approach. The chapter advocates for equal rights and opportunities for Buddhist nuns across all Buddhist traditions. The empowerment and social development of Buddhist nuns cannot rely on the voices of religious leaders who are behind discriminatory religious gender practices.[46] Failure to recognise the important discriminatory practices and discourses coming from conservative religious institutions in gender development is a serious flaw in the current United Nations SDGs. For this reason, the objective to eliminate discrimination against women by 2030 is unlikely to take place, and the use of the term *empowerment* is at risk of losing its significance.

As suggested by Kim,[47] development policies, to be effective, have to present a balance between accountability, empowerment, and participation. This study goes further and adds the idea that they must be rooted in religious values. Some pertinent questions to address for political and social realities of Southeast Asia in order to move forward include: Do the SDGs seek to increase activism? How comfortable are the governments in the ASEAN with tolerating new, unheard voices and inviting them to the table? How open are the monks to collaborating with the nuns in recognizing and actively promoting them as equal spiritual achievers? How can religious and secular groups write and promote the message on the social benefits of empowering women in religious traditions? The question is not when, but how, as there is currently a growing number of Bhikkhunis across South (Sri Lanka) and Southeast Asia.

The SDGs as an Agenda should recognise its will to change and fix problems connected to gender equality and gender empowerment in the religious sphere, not only in the secular one. That brings us to a core problem: how common is encouraged freedom of speech in the region? Is there a need to reinforce measures on religious and political immunity from marginalization in the name of social development and gender empowerment? According to Kim,[48] the SDGs currently presume that poverty reduction and improvement of social and economic development will bring forth gender equality, gender-based access, and full participation. The Agenda misses the importance of a cultural, religious and social context to bring about gender equality in Southeast Asia. Education, employment, and empowerment are insufficient without proper knowledge of all contextual religious and cultural constraints.

BIBLIOGRAPHY

Adam, Martin T. "Buddhism, Equality, Rights." *Journal of Buddhist Ethics* 20 (2013): 422–43.
Beek, Kurt Alan Ver. "Spirituality: A Development Taboo." *Development in Practice* 10, no. 1 (2000): 31–43.
Bowie, Katherine. "Standing in the Shadows: Of Matrilocality and the Role of Women in a Village Election in Northern Thailand." *American Ethnologist* 35, no. 1 (February 1, 2008): 136–53.

Cao, Huhua. "Introduction." In *Ethnic Minorities and Regional Development in Asia: Reality and Challenges*, 13–16. Amsterdam: Amsterdam University Press, 2009.
Chung, Ji-Sun. "Women's Unequal Access to Education in South Korea." *Comparative Education Review* 38, no. 4 (1994): 487–505.
Collins, Steven, and Justin McDaniel. "Buddhist 'Nuns' (Mae Chi) and the Teaching of Pali in Contemporary Thailand." *Modern Asian Studies* 44, no. 6 (2010): 1373–1408.
Cook, Sarah. "Structural Change, Growth and Poverty Reduction in Asia: Pathways to Inclusive Development." *Development Policy Review* 24, no. 1 (2006): 51–80.
Daskon, Chandima, and Tony Binns. "Practising Buddhism in a Development Context: Sri Lanka's Sarvódaya Movement." *Development in Practice* 22, no. 5–6 (2012): 867–74.
"Editorial." *Gender and Development, Gender, Religion and Spirituality* 7, no. 1 (1999): 2–6.
Esping-Andersen, Gøsta. *Social Foundations of Postindustrial Economies*. Oxford: Oxford University Press, 1999.
Falk, Monica Lindberg. *Making Fields of Merit: Buddhist Female Ascetics and Gendered Orders in Thailand*. Gendering Asia. Copenhagen: NIAS, 2007.
Gupta, Joyeeta, and Courtney Vegelin. "Sustainable Development Goals and Inclusive Development." *International Environmental Agreements: Politics, Law and Economics* 16, no. 3 (2016): 433–48.
Hastings, David A. "The Human Security Index: Pursing Enriched Characterization of Development." *Development* 56, no. 1 (2013): 66–78.
Haynes, Jeffrey. *Religion and Development: Conflict or Cooperation?* New York: Palgrave Macmillan, 2007.
Hicken, Allen. *Building Party Systems in Developing Democracies*. New York: Cambridge University Press, 2009.
Hjelm, Titus. "Religion and Social Problems: Three Perspectives." In *Religion and Social Problems*, 1–11. London: Routledge, 2011.
Inglehart, Ronald, and Pippa Norris. *Rising Tide: Gender Equality and Cultural Change Around the World*. New York: Cambridge University Press, 2003.
Kabilsingh, Chatsumarn. *Thai Women in Buddhism*. Berkeley, CA: Parallax Press, 1991.
Kawanami, Hiroko. *Renunciation and Empowerment of Buddhist Nuns in Myanmar-Burma: Building a Community of Female Faithful*. Leiden, the Netherlands: Brill, 2013.
Kim, Eun Mee. "Gender and the Sustainable Development Goals." *Global Social Policy* 17, no. 2 (2017): 239–44.
King, Sallie B. "Buddhism and Human Rights." In *Religion and Human Rights: An Introduction*, 103–18. Oxford: Oxford University Press, 2012.
Klug, Anja. "Enhancing Refugee Protection in the Asia-Pacific Region." *Proceedings of the Annual Meeting (American Society of International Law)* 107 (2013): 358.
Litalien, Manuel. *La Philanthropie Religieuse En Tant Que Nouveau Capital Démocratique, Développement Social et Régime Providentiel En Thaïlande*. Québec: Presses de l'Université Laval, 2016.
———. "Social Inequalities and the Promotion of Women in Buddhism in Thailand." *Journal of Buddhist Ethics*, 25 (August 2018): 569–606.
———. "Le Statut Des Religieuses (Mae-Chi/Mae Ji) Dans l'institution Bouddhique Contemporaine En Thaïlande: Vers Un Changement de Paradigme." M.A. Littérature comparée, Université de Montréal, 2001.
Muntarbhorn, Vitit. *The Status of Refugees in Asia*. Oxford: Clarendon Press, 1992.
Ockey, James. *Making Democracy: Leadership, Class, Gender, and Political Participation in Thailand*. University of Hawaii Press, 2004.
Pandey, Shanta. "The Road from Millennium Development Goals to Sustainable Development Goals by 2030: Social Work's Role in Empowering Women and Girls." *Journal of Women and Social Work* 32, no. 2 (2017): 125–32.
Park, Kyung Ae. "Women and Development: The Case of South Korea." *Comparative Politics* 25, no. 2 (1993): 127–45.
Parpart, Jane. "Rethinking Gender and Empowerment." In *The Companion to Development Studies*, 407–11. London: Routledge, 2014.
Pew Research Center. 2012.

"Progress of the World's Women 2015–2016: Transforming Economies, Realizing Rights." New York: UN Women, 2015. http://progress.unwomen.org.

Salgado, Nirmala S. *Buddhist Nuns and Gendered Practice: In Search of the Female Renunciant*. Oxford: Oxford University Press, 2013.

Schnabel, Landon. "Religion and Gender Equality Worldwide: A Country-Level Analysis." *Social Indicators Research* 129, no. 2 (November 2016): 893–907.

Selinger, Leah. "The Forgotten Factor: The Uneasy Relationship between Religion and Development." *Social Compass* 51, no. 4 (December 2004): 523–43.

Stevens, Casey, and Norichika Kanie. "The Transformative Potential of the Sustainable Development Goals (SDGs)." *International Environmental Agreements: Politics, Law and Economics* 16, no. 3 (June 2016): 393–96.

Tan, Paige Johnson. "Anti-Party Attitudes in Southeast Asia." In *Party Politics in Southeast Asia: Clientelism and Electoral Competition in Indonesia, Thailand and the Philippines*, 80–100. London: Routledge, 2013.

World Economic Forum. "The Global Gender Gap Report 2016." Global Gender Gap Report. Geneva: World Economic Forum, 2016.

Tomalin, Emma. "Buddhist Feminist Transnational Networks, Female Ordination and Women's Empowerment." *Oxford Development Studies* 37, no. 2 (2009): 81–100.

———, ed. *Gender, Faith and Development*. Oxford: Practical Action Publishing, 2011.

———. *Religions and Development. Routledge Perspectives on Development*. New York: Routledge, 2013.

———. "Religion and a Rights-Based Approach to Development." *Progress in Development Studies* 6, no. 2 (2006): 93–108.

Tsomo, Karma Lekshe. "Introduction." In *Bridging Worlds: Buddhist Women's Voice Across Generations*, 1–12. Taipei: Yuan Chuan Press, 2004.

United Nations Development Goals. "Mixed Results on Millennium Development Goals in Caucasus and Central Asia: UN Report 2014." The Millennium Development Goals Report 2014. Moscow/Almaty: United Nations, July 7, 2014.

UN Secretary-General's High-Level Panel on Women's Economic Empowerment. "Leave No One Behind: A Call to Action for Gender Equality and Women's Economic Empowerment," 2016.

United Nations. "Transforming Our World: The 2030 Agenda for Sustainable Development." Resolution. New York: United Nations, 2015.

Willis, Katie. *Theories and Practices of Development*. New York: Routledge, 2011.

Zakaria, Fareed. "Asian Values." *Foreign Policy*, no. 133 (November–December 2002): 38–39.

NOTES

1. Tomalin, *Religions and Development*, 148–49.
2. United Nations, "Transforming Our World," 7–10, 18, 20, 22, 25. See also: Pandey, "The Road from Millennium Development Goals," 129–30.
3. Kim, "Gender and the Sustainable Development Goals," 80.
4. According to the Global Gender Gap Report (2016), the Gender Gap is an index that seeks to quantify "the magnitude of gender-based disparities and tracks their progress over time." It focuses on four different areas: health, education, economy, and politics. The objective of the report is to measure a "consistent and comprehensive measure for gender equality that can track a country's progress over time." The report does not, however, measure the relative gap between men and women in religion. This contrasts with the argument supporting the importance of recognizing how the religious sphere affects gender equality (Tomalin 2006, 2011, 2013). Religion has been acknowledged in the literature as a facilitator or inhibitor of development (Hjelm 2011). The questions summarised by Hjelm follow: Is religion a solution of social problems or is religion a source of social problems? Considering how gender inequality is perceived as a social development problem, one may wonder why religion, gender, and social problems are not more emphasized in the various indexes measuring gender and devel-

opment. The same observation applies to the Gender Empowerment Measure or the Gender-related Development Index where religion is not acknowledged.

5. UN Secretary-General, "Leave No One Behind," 1–3.

6. Parpart, "Rethinking Gender and Empowerment," 409–10.

7. See UN Women, "Asia and the Pacific," http://www.unwomen.org/en/where-we-are/asia-and-the-pacific, accessed 19 July 2016. According to the United Nations Millennium Project, however, the Sub-Saharan region is at the epicentre of the crisis. See http://www.unmillenniumproject.org/goals, accessed 22 July 2016.

8. World geographic distribution of religious groups in Asia and the Pacific region: Hindu 99%, Buddhist 99%, Muslim 62%, folk religions 90%, members of other world religions, excluding Christianity and Judaism 89% (Pew Research Center 2012, 10, 38). The region is also where 76 percent of the world's religiously unaffiliated reside.

9. Schnabel, "Religion and Gender Equality Worldwide," 904.

10. The SDGs are formulated in the United Nations "Transforming our World: The 2030 Agenda for Sustainable Development." This resolution (A/RES/70/1) was adopted in 25 September 2015.

11. Willis, *Theories and Practices of Development*, 147.

12. See "ASEAN to Enhance Economic Opportunities for Women," http://asean.org/asean-to-enhance-economic-opportunities-for-women, accessed 22 January 2018.

13. See "ASEAN, UN to Promote Gender Equality through HeForShe Campaign," http://asean.org/asean-un-to-promote-gender-equality-through-heforshe-campaign, accessed 22 January 2018.

14. United Nations Development Program (Gender Development Index): http://hdr.undp.org/en/content/gender-development-index-gdi, accessed January 4, 2018

15. Inglehart and Norris, *Rising Tide*, 36, 43, 95.

16. See the editorial of the March 1999 special edition of the journal *Gender and Development* on Religion. See also Selinger, "The Forgotten Factor," 539; Haynes, *Religion and Development: Conflict or Cooperation?* 108; Tomalin, *Religions and Development*, 1–14; Beek, "Spirituality: A Development Taboo," 36; Litalien, *La Philanthropie Religieuse En Tant Que Nouveau Capital Démocratique, Développement Social et Régime Providentiel En Thaïlande*, 331–32; Litalien, "Social Inequalities and the Promotion of Women in Buddhism in Thailand," 576–79.

17. Tsomo, "Introduction," 7. In Buddhism, temples and some meditation centres depend on donations from the lay communities to survive. By refusing higher (full) ordination to women, the Buddhist clergies enjoy a relative financial and moral monopoly, despite their intention to endorse community projects initiated by nuns, or their meditation prowess (Collins and McDaniel 2010, 1375, 1390). Wealthy religious communities can be associated with good karma, and attract more donations. Consequently, the portrayal of Buddhist nuns as being only poor can be problematic, as wealthy nuns do exist; however, their financial resources usually stand in sharp contrast with the monks and need to be emphasized (Collins and McDaniel 2010, 1392). Success stories are few, such as Mae Chi Sansanee, the late Mae Chi Kanitha, or the late Khun Yai Chan (Kabilsingh 1991; Kawanami 2013; Lindberg Falk 2007; Litalien 2001; Salgado 2013). Nuns are often perceived as a "digression from [the] traditional notion of femininity," whether in Thailand, Cambodia, or Myanmar (Kawanami 2013, 52). They have often been portrayed as working in fields of lesser merit, and as a consequence, receive fewer donations from the Buddhist lay community than the monks, which negatively affects the social opportunities of Buddhist nuns. This perception is, however, slowly changing due in part to well-respected nuns' community projects, respected meditation teachers, and the corruption associated with traditional male Buddhist institutions.

18. United Nations, "Transforming Our World," 12.

19. Yamakage, "The Construction of an East Asian Order," 4–6. ASEAN has opted for protective strategies rather than a critical one in the past, when the international community condemned certain behaviour, such as in the case of atrocities in Myanmar, Cambodia, or Philippines.

20. Daskon and Bins, "Practising Buddhism in a Development Context," 871; Adam, "Buddhism, Equality, Rights," 440–41. See United Nations Development Programme Human De-

velopment Reports: Gender Development Index, http://hdr.undp.org/en/indicators/137906, accessed 4 January 2018.

21. UN Women, "Progress of the World's Women 2015–2016," 31, 51.

22. The term comes from Esping-Andersen, and refers to welfare obligations that rest on household members rather than the state (1999, 45). It is at times referred to as a "male-bread winner" model.

23. King, "Buddhism and Human Rights," 103–107, 116.

24. Zakaria, "Asian Values," 38–39.

25. UN Women, "Progress of the World's Women 2015–2016," 3, 60, 72, 221.

26. Gupta and Vegelin, "Sustainable Development Goals and Inclusive Development," 445.

27. Ockey, *Making Democracy: Leadership, Class, Gender, and Political Participation in Thailand*, 2004; Bowie, "Standing in the Shadows: Of Matrilocality and the Role of Women in a Village Election in Northern Thailand," 2008; Hicken, *Building Party Systems in Developing Democracies*, 2009; Tan, "Anti-party Attitudes in Southeast Asia," 2013; Hutchcroft, "Linking Capital and Countryside: Patronage and Clientelism in Japan, Thailand, and the Philippines," 2014.

28. Muntarbhorn, *The Status of Refugees in Asia*, 1992; Cao, "Introduction," 2009; Klug, "Enhancing Refugee Protection in the Asia-Pacific Region," 2013.

29. Tomalin, "Religion and a Rights-based Approach to Development," 385.

30. Gupta and Vegelin (2016, 442) provide the following definition of relational inclusiveness: "Inclusion refers to closing the income gap between the rich and poor, eliminating discriminatory laws and implementing social protection to enhance equality." It also "questions the need for continuous economic growth in a business-as-usual paradigm." It is development that focuses on the social and ecological aspects. Cook (2006) also looks at the key role government policies should assume in inclusive and equitable development, where strong representative and rule-of-law institutions guarantee the rights of participation to marginalised groups. This notion of recognised inclusive citizenship participation is crucial toward assisting Buddhist nuns of all traditions with getting out of poverty and attaining social recognition.

31. United Nations, "Transforming Our World: The 2030 Agenda for Sustainable Development," Resolution (New York: United Nations, 2015), 10.

32. United Nations, "Transforming Our World," 10.

33. United Nations, "Transforming Our World," 25.

34. United Nations, "Transforming Our World," 6.

35. See https://www.bangkokpost.com/archive/nuns-seek-nhrcs-help-to-win-legal-recognition-fight/1194005, accessed 22 January 2018.

36. See https://www.bangkokpost.com/archive/bhikkhuni-protest-palace-ban/1179101, accessed 22 January 2018.

37. Gupta and Vegelin, "Sustainable Development Goals and Inclusive Development," 433.

38. Gupta and Vegelin, "Sustainable Development Goals and Inclusive Development," 444.

39. Kim, "Gender and the Sustainable Development Goals," 2017; Chung, "Women's Unequal Access to Education in South Korea," 1994; Park, "Women and Development: The Case of South Korea," 1993.

40. Kim, "Gender and Sustainable Development Goals," 242.

41. Kabilsingh, *Thai Women in Buddhism*, 1991; Litalien, "Le statut des religieuses (maechi/mae ji) dans l'institution bouddhique contemporaine en Thaïlande: vers un changement de paradigm," 2001; Tsomo, "Introduction," 2004; Tomalin, "Religion and a Rights-based Approach to Development," 2006; Tomalin, "Buddhist Feminist Transnational Networks, Female Ordination and Women's Empowerment," 2009.

42. Tsomo, "Introduction," 11. These proportions are likely to change rapidly, as the Chinese government seeks to further promote and protect Buddhism. Since China officially recognises the ordination of nuns, the disparity ratio is likely to change over time, therefore reducing this gap.

43. See Collins and McDaniel, "Buddhist 'Nuns' (mae chi) and the Teaching of Pali in Contemporary Thailand," 2010; Linberg Falk, *Making Fields of Merit: Buddhist Female Ascetics and Gendered Orders in Thailand*, 2007.

44. Kabilsingh, *Thai Women in Buddhism*, 1991; Litalien, "Le statut des religieuses (mae-chi/mae ji) dans l'institution bouddhique contemporaine en Thaïlande: vers un changement de paradigm," 2001; Tomalin, "Buddhist Feminist Transnational Networks, Female Ordination and Women's Empowerment," 2009.

45. Stevens and Kanie, "The Transformative Potential of the Sustainable Development Goals (SDGs)," 395.

46. See http://www.atimes.com/article/liberation-struggle-thai-buddhist-nuns, accessed 22 January 2018.

47. Kim, "Gender and Sustainable Development Goals."

48. Kim, "Gender and Sustainable Development Goals."

II

Genocidal Fractures: The Eternal Return of the Past

Laurie Kruk

We humans are the storytelling beings. Two decades into the twenty-first century, we continue to need, crave, teach, discuss, read, and write stories about our deepest fears, darkest feelings, and questions about our future. Where do these fears come from? For our future survival, we have no choice but to survey the past.

One story we must confront is the perennially shocking event of the Holocaust, or *Shoah*, of World War II. What can we learn from this darkest moment of genocide, this challenge to our highest humanist ideals of reason? In her chapter, Gillian McCann declares, "Within the history of the western world, the Holocaust exists as a point of rupture." Furthermore, "there is 'no choice but to confront the Holocaust.' This unprecedented attempt at genocide has had a profound impact on understandings of religion, human rights, and the impact of modernity itself." More than seventy years later, this fact seems undeniable. The Holocaust survivor Elie Wiesel, winner of the Nobel Peace Prize for his memoir, *Night* (1958), ponders his motivation as follows:

> Did I write it so as not to go mad, or on the contrary, to go mad in order to understand the nature of madness, the immense, terrifying madness that had erupted in history and in the conscience of mankind?
>
> Was it to leave behind a legacy of words, of memories, to help prevent history from repeating itself?

Or was it simply to preserve a record of the ordeal I endured as an adolescent, at an age when one's knowledge of death and evil should be limited to what one discovers in literature? ("Preface," vii).

In Part II, chapters by Gillian McCann, Pavlina Radia, and Aaron Weiss consider our relationship as readers, writers, and witnesses to this genocidal narrative of our history. Within it, we have two chapters about space (McCann, Radia), and another about time (Weiss). McCann's chapter considers the recent phenomenon of "death tourism" to concentration camps of Eastern Europe in the context of the religious concepts of "atonement" and "pilgrimage." She writes, "The year 2016 saw record attendance to the site of Auschwitz-Birkenau with over two million visitors making the journey to Poland. The majority of these came mostly from areas directly involved in World War II, including Poland, the United Kingdom, the United States, Germany, France, and Israel." McCann tries to distinguish between "tourist" and "pilgrim" in her overview of accounts of such journeys, bringing to light the possibility of atonement, witnessing, and reconciliation. Pilgrimage, she argues, "can be defined as a journey to a special place of spiritual significance. . . . Traditional reasons for going on a pilgrimage might include fulfilling a vow, visiting a place of historical significance for one's tradition, being healed, making a petition, atoning for a transgression, and being cleansed of sin." Witnessing may also be viewed in a more political light, as McCann suggests.

Radia's chapter bridges this legacy of war with the turn-of-the-millennium's struggle with terrorism and our attempt as North Americans to memorialize the attacks of 11 September 2001 in New York, Washington, DC, and Pennsylvania. In 2018, the Holocaust Memorial Museum finds its dark twin in the 9/11 Memorial Museum and annual gatherings at the Ground Zero site. In readings of recent books—the memoir *American Widow* by Alissa Torres and the novel *Hope: A Tragedy* by Shalom Auslander—Radia challenges the easy answer of "commodifying" survivors' stories for quick consumption. As she writes, "the texts by Torres and Auslander ponder the future of postmemory in the posthuman age, where the emphasis on experientiality and trauma are blended with national politics and an imperative of instant closure and gratification." Alissa Torres, a woman widowed, while pregnant, by the terrorist attacks of 2001, has her own story to tell in *American Widow* and it is not a simple one. In *Hope*, Auslander's protagonist contemplates the national celebrations of 1 July, and the making of national memory, haunted by the ghost of the Holocaust, represented by a spectral Anne Frank typing out her diary in his attic. In their writing, Radia argues, both Torres and Auslander critique "death tourism" and its wishful desire for closure or cure. Buying a "Never Forget" souvenir, from either site, they suggest, is not, and never can be, enough. Radia draws on Judith Butler's theory of assembly as an "embodied performance" of the "claim to the political" to examine the challenges of bearing witness as collective witnessing. She also engages with Marianne Hirsch's notion of "postmemory as 'retrospective witnessing' that repositions traumatic memory in the quest of reintegrating past experiences of previous generations into the fabric of everyday life." Unlike monuments and memorials that are frequently teleological, Radia argues, literary texts by Torres and Auslander ponder the more complex topographies of "retrospective witnessing" that refuse full closure and explore fractures instead. Citing Hirsch, Radia contends that such narratives present "'the impulse to return as a fractured encounter.'" According to Shoshana Felman, "this fracture is . . . 'a situation with no cure,' but also the very medium that transmits the estranging effects and affects of memory." However, as Radia shows, while there is no simple "cure," art can provide an important platform for examining the challenges that retrospective witnessing inevitably poses.

Weiss's chapter narrows the focus of this "retrospective witnessing" to a narrative of one woman's journey through time—the wrong time, World War II—as a Jewish child in hiding. In a deeply personal and subjective account of the experience of "Rachel," Weiss invokes both interviewing and art analysis to provide a unique lens on this traumatic testimony. Three drawings—"Mother and Son," "Elderly Bearded Man," and "Elderly Man with Hat"—are examined "through a content analysis of the visual vocabulary." Biographical information from interviews that Weiss conducted with Rachel, as well as her interview with the Shoah Foundation (started in 1994 by famed Jewish-American director Steven Spielberg), inform this chapter's analysis. Rachel's personal trauma has had ripple effects that shape not only her long life, but the lives of her four children. Art, however, serves as an important through line in her life. As Weiss notes, "the threads displayed in her art (religion, family, Holocaust, her childhood, comfort objects) function as a partial roadmap for communicating her experiences during the Holocaust from multiple viewpoints." An inevitable legacy of World War II is the challenge of engaging with traumatic memory and its transgenerational influence. Although Weiss highlights the therapeutic aspects of art, he acknowledges the fractures that remain, the silences that can never be bridged. Yet as Radia has cautioned, Weiss also reminds us that "art as a mediator for trauma is a complicated notion." Nevertheless, this moving chapter of one woman's difficult journey is a strong reminder that "art can be a powerful mechanism for addressing trauma and anxiety even if the person does not wish to view it as such." The power of art, like the power of storytelling, lies in its ability to address the past through the gaze of the present. To bear witness, as Wiesel insisted on doing, is a crucial imperative "for the youth of tomorrow, for the children who will be born tomorrow" ("Preface" xv). For he did not want his past to become their future.

BIBLIOGRAPHY

Wiesel, Elie. *Night*. 1958. Translated by Marion Wiesel. With a New Preface by the Author. New York: Hill and Wang, 2006.

Chapter Four

The Pilgrimage to Auschwitz

Making Meaning in Late Modernity

Gillian McCann

Within the history of the Western world, the Holocaust exists as a point of rupture. Greenberg refers to it as an orienting event and argues that there is "no choice but to confront the Holocaust."[1] This unprecedented attempt at genocide has had a profound influence on understandings of religion and human rights, and of modernity itself.[2] Certainly for Jews and Christians, the necessity of grappling with the implications of the Holocaust are clear.

Social scientists, psychologists, and historians have all attempted to analyse and understand the events of the Holocaust. Theologians such as Emil Fackenheim, Richard Rubenstein, and Abraham Joshua Heschel developed varying responses while agreeing that the Holocaust was a watershed in Jewish history. These struggles with the idea of making meaning have also been extremely important in changing the tenor of Jewish–Christian relationship, and yet the sense of a horrific void remains.

The recognition of both the necessity and the impossibility of coming to terms with this history is expressed in the design of the United States Holocaust Memorial Museum in Washington, DC. The Hall of Remembrance, which is the last stop in the museum tour, is a space characterised by emptiness. In *An Architect's Journey*, James Ingo Freed writes that "the void in the middle of the room becomes the core of remembrance."[3] This hall attempts to depict spatially the fissure created by the events of the Holocaust while accepting its essential inexpressibility. The tension created by the need to recognise and memorialise the Holocaust and the impossibility of doing so adequately has resulted in controversy around various forms of commemoration.

Despite this inevitable strain, people continue to visit the places dedicated to remembrance in large numbers. The year 2016 saw record attendance to the site of Auschwitz-Birkenau with over two million visitors making the journey to Poland. The majority of these came mostly from areas directly involved in World War II, including Poland, the United Kingdom, the United States, Germany, France, and Israel.[4] The ever-increasing number of visitors can be understood as an expression of an ongoing effort to create meaning from the events of the Holocaust through material practice.

In the context of the struggle to make sense of history, the site of Auschwitz-Birkenau has emerged as the most important symbol of the Holocaust. Although Snyder's monograph *Bloodlands* (2010) has demonstrated that a large number of Jews were murdered farther east by the *Einsatzgruppen*, the death camp has retained its place in the public imaginary. The process of creating a field of meaning continues and the Ukrainian government has indicated that it will finally be memorializing the site of Babi Yar where more than one hundred thousand people, mostly Jews, were murdered and buried in mass graves.[5]

Despite an expanding number of destinations related to Holocaust remembrance, Auschwitz-Birkenau remains the most important. The reason for this is related to the nature of the site, which has retained the features of barracks, fences, railway, and crematoria that allow for a form of site-specific memory that is not possible in other sites. Babi Yar, Yad Vashem, and the United States Holocaust Memorial Museum are also important nodes in this field of meaning but Auschwitz-Birkenau sits at the centre. As the official website for the former concentration and extermination camp notes, "All over the world, Auschwitz has become a symbol of terror, genocide, and the Holocaust."[6]

The Polish parliament created the Auschwitz-Birkenau State Museum on July 2, 1947, and includes the grounds of two extant parts of the Auschwitz I and Auschwitz II-Birkenau concentration camps. In 1979, the site of Auschwitz-Birkenau concentration camp was entered on the UNESCO international list of world heritage sites. This decision signalled that Auschwitz-Birkenau was a place of international importance representing a history with implications for the entire world community.

The ever-increasing number of visitors to Auschwitz indicates that the vital importance of the site is widely recognised. A 2015 newspaper article referring to the exponential increase in visitors to Auschwitz-Birkenau described the site as the "most unlikely tourist hotspot."[7] However, when understood through the lens of religious studies, it is not unlikely at all. The journey to Auschwitz-Birkenau has become for many, even though often unconsciously, a pilgrimage.

Typical practices performed by those who visit the concentration and death camp range from the traditional kaddish to lighting of candles and individual and group prayer. All these rituals and observances are drawn from within the Jewish and Christian traditions. These material practices also mirror and work in tandem with the changes clergy are creating at the theological level. As is often the case with many places of pilgrimage, it is the requirements and practices of the laity that have been central in the creation of meaning at the site.[8]

While official theologies emerging from the Holocaust are well documented and studied, much less attention has been paid to material practices that have developed in the period following World War II. As Morgan writes of religion in general, rather than through philosophical discourse, most people live their beliefs "in the grit and strain of a felt-life."[9] The meaning-making occurring on the ground at various sites of remembrance, then, becomes a form of popular theology created by the pilgrims themselves through their actions and understanding of the journey.

Through the toil of their travel and the rituals enacted once they arrive, visitors to Auschwitz construct public liturgies that have vitally important implications. The site, unsurprisingly, has also been the subject of ongoing controversy. As Michael Rothberg notes, Auschwitz has been contested ground since the first Soviet soldiers arrived there at the end of January 1945.[10] However, when viewed as a form of pilgrimage, the journey of so many to Auschwitz-Birkenau begins to come into focus both from a secular and a religious point of view.

TOURIST OR PILGRIM?

Journeys to Auschwitz-Birkenau take place within the larger context of a worldwide increase in travel and tourism more generally. In his article on the growing popularity of pilgrimage, Robert Macfarlane notes that these trips are undertaken for a variety of reasons, including "religious, cultural or personal."[11] The pilgrimage revival encompasses the traditional routes such as the Santiago de Compostela and the back-to-nature hikes described in books like Cheryl Strayed's *Wild*.

According to Davidson and Gitlitz, three fundamental beliefs are held by pilgrims: (1) powers infinitely larger than ourselves, including gods, superheroes, and the tectonic plates of history, have the ability to influence one's life; (2) we can initiate a meaningful relationship with these forces; and (3) there are certain special places where remote or transcendent powers are closer.[12] *Pilgrimage*, then, can be defined as a journey to a special place of spiritual significance, or to what Di Giovine calls spaces of "hyper meaning."[13] Traditional reasons for going on a pilgrimage include fulfilling a vow, visiting a place of historical significance for one's tradition, being healed, making a petition, atoning for a transgression, and being cleansed of sin.[14]

Arguments over the status of those who travel to sites has been ongoing, particularly between those in pilgrimage and tourist studies. The famous pronouncement of anthropologists Victor and Edith Turner that "a tourist is half a pilgrim"[15] has resulted in a great deal of spilled ink over the years. However, as Di Giovine concludes, it is perhaps impossible to categorise the participants in this "special form of modern, global mobility" and, in fact, a person's sense of identity can shift in the course of the journey.[16]

In the case of survivors returning to Auschwitz-Birkenau, this shift may be self-protective. Holocaust survivor Rene Chernoff told an interviewer that she was determined to interact with the site strictly as an American tourist. However, as Cole recounts in his article, upon reaching the former death camp, she found herself reacting as "mourning sister, survivor mother, acting as expert guide, and American Jew concerned about the contemporary politics of memory."[17]

The toggling back and forth between tourist and pilgrim seems to be particularly heightened in the case of visitors to Auschwitz-Birkenau. There may be a variety of motivations for making the journey, including to become more educated, to honour the memory of the dead, and to understand their personal histories. As Keil notes, an innate tension between secular and transcendent, sacred and profane, is present in the very notion of tourism as the site is "a shrine but it is also a point on a tourist itinerary."[18] In their book *Dark Tourism*, Lennon and Foley note with some unease the attraction of tourists to sites such as Auschwitz-Birkenau and argue that this form of travel expresses the "anxieties and doubts inherent in modernity."[19]

In "Sightseeing in the Mansions of Death," Chris Keil takes a critical look at "death tourism" and the ways in which it is often commercialised and commodified. He notes that trips to death camps reveal an overlap between cultural and heritage tourism. The camps also are highly charged spaces of collective memory and meaning, and are "iconic points of shared reference filled with symbolic value." He refers to Auschwitz-Birkenau as "one of the most symbolically charged and highly cathected places on earth."[20]

Jewish commentators commonly refer to the journey to Auschwitz as a *pilgrimage*, this regardless of whether the traveller is religiously observant or not. In his 2015 article for *The Telegraph*, Michael Goldfarb argues that Auschwitz-Birkenau should be recognised as place of pilgrimage, referring to the site as hallowed ground. Despite his own secular identity, Goldfarb states that Auschwitz speaks to what it means to be Jewish post-Holocaust, and to be "both chosen and forsaken."[21]

WITNESSING

One of the most commonly expressed reasons for visiting Auschwitz is related to the desire to bear witness. This formulation is used by both the religious and the nonreligious in explaining their motives for going. This concept is multivalent in its meaning and has a complex history within the Jewish and Christian traditions. The term *witness* was also used explicitly in the application of the Polish government to have Auschwitz-Birkenau added to the World Heritage List.[22]

The most important source of inspiration for this common practice is Elie Wiesel's statement in his Nobel Prize–winning book *Night*:

> My life as a writer—or my life period—would not have become what it is: that of a witness who believes he has a moral obligation to prevent the enemy from enjoying one last victory by allowing his crimes to be erased from human memory.[23]

Wiesel and other survivors who experienced the camps firsthand were of course among the first who witnessed the events of the Holocaust. In a sense, then, the acts of those who follow after form a lineage of witness, creating a chain of memory committed to ensuring that the events are never forgotten.

The Hall of Witness in the United States Holocaust Memorial Museum recapitulates this idea. The words "You are my witnesses" from Isaiah 43:10 are etched in black granite, acting as an exhortation to visitors; the words are described by Freed as a "momentous charge."[24] For many who participate in the pilgrimage to Auschwitz, whether they fully understand the source of this charge, they are taking up of this moral duty of remembrance.

Christianity's conception of witness stretches back to the very beginning of the tradition. According to Acts in the New Testament, the Apostles were commissioned by Jesus to act as his witnesses to "the ends of the earth."[25] This understanding of each Christian as a witness has been central to the tradition as it has developed around the world. However, the meaning of the term has also evolved.

The concept of witnessing has developed within the Christian tradition to encompass an approach to social justice that resonates with Wiesel's call to witness. For Protestant Christian theologian Karl Barth, who lived through the Nazi rise to power and the Second World War, this idea became central. For Barth, the action of witnessing is based on a "relational ethic" and overrules the obligations of any other ideology, including that of nationalism. From Barth's point of view, every Christian is "a responsible agent of peace and justice in the world."[26] The Quaker understanding of witness has highlighted the social justice aspect and, as Weyler notes, the Quakers believe "[t]hat a witness to atrocity becomes an agent of change."[27]

These understandings of witnessing as a moral imperative post-Holocaust have percolated into the general consciousness. In the comments section under an article describing the increasing number of visitors to Auschwitz-Birkenau, a writer who evinced the wish to go to the site used the moniker "Silent Witness."[28] Whether Jewish, Christian, or secular, many visitors to Auschwitz-Birkenau understand themselves as bearing witness both to ensure the events are not forgotten and that that they do not happen again.

ATONEMENT

The concept of atonement is also a central feature of both Judaism and Christianity. However, it possesses a special place in pilgrimages to Auschwitz. While as Lewis notes, Nazi anti-Semitism had shifted from religious to racial, the enabling background of a long history of Christian anti-Semitism is clear.[29] As David I. Kertzer's book, *The Popes Against the Jews* (2001), demonstrates, the churches played a significant role in creating a climate that made the Final Solution possible. According to Kertzer, the historical record reveals plainly the role that the churches, both Catholic and Protestant, played in "dehumanizing the Jews."[30] Probst concludes that Protestant clergy and theologians in Nazi Germany largely shared Luther's attitude towards the Jews, often associated them with Bolshevism, and viewed them as a threat to the German *volk*.[31]

The postwar period required a reckoning with the silence and inaction of both Catholics and Protestants during the Third Reich. This acceptance of culpability has resulted in both denominations engaging in forms of collective soul searching. As Irving Greenberg writes, both traditions posit human life as being of infinite value and so the Holocaust "poses the most radical counter-testimony to both Judaism and Christianity."[32] Because of this, the need to respond reverberates through the whole community of both Jews and Christians and is not solely the concern of theologians, rabbis, and priests.

During Vatican II part of the mandate of the historic meeting was a commitment to facing this tragic history. The council moved decisively away from the former "fortress mentality" and into dialogue with other religious communities. According to D'Costa, the council rejected the Christian doctrine that held the Jewish community collectively responsible for the death of Christ.[33] Controversies around the inclusion of prayers for the conversion of the Jews in the Good Friday Prayer continue to be hotly debated in the Orthodox, Catholic, and Protestant churches. Building from *Nostra Aetate* and a growing recognition of the need to change the material practice of the tradition, clergy has attempted to "excise anti-Semitic passages from its liturgy."[34]

Another example of visits to Auschwitz as a form of atonement can be seen in the antifascist pilgrimages from Germany by Aktion Suhnezeichen and Sozialistische Jugend beginning in the 1960s. These visits are described by Heuner as representing a desire to confront the past "on-site."[35] The language used to describe these trips is explicitly religious and Huener refers to them as seeking contrition, expiation, and a desire for reconciliation.[36]

The physical presence at Auschwitz of those who are actively or culturally Christian can be viewed as a powerful act of atonement. These journeys are an embodied rejection of denial as a mode for responding to the Holocaust. The visit also represents a direct, and often uncomfortable, recognition of complicity. This is not only true for those from European nations but also for Canadians, as it now widely recognised that the Canadian government largely ignored the call to take in Jewish refugees both before and during World War II.[37]

RECONCILIATION

Following logically on the heels of the recognition of the requirement for atonement on the part of Christians has been the movement towards reconciliation. These efforts are various and have been spearheaded by members of both communities, as can be seen in the creation of the International Council of Christians and Jews in 1987. In a similar spirit, in 1968 Spain formally revoked the Alhambra Decree of 1492 and in 2012 granted automatic Spanish citizenship to all Sephardic Jews.[38] Portugal followed suit in 2015, granting dual citizenship to the descendants of Portuguese Sephardic Jews.[39]

Christian reactions took a variety of forms, including changes adopted as a result of the Second Vatican Council 1962–1965. These included the ecumenical movements that attempted to bridge the gap between Jews and Christians and between Catholics and Protestants. While these already had a precedent in events such as the World Parliament of Religion in 1893, in the aftermath of World War II, the movement took on a new urgency.

The most dramatic demonstration of this change in attitude was the visit of Pope John Paul II to Rome's central synagogue in April 1986. This first visit in recorded history of a Pope to a synagogue was carefully orchestrated to emphasise the unity of the two communities; the visit was scheduled to fall on Pesach (Passover) and during the Easter season for Christians.

During the visit the Pope categorically denounced all forms of anti-Semitism, and emphasized the "equal dignity" of the two religious communities. These statements were underscored by reading and singing the Psalms revered by both Jews and Christians.[40] This was an implicit rejection of the traditional teaching that Christianity represented the supersession of Judaism and established their connection as related but distinct traditions.

This visit by Pope John Paul demonstrates the necessity of paying attention to material practice and ceremony along with theological approaches. As leader of the Catholic Church, the Pope's physical presence in a synagogue was both deeply symbolic but also directly tied to substantive changes. The recent visit of Pope Francis to Israel, during which he laid a wreath on the grave of Theodor Herzl and prayed at the Wailing Wall, has continued the papal commitment to rapprochement with the worldwide Jewish community and recognition of the state of Israel.[41]

The magnitude of the challenges faced in attempting reconciliation is recognised by both Jews and Christians. In his chapter "Crosses in Auschwitz: Crisis and Turning," Jacob Neusner discusses the long history of Polish anti-Semitism and the complicated shared history of the two communities. However, he concludes his analysis with a recognition of the opening created by Polish Pope John Paul II and concludes by writing that "Poland is the place for dialogue."[42]

"I TURNED TO THE ASHES BUT THEY WERE SILENT"[43]

An account of the ways in which these processes happen in practice can be found in Robert E. Kennedy's 2005 article "Rituals at Auschwitz-Birkenau."[44] A Catholic theologian and Jesuit priest, Kennedy writes about his own pilgrimage experience at Auschwitz-Birkenau. Kennedy travelled to Poland with an international peacemakers group made up of Jews and Christians. At various locations, the groups performed a series of rituals culminating in those performed at the site of the death camp. He writes, "It was my participation in a number of rituals at Auschwitz-Birkenau that built upon one another that brought me to a truth I would otherwise never have imagined."

In the course of his pilgrimage, while sitting in a restaurant in Krakow Kennedy is faced with the culpability of Christians in the Holocaust and is told that his church is to blame. With a growing sense of anxiety, he continues with his rituals, but finds himself paralysed when asked to perform the Eucharist while standing at the site of the mass burial of the ashes of the dead. Kennedy asks the rabbi present if it is appropriate to lead a prayer there. The rabbi replies: "Of course you can pray, just don't build a cathedral."

The article ends with the shaken priest attending a final gathering for a farewell dinner. Sitting in a dejected state while others danced, he writes:

> Suddenly the dancing across the room stopped and the rabbi stepped forward and blessed new wine and poured it, and then he took up the first glass and he walked across the room and he offered it to me. And so my many rituals and

my many voiceless brothers and sisters led me to another truth: there is no forgiveness at Auschwitz-Birkenau, but there is rich humanity.[45]

In this description of his experience at Auschwitz-Birkenau, Kennedy demonstrates that no sense of closure or absolute reconciliation is possible. The pilgrimage and its attendant rituals served to highlight the void and impossibility and yet allowed a space for meaningful encounter.

This acceptance of the ultimate impossibility of resolution does suggest a way forward that would allow for ambivalence and ambiguity that is part of the ongoing process of reconciliation.

CONCLUSION

Ritualised journeys to Auschwitz, whether made by university or high school classes, rabbis or priests, or individual tourists, can be understood as forms of popular theology and pilgrimage. Like many pilgrimage sites, Auschwitz-Birkenau seems to have been created at least partly out of a collective necessity. The pilgrimage to Auschwitz-Birkenau has been created by people who have voted (literally) with their feet and made their way to the site for perhaps often obscure emotional reasons. This site continues to grow in popularity as a destination for pilgrim–tourists, maintained because it serves a vital cultural and religious function. Auschwitz-Birkenau is a symbolically charged physical space that acts as a locus of memory and serves a variety of purposes, including allowing for acts of contrition, atonement, and reconciliation.

The meanings made within the site have also evolved with time. Memorial and education remain central to the stated aims of those who oversee the sites of "death tourism." Auschwitz-Birkenau now attracts people from a wide variety of religious backgrounds. In 2010, a joint trip of a group of Muslim imams and Jewish rabbis to Auschwitz-Birkenau was sponsored by the Center for Intercultural Understanding in New Jersey. This trip was meant to mitigate anti-Semitism and Holocaust denial within the Muslim community. After the trip, the imams released a joint statement that "denials of this tragedy are against the Islamic code of ethics." They also stated that sixty years of complex history between Jews and Muslims in the Middle East should in no way influence the Muslim view of the Holocaust.[46]

The contestation that surrounds the creation of Auschwitz as a pilgrimage site is not an indication of failure. Rather, as Di Giovine argues, these disagreements are necessary and are typical of all pilgrimage sites.[47] In light of millennia of tension between the Jewish and Christian communities, this is unavoidable and so this site has become a physical zone in which this difficult history can be memorialised and reimagined. Viewed through a religious lens and understood as a pilgrimage, it is inevitable that individuals and groups will all have their own reasons for going to, and understandings of, Auschwitz-Birkenau.

The "crisis of the crosses" and the controversy over the building of a Carmelite convent on the site have what Prosono refers to as a conflict over "symbolic territoriality."[48] Viewed within the context of the complex and difficult history of Polish–Jewish and Jewish–Christian relations, these conflicts were inevitable.

Resurgent forms of fascism and anti-Semitism, including in countries such as Canada and the United States, have only rendered the need for this site clearer. It is likely that these sites will continue to grow in importance and expand as sites such as Babi Yar in Ukraine become part of the mapping of this history of the Holocaust. The expansion and remapping of meaning will only continue as these parts of Europe become more accessible to visitors.

Auschwitz-Birkenau also attracts visitors who identify as nonreligious. However, this can be understood as a form of secular pilgrimage. As Zygmunt Bauman[49] has convincingly argued, the Holocaust was an example of the logical end of modernity itself. Secular as well as religious activists continue to be galvanised in their commitment to welcoming refugees by their knowledge of the history of the Holocaust.

Despite the dictums of philosophers like Adorno, and the many criticisms of "death tourism," the public has stubbornly continued to travel to Auschwitz-Birkenau in an attempt to make meaning within the void created by the Holocaust.[50] Faced with the uncanny silence at the heart of the twentieth century, they have stepped into the empty space in order to bear witness.

The general public and clergy have created rituals that emphasize witnessing, atonement, and reconciliation. Central to these actions is the belief in the duty of remembrance. These practices have been deployed to prevent Holocaust denial and to continue to oppose fascism and anti-Semitism. Sadly, the need for this sort of vigilance has only become more important in the early twenty-first century.

BIBLIOGRAPHY

Auschwitz-Birkenau Memorial and Museum. "History." Accessed 27 April 2019. http://auschwitz.org/en/history/.

———. "Over 2 Million Visitors at the Auschwitz Museum in 2016." Accessed 27 April 2019. http://auschwitz.org/en/museum/news/over-2-million-visitors-at-the-auschwitz-memorial-in-2016,1232.html.

Bauman, Zygmunt. *Modernity and the Holocaust*. Ithaca: Cornell University Press, 1989.

Ben Ezra, Daniel Stökl. *The Impact of Yom Kippur on Early Christianity: The Day of Atonement from Second Temple Judaism to the Fifth Century*. Tübingen, Germany: JCB Mohr, 2003.

Carosa, Alberto. "Controversy over Good Friday Prayer Flares Again." *Catholic World Report*, 18 January 2016.

Cole, Tim. "Crematoria, Barracks, Gateway: Survivor's Return Visit to the Memory Landscapes of Auschwitz." *History and Memory* 25, no. 2 (Fall/Winter 2013): 102–31.
Csillag, Ron. "Politician Ron Atkey Opened Canada's Doors to Boat People." *Globe and Mail*, 24 May 2017. https://beta.theglobeandmail.com/news/politics/politician-ron-atkey-opened-canadas-doors-to-boat-people/article35108399/?ref=http://www.theglobeandmail.com&
Davidson, Linda Kay, and David M. Gitlitz. *Pilgrimage: From the Ganges to Graceland. An Encyclopedia.* Santa Barbara: ABC-Clio, 2002.
D'Costa, Gavin. *Vatican II. Catholic Doctrines on Jews and Muslims.* London: Oxford University Press, 2014.
Di Giovine, Michael A. "Pilgrimage: Communitas and Contestation, Unity and Difference—An Introduction." *Tourism* 59, no. 3 (2011): 247–69.
Diamant, Jeff. "N.J. Rabbi Leads Jews, Muslims on Interfaith Trip to Nazi Concentration Camps." *Star-Ledger*, 15 August 2010.
Dionne Jr., E. J. "Pope Speaks in Rome Synagogue in the First Such Visit on Record." *New York Times*, 13 April 1986.
Finlan, Stephen. *Option on Atonement in Christian Thought.* Collegeville, MN: Liturgical Press, 1989.
Freed, James Ingo. *Designing the United States Holocaust Memorial Museum: An Architect's Journey*, edited by Janet Adams Strong. New York: Piloti Press, 2012.
Goldfarb, Michael. "Auschwitz Should Be a Place of Pilgrimage." *The Telegraph*, 26 January 2015.
Greenberg, Irving. "Cloud of Smoke, Pillar of Fire. Judaism, Christianity and Modernity after the Holocaust." In *The Holocaust Reader, Response to the Nazi Extermination*, edited by Michael L. Morgan. New York: Oxford University Press, 2001.
Haddorff, David. *Christian Ethics as Witness. Barth's Ethics for a World at Risk.* Eugene, OR: Cascade Books, 2010.
Harri, Ruth. *Lourdes: Body and Spirit in the Secular Age.* London: Penguin Books, 1999.
Huener, Jonathan. "Antifascist Pilgrimage and Rehabilitation at Auschwitz: The Political Tourism of Aktion Suhnezeichen and Sozialistische Jugend." *German Studies 24*, no. 3 (October 2001): 513–32.
Keil, Chris. "Sightseeing in the Mansions of the Dead." *Social and Cultural Geography* 6, no. 4 (August 2005).
Kennedy, Robert E. "Rituals at Auschwitz-Birkenau." *America: The Jesuit Review*, 10 October 2005.
Kertzer, David I. *The Popes against the Jews: The Vatican's Role in the Rise of Modern Anti-Semitism.* New York: Random House, 2001.
Kintsler, Linda. "No Monument Stands over Babi Yar." *Atlantic*, 30 September 2016. https://www.theatlantic.com/international/archive/2016/09/ukraine-jewish-babi-yar-russia-holocaust-germany-poroshenko/502517/.
Lefkovitz, Etgar. "Priests Remove Anti-Semitic Liturgy," *Jerusalem Post*, 20 April 2007.
Lennon, John, and Malcolm Foley. *Dark Tourism: The Attraction of Death and Disaster.* London: Thomson, 2006.
Lewis, Bernard. "Anti-Semites." In *The Holocaust: A Reader*, edited by Simone Gigliotti and Berel Lang. London: Blackwell Publishing, 2005.
Macfarlane, Robert. "Rites of Way: Behind the Pilgrimage Revival." *The Guardian*, 15 June 2012.
Maltz, Judy. "Pope Francis Calls for Peace in First Visit to Israel." *Haaretz*, 25 May 2014.
Morgan, David. *Religion and Material Culture: The Matter of Belief.* New York: Routledge, 2010.
Neusner, Jacob. "Crosses at Auschwitz: Crisis and Turning." In *The Continuing Agony: From the Carmelite Convent to the Crosses at Auschwitz*, edited by Alan L. Berger, Harry J. Cargas, and Susan E. Nowak. Binghamton, NY: Global Academic Publishing, 2002.
Payne, Emily. "So Popular They're Turning People Away: Auschwitz becomes the World's Most Unlikely Tourist Hot Spot Thanks to 40% Surge in Visitor Numbers." *Mail Online*, 23 April 2015. Accessed 27 April 2018. https://www.dailymail.co.uk/travel/travel_news/

article-3052542/So-popular-turning-people-away-Auschwitz-world-s-unlikely-tourist-hot-spot-40-increase-visitors.html.

"Portugal to Grant Citizenship to Descendants of Persecuted Jews." *The Guardian*, 29 January 2015.

Probst, Christopher J. *Demonizing the Jews: Luther and the Protestant Church in Nazi Germany*. Bloomington: Indiana University Press, 2012.

Prosono, Marvin. "Cross Purposes: The Conflict over Symbolic Territory between Poles and Jews at Auschwitz." In *The Continuing Agony: From the Carmelite Convent to the Crosses at Auschwitz*, edited by Alan L. Berger, Harry J. Cargas, and Susan E. Nowak. Binghamton, NY: Global Academic Publishing, 2002.

Rothberg, Michael. "After Adorno: Culture in the Wake of Catastrophe." *New German Critique* 72 (Autumn 1997): 45–81.

Röttjer, Julia. "Safeguarding Negative Historical Values for the Future? Appropriating the Past in the UNESCO Cultural World Heritage Site Auschwitz-Birkenau." *Ab Imperio* 4 (2015): 130–65.

Stavans, Ilan. "Repatriating Spain's Jews." *New York Times*, 1 April 2014.

Troper, Harold, and Irving Abella. *None is Too Many: Canada and the Jews of Europe 1933–1948*. Toronto: University of Toronto Press, 2012.

Turner, Victor, and Edith Turner. *Image and Pilgrimage in Christian Culture*. New York: Columbia University Press, 1978.

Weyler, Rex. *Greenpeace: How a Group of Ecologists, Journalists and Visionaries Changed the World*. Vancouver: Raincoast Books, 2004.

Wiesel, Elie. "Preface." In *The Night Trilogy*, translated by Marion Wiesel. New York: Hill and Wang, 2008.

Younan, Munib. *Witnessing for Peace: In Jerusalem and the World*. Minneapolis: Fortress Press, 2003.

ACKNOWLEDGMENT

This article is dedicated to my friend and mentor Judy Cohen.

NOTES

1. Irving Greenberg, "Cloud of Smoke, Pillar of Fire. Judaism, Christianity and Modernity after the Holocaust," in *The Holocaust Reader: Response to the Nazi Extermination*, ed. Michael L. Morgan (New York: Oxford University Press, 2001), 107.

2. Zygmunt Bauman, *Modernity and the Holocaust* (Ithaca: Cornell University Press, 1989).

3. James Ingo Freed, *An Architect's Journey*, ed. Janet Adams Strong (New York: Piltoti Press, 2012), 50.

4. "Over 2 Million Visitors at the Auschwitz Memorial in 2016," Auschwitz-Birkenau Memorial and Museum, http://auschwitz.org/en/museum/news/over-2-million-visitors-at-the-auschwitz-memorial-in-2016,1232.html.

5. Linda Kintsler, "No Monument Stands over Babi Yar," *Atlantic*, 30 September 2016, https://www.theatlantic.com/international/archive/2016/09/ukraine-jewish-babi-yar-russia-holocaust-germany-poroshenko/502517/.

6. "History," Auschwitz-Birkenau Memorial and Museum, http://auschwitz.org/en/history.

7. Emily Payne, "So Popular They're Turning People Away: Auschwitz becomes the World's Most Unlikely Tourist Hot Spot Thanks to 40% Surge in Visitor Numbers," *Mail Online*, 23 April 2015, https://www.dailymail.co.uk/travel/travel_news/article-3052542/So-popular-turning-people-away-Auschwitz-world-s-unlikely-tourist-hot-spot-40-increase-visitors.html.

8. Ruth Harri, *Lourdes: Body and Spirit in the Secular Age* (London: Penguin Books, 1999). In the case of Lourdes, the Catholic authorities actively attempted to prevent the creation of the pilgrimage site. Despite this the pilgrims simply ignored these directives from above.

9. David Morgan, *Religion and Material Culture: The Matter of Belief* (New York: Routledge, 2010), 8.

10. Michael Rothberg, "After Adorno: Culture in the Wake of Catastrophe," *New German Critique* 72 (Autumn 1997): 45.

11. Robert Macfarlane, "Rites of Way: Behind the Pilgrimage Revival," *The Guardian*, 15 June 2012.

12. Linda Kay Davidson and David M. Gitlitz, *Pilgrimage: From the Ganges to Graceland: An Encylopedia* (Santa Barbara: ABC-Clio, 2002), xvii.

13. Michael A. Di Giovine, "Pilgrimage: Communitas and Contestation, Unity and Difference—An Introduction," *Tourism: An International Interdisciplinary Journal* 59, no. 3 (2011): 249.

14. Davidson and Gitlitz, *Pilgrimage*, xxi.

15. Victor Turner and Edith Turner, *Image and Pilgrimage in Christian Culture* (New York: Columbia University Press, 1978), 20.

16. Di Giovine, "Pilgrimage," 249.

17. Tim Cole, "Crematoria, Barracks, Gateway: Survivor's Return Visit to the Memory Landscapes of Auschwitz," *History and Memory* 25, no. 2 (Fall/Winter, 2013): 103.

18. Chris Keil, "Sightseeing in the Mansions of the Dead," *Social and Cultural Geography* 6, no. 4 (August 2005): 491.

19. John Lennon and Malcolm Foley, *Dark Tourism: The Attraction of Death and Disaster* (London: Thomson, 2006).

20. Keil, "Sightseeing," 491.

21. Michael Goldfarb, "Auschwitz Should Be a Place of Pilgrimage," *The Telegraph*, January 26, 2015.

22. Julia Röttjer, "Safeguarding Negative Historical Values for the Future? Appropriating the Past in the UNESCO Cultural World Heritage Site Auschwitz-Birkenau," *Ab Imperio* no. 4 (2015): 146.

23. Elie Wiesel, "Preface," in *The Night Trilogy*, trans. Marion Wiesel (New York: Hill and Wang, 2008), 6.

24. Freed, *Designing the United States Holocaust Memorial Museum*, 33.

25. Munib Younan, *Witnessing for Peace: In Jerusalem and the World* (Minneapolis: Fortress Press, 2003), 3.

26. David Haddorff, *Christian Ethics as Witness: Barth's Ethics for a World at Risk* (Eugene, OR: Cascade Books, 2010), 100.

27. Rex Weyler, *Greenpeace: How a Group of Ecologists, Journalists and Visionaries Changed the World* (Vancouver: Raincoast Books, 2004), 28.

28. Payne, "So Popular."

29. Bernard Lewis, "Anti-Semites," in *The Holocaust: A Reader*, ed. Simone Gigliotti and Berel Lang (London: Blackwell Publishing, 2005), 17.

30. David I. Kertzer, *The Popes against the Jews: The Vatican's Role in the Rise of Modern Anti-Semitism* (New York: Random House, 2001), 16.

31. Christopher J. Probst, *Demonizing the Jews: Luther and the Protestant Church in Nazi Germany* (Bloomington: Indiana University Press, 2012), 173.

32. Greenberg, "Cloud of Smoke," 23.

33. Gavin D'Costa, *Vatican II. Catholic Doctrines on Jews and Muslims* (London: Oxford University Press, 2014), 6.

34. Etgar Lefkovitz, "Priests Remove Anti-Semitic Liturgy," *Jerusalem Post*, 20 April 2007; Alberto Carosa, "Controversy over Good Friday Prayer Flares Again," *Catholic World Report*, 18 January 2016.

35. Jonathan Heuner, "Antifascist Pilgrimage and Rehabilitation at Auschwitz: The Political Tourism of Aktion Suhnezeichen and Sozialistische Jugend," *German Studies* 24 no. 3 (October 2001), 515.

36. Heuner, "Antifascist Pilgrimage," 521.

37. Harold Troper and Irving Abella, *None Is Too Many: Canada and the Jews of Europe 1933–1948* (Toronto: University of Toronto Press, 2012). The recognition of this guilt has had substantive influence on Canadian attitudes towards refugees. During the so-called Boat People crisis of 1979, historians Irving Abella and Harold Troper sent an early version of the book to then-Deputy Immigration Minister Ron Atkey. This contributed to his decision to open Canada's door to more refugees and he went on to push for an increase in the number of Syrian refugees in the contemporary period. Also see Ron Csillag, "Politician Ron Atkey Opened Canada's Doors to Boat People," *Globe and Mail*, 24 May 2017, https://beta.theglobeandmail.com/news/politics/politician-ron-atkey-opened-canadas-doors-to-boat-people/article35108399/?ref=http://www.theglobeandmail.com&

38. Ilan Stavans is sceptical of the sincerity of this gesture in "Repatriating Spain's Jews," *New York Times*, 1 April 2014.

39. "Portugal to Grant Citizenship to Descendants of Persecuted Jews," *The Guardian*, 29 January 2015.

40. E. J. Dionne Jr., "Pope Speaks in Rome Synagogue in the First Such Visit on Record," *New York Times*, 13 April 1986.

41. Judy Maltz, "Pope Francis Calls for Peace in First Visit to Israel," *Haaretz*, 25 May 2014.

42. Jacob Neusner, "Crosses at Auschwitz: Crisis and Turning," in *The Continuing Agony: From the Carmelite Convent to the Crosses at Auschwitz*, ed. Alan L. Berger, Harry J. Cargas, and Susan E. Nowak (Binghamton, NY: Global Academic Publishing, 2002), 77.

43. Robert E. Kennedy, "Rituals at Auschwitz-Birkenau," *America: The Jesuit Review*, 10 October 2005.

44. Kennedy, "Rituals at Auschwitz-Birkenau."

45. Kennedy, "Rituals at Auschwitz-Birkenau."

46. Jeff Diamant, "N.J. Rabbi Leads Jews, Muslims on Interfaith Trip to Nazi Concentration Camps," *Star-Ledger*, 15 August 2010.

47. Di Giovine, "Pilgrimage," 263

48. Marvin Prosono. "Cross Purposes: The Conflict Over Symbolic Territory Between Poles and Jews at Auschwitz," in *The Continuing Agony: From the Carmelite Convent to the Crosses at Auschwitz,* ed. Alan L. Berger, Harry J. Cargas, and Susan E. Nowak (Binghamton, NY: Global Academic Publishing, 2002), 80.

49. Bauman, *Modernity and the Holocaust*.

50. Adorno, Theodor W. 1983. "Cultural Criticisms and Society" in *Prisms*, 17–34. Cambridge: MA: MIT Press..

Chapter Five

From Gas Chambers to 9/11

The Future of Postmemory and Contemporary America's Commodity Grief Culture

Pavlina Radia

On 15 March 2002, about six months after the tragedy of 11 September 2001, Alissa Torres, a 9/11 widow—who would become the author of *American Widow*[1]—sent an article, "Wrath of a Terror Widow," to the *Salon* Media Group asking, "Why, oh why, do we unearth the graphic sights and sounds of the day, hold ceremonies before hundreds of cameras with Ground Zero the background in every shot? To make sure 'the rawness' doesn't fade, according to one CBS executive producer. This is a worthy goal?"[2] Her article not only reacted to the post-9/11 hype of mass advertising, the "Never Forget" merchandise, and the tourists flocking to the Ground Zero site, but also to the increasing commodification of the personal grief of 9/11 victims' families. In the article, Torres explores the early post-9/11 iteration of what critics have been calling *tragic* or *death tourism*, a tourism to "sites of violent death, such as concentration camps, prisons, battlegrounds, killing fields, places of terror attacks, plane crashes and natural disasters,"[3] to use Brigitte Sion's terms. In *American Widow*,[4] a graphic novel, Torres further expands on the challenges of losing her husband in the 9/11 attacks, while pregnant, and critiques the ways in which the 9/11 memory has been subjected to (inter)national reframing and commodification.

In his 2012 novel, *Hope: A Tragedy*, Shalom Auslander[5] similarly ponders America's historical obsession with memorialisation as essential to America's collective nation-building, but also as a form of personal identification with trauma that blurs the line between fact and fiction, memory and postmemory, the individual and collective. Similar to Torres, Auslander explores the ethical challenges of bearing witness in the posthuman and postmemory age, specifically as it pertains to the generation that has not experienced the Holocaust or 9/11. As Marianne Hirsch has recently argued, the postmemorial paradigm exposes "the multiple ruptures and breaks introduced by trauma and catastrophe" through "a generational structure of transmission embedded in multiple forms of mediation."[6] This mediation highlights memory as a nonteleological, multivalent construct, shaped by diverse cultural and affective topographies. Similarly, the posthuman age invites us to consider the human as a conglomerate of human and nonhuman relationships that are decentralized rather than centred in and around the individual subject (man). The posthuman is a multidimensional concept that consists of a "flow of relations with multiple others,"[7] to put it in Rosi Braidotti's terms. The multidimensionality of these relations thus also forces us to reconsider the complex relationship between the past and the present, not to mention its influence on history and humanity's future.

Through his characters, Auslander, echoing some of Torres's concerns, queries the relationship between trauma and memory, individual and national history. He asks, "What does remembering do?"[8] His protagonist, Kugel, reflects on the commodification of the Fourth of July and all the flags and symbols that "seemed now as the basest form of patriotism; not pride, but fear,"[9] while simultaneously dealing with his mother's identification with the Holocaust memory and the ghostly visitor of Anne Frank typing away in his attic. While Torres's graphic novel is both a memoir and a sociocultural critique of the grief culture of contemporary America and its increasing commodification, Auslander's novel provides an intriguing insight into the American preoccupation with memory and memorialisation not only as a national(ist) form of becoming-the-nation, but also as a means of containing public trauma through a particular framing of events.

Questioning America's obsession with memorialisation as a public discourse and national identification, the texts by Torres and Auslander ponder the future of postmemory in the posthuman age where the emphasis on experientiality and trauma are blended with national politics and an imperative of instant closure and gratification. In what follows, this chapter explores contemporary America's commodity grief culture and the future of postmemory as a form of assembly where the public and private memories are not only blurred, but also exposes the challenges of bearing witness in the posthuman age. In parsing the ethical questions surrounding postmemory, death tourism, and grief commodification, this chapter draws on Judith Butler's theory of assembly as an "embodied performance" of the "claim to the political"[10] and an "ethical solicitation,"[11] while not necessarily circumventing the exclusion of those whose voices cannot be heard, or whose voices are silenced. It also engages with Marianne Hirsch's notion of postmemory as "retrospective witnessing"[12] that repositions traumatic memory in the quest of reintegrating past experiences of previous generations into the fabric of everyday life. Such repositioning, in Hirsch's terms, is an "embodied and affective experience"[13] that can be as "engaging as it is troubling."[14] Both Butler and Hirsch raise important questions about the challenges of bearing witness in the posthuman age, noting the dangers of appropriation and commodification that may come with such repositioning.

Even though America's increasing interest in memorialisation can be seen as an attempt to "promote human rights, democracy, reconciliation, and peace,"[15] as Amy Sodaro suggests, it also relies on engaging experiential affectivity in a fairly formulaic manner that evokes and legitimates "the political priorities and goals of the regimes that build them."[16] As a form of assembly, death tourism is highly performative as an expression and embodiment of postmemory. Consisting of a palimpsest of memories and memorial narratives of generations who have not experienced or witnessed the tragic event, postmemory (in the service of various death tourist agendas) thus inevitably participates in distinct forms of political (and national) legitimation that can be democratic but also exclusionary, commodifying, and ideological. Taking a cue from the literary texts by Torres and Auslander, this chapter asks what role literature can play in mobilizing memory as a call to ethics rather than a public assembly where the personal can be lost or excluded. Expanding on my previous work on memorialisation,[17] this chapter explores contemporary America's grief culture as tied up in the work of postmemory whose "future" depends on the kind of postmemorial work the American postmillennial generation is willing to do.

AMERICANIZING MEMORY: GRIEF COMMODITY CULTURE 101

In the posthuman culture associated with digital media, mass marketing, and commodification, a constant barrage of news outlet content, Facebook posts, and tweets that essentialize, memorialise, and commodify genocide and violent events have become our new reality. Online websites from *Viator* to *Tripadvisor* offer cheap packages and tours to the United States Holocaust Memorial Museum (USHMM), the 9/11 Memorial Museum, and many others. Each year, visitors from all over the world gather around the 9/11 memorial and visit the museum to pay homage to the victims of the great American tragedy while some honour the tragic memory by taking selfies or purchasing "Never Forget" souvenirs from the 9/11 Memorial Museum gift shop.

From what Daniel Levy and Natan Sznaider (2006) have called "the Americanization of the Holocaust"[18] to the increasing commodification of 9/11, contemporary America's culture is "marked by emotional appeals and investments"[19] and what Erica Doss (2010) has recently called "memorial mania."[20] Amy Sodaro argues that memorialisation through tourism as a form of educational pilgrimage participates in the spread of democratic values and thus, in spite of its national(ist) agendas, provides an opportunity to learn about past atrocities.[21] Mark Pendleton, on the other hand, questions the increasing commodification of "traumascapes" as sites of pilgrimage by suggesting that the call to never forget traumatic events frequently encourages "wilful acts of forgetting."[22] Generally, critics remain divided on the subject of what can be called the future of postmemory and its relationship to national and global, but also personal, individual agendas, noting that most memorials and museums, and increasingly memorial museums, tend to privilege a particular way of framing the violent past that, specifically in the American context, highlights American sovereignty and prowess, and thus leaves out important voices from the process of memorialisation and its narrativization.

As critics like Doss,[23] Sion,[24] and Sodaro[25] have emphasized, American memorials like the USHMM and the 9/11 Memorial Museum rely on memory tropes that engage the visitors' affect by highlighting the experiential component of the exhibitions. Their architecture is minimalist and designed to house "carefully orchestrated narratives of select traumas" whereby trauma becomes a "national project."[26] The USHMM exhibition is mostly chronological and performative. Upon entry, the visitors are given an identification card, providing a history of a particular Holocaust victim or survivor. The USHMM emphasizes the experiential through an intense simulation of the Holocaust events with transplanted bunks and other artefacts from Auschwitz, for example.[27] Not surprisingly, a well-known article by Philip Gourevitch, published in 1993 in *Harper's* magazine, denounced the museum's "peep-show" format and questioned its playing into "the viewer's fascination" with tragic atrocities.[28] While suggesting that the USHMM plays a role in advocating democracy and human rights, Sodaro also concludes that, in sum, "the Holocaust in the museum is packaged like a Hollywood movie—scripted, well-designed, and widely accessible."[29] Similarly, the 9/11 Memorial Museum has invited its own share of critics, from both the public and the victims' families. The construction costs reached over $1 billion and the annual operating costs are around $57 million.[30] The Memorial Museum highlights the heroism of American ideals and is deeply "nationalistic and divisive" in its carefully controlled narrative of the 9/11 events.[31] Both exemplify what Doss has called America's "memorial mania," or America's obsession with appropriating grief as a national trauma and as a means of reaffirming American national identity.[32]

So how can we live up to the limits of memory and its influence on our sense of future? According to the Holocaust scholar Geoffrey Hartman, distortion, fragmentation, and nonlinearity are all part and parcel of memory retrieval; therefore, "we should not underestimate the counter-force of literature as it combines with testimony."[33] As the narratives by Torres and Auslander demonstrate, contemporary American literature can provide interesting insights into the complex, and frequently nationalist and political agendas of memorialisation. In *American Widow*, Alissa Torres outlines the traumatic realities of being a 9/11 widow, pregnant with her first child and coping with the tragedy of losing her husband while navigating the post-9/11 government and resulting media frenzy. But she also exposes the ways in which the American government's emphasis on framing the 9/11 event as a national grief further complicated, and frequently erased, the individual grieving process of the victims' families and relatives. Detailing the media's, and the Bush administration's, framing of the trauma narrative as an event of national grief but also heroic survival that was marketed or "sold," to paraphrase Dana Heller's words, as "a new kind of national identification—or national branding awareness,"[34] Torres asks, "How do I choose a headstone for you?"[35] Exposing the deeply personal trauma of losing her husband, Torres presents the reader with the dialectics of memory and anger, grief and the impossibility of grief through a juxtaposition of sparse, fragmented narrativization and the mainly blue-black-and-white visual framing of the narrative. The illustration on the next page of the labyrinthine cemetery overtakes the process of any kind of identification—national or personal. Sitting on the ground, Alissa is overwhelmed by the seemingly infinite landscape of grief.[36]

In her critique of the nationalization of 9/11 through her personal grief, Torres provides an intriguing social commentary on the ethics of remembrance and its challenges when she echoes the pandemonium of the ABC's "Babies of 9/11" segment, airing on 20 December 2001, and its follow-up on 29 August 2002, in her depiction of the Independent Women's Forum Luncheon. Chapter 18 examines the public and media appropriation of the widows' grief. While some widows allow the media in, Torres resists being interviewed, only to be duped by the Independent Women's Forum. The media and photographers surround the luncheon and the babies are taken to the nursery so that the mothers can "enjoy" themselves.[37] The public's appropriation of post-9/11 as a national grief not only becomes divisive but also exclusionary in that it imposes a particular way of grieving and dealing with the loss on widows like Torres.

The emphasis on psychological closure as healing and redemptive pervades the post-9/11 memorial(ization) process. As Dana Heller notes, "closure through consumption" continues to dominate the 9/11 (post)memory.[38] Heller points to the increased sales of American flags and 9/11 souvenirs. In 2001, retailers sold more than $51.7 million worth of American flags.[39] The persistent retelling and revisiting of the event through media segments and annual markings of the event can be seen as an attempt to "recenter" what was a "decentering" sequence of events, to use the words of Judith Butler.[40] According to Butler, the compulsive retelling of the 9/11 tragedy served as a mechanism to "compensate for the narcissistic wound opened up by the public display of our physical vulnerability."[41] Butler speaks to the Bush administration's push for a national closure through patriotic appeals and their refocusing on the justification of the Iraqi war. In *Selling 9/11*, Heller anticipates Butler's critique when she suggests that the 9/11 anniversary celebrations embody the very irony of the trauma and its presumed "closure" through postmemory's performative lens. In Heller's words, the nationalizing of the grieving process became a "centerpiece of the strategy that would help 'sell' the idea of an Iraqi war to the American people," but also "an amplification of the opportunism that had already transformed 9/11 into a commercial pitch."[42] This form of ecstatic commodification of trauma as a tokenized narrative of grief is what Torres's graphic memoir strives to decenter through a juxtaposition of the mostly black-white-and-blue frames, monotone imagery, and fragmented narrative.[43] The frames refuse to explain; instead, the drawings and the text speak to postmemory's unreliability, or what Hirsch (2012) calls "the multiple ruptures and radical breaks introduced by trauma."[44] Visual and textual fragmentation thus becomes a crucial mechanism of questioning the increasing nationalization of the 9/11 tragedy, but also a means of honouring the personal as an embodied fragment.

For example, Torres critiques the collusion of the patriotic imperative to affirm America's national identity and the 9/11 tragedy by refusing to use the American flag as a commodity symbol. Instead, her use of red, white, and blue roses indicates the plurality and diversity of America's population and its complex history. To disrupt the post-9/11 spectacle, she zooms in on the financial dire straits of the victims' families and the government's assessment of the victims' "economic value."[45] She exposes the House Resolution 2926, dubbed the Feinberg Compensation Fund, as inequitable and exclusive, measuring victims' pain and suffering based on their employment, class, race, and religion. Torres notes, "When the statute finally talked about compensating the victims and their families, it described what it would give . . . and what it would take away."[46] The graphic frames describe Kenneth Feinberg's dismissive attitude, saying to a victim's relative, "Your wife certainly worked well beyond her years. So the bad news is that her actual economic value is minimal."[47] Feinberg's economic commodification of the victims led to a lot of backlash. As Torres notes, the families were insulted by the emphasis on the economic and thus national value of their beloveds and, not surprisingly, felt betrayed by the government.[48] The public was also outraged, but their outrage had to do with their perception of the compensation itself. Torres cites a whole list of public litanies aimed at the victims' families and widows in her book, ranging from accusations of greediness to outright racism. One "legal citizen's" comment states, "Don't give my money to illegals. Bad enough they take jobs. Now cause their loved ones died, we are giving them even more of my tax dollars."[49] The complaints are then juxtaposed with snapshots from newspapers and editorial commentaries, affirming the controversial responses of the public.

Torres's emphasis on the public "burning" of the victims' families speaks to the complex politics surrounding 9/11, specifically the fact that the victims of 9/11 came from diverse backgrounds—ethnic, racial, and religious; some were illegal immigrants. This diversity remains largely unaddressed by the 9/11 Memorial Museum. As Sodaro (2017) correctly points out, the memorial museum's chronological narrative, the predomination of blue (as indicative of the blue skies of 11 September), and the emphasis on American ideals "avoid confrontation with the politics behind the cause and consequences of the 9/11" and "instead creat[e] a hegemonic and monolithic memory of the event that is deeply political and problematic."[50] It is a form of assembly that performs its own call to inclusion by being exclusionary. As Butler reminds us, "every determination of the 'people' involves an act of demarcation,"[51] which limits and circumscribes the narrative of inclusion. Instead, the demarcation dictates who can be heard and who must be silenced. Such erasures merely contribute to the weight of the traumatic event and raise the question of what it means to remember in a public forum.

In "Wrath of a Terror Widow," Torres addresses this dictate as she comments on the Circle Line Boat Tour, arranged in honour of the 9/11 victims and their families on 11 March 2001, to mark the deaths of their loved ones.[52] As well-meaning as the tour might have been, its patronizing underpinnings were a far cry from honourable remembrance. Not only were the media outlets allowed on board, but the tour guide's "incongruously happy-go-lucky" attitude, "reminding [the families] that the snacks are free" and saying "It doesn't get better than that!" evoked the more global, national reframing of grief as a literal act of consumption. This reframing as a public discourse produced "a new kind of national identification—or national branding awareness," to put it in Dana Heller's words, that merely "refashion[ed] fantasies of coherent, monolithic nationhood and consensual nationalism" propagated by the George W. Bush administration.[53] As Torres emphasizes in her article, the monolithic reframing contributes to a particular retelling of 9/11 events that often eliminates the individual, and deeply personal, meaning of the pain and grief that the victims' families experienced and continue to experience.

Memorials—be they mobile, static, or temporary—are, by definition, translations and representations of historical events. Since memory is fluid, it is an unreliable narrative that blends fact, fiction, and affect in ways that depend on time, space, and, of course, cultural context. As Mark Shaming, who was an employee of the New York State Museum at the time of the 9/11 attacks, reveals, the unfolding of the days and weeks after the event demonstrated the unreliability of memory and its ethical challenges.[54] In his words, "Information was unstable, in many cases, emotions—grief, anger, sympathy—were shaping actions and history."[55] What Torres's book and her article speak to, however, is the very limit of translatability and what Giorgio Agamben in *Remnants of Auschwitz* describes as the "paradox of testimony."[56] According to Agamben, only those who perished are the true "witnesses" and hence the survivors can only "speak in their stead, by proxy, as pseudo-witnesses; they bear witness to a missing testimony."[57] Throughout her graphic novel memoir, Torres refers to this untranslatability by outlining the painful ordeal of piecing together a narrative of her husband's tragic and unexpected death.

American Widow rejects chronology or linearity; instead, it persistently disrupts the narrative through and by the visual barrage of the images and graphic frames that reiterate the physical fragmentation of Torres's young family but also her husband's physical body as Torres shares the coroner's clinical cataloguing: "Long Body Notes 1: upper-torso, left arm, hand."[58] In her emphasis on the untranslatable and the narrative lacunae of the grieving process, Torres echoes Agamben's notion that testimony can only speak to "the disjunction between two impossibilities of bearing witness."[59] Consequently, it can be said that postmemory, as a testimony to the linguistic, but also nonverbal, lacunae of historical and personal events, is an unreliable narrative that embodies the lack it cannot represent while simultaneously being in excess of the very lack it represents.

While death tourism relies on the promise of closure—with exhibitions frequently organised in a mostly linear, chronological manner, Torres's *American Widow* persistently subverts any possibility of an organised narrative that affirms the possibility of "cure." As she shows through the juxtaposition of textual and visual frames wedded by narrative lacunae, her testimony is a form of confrontation and displacement. Not only does it speak to the psychology of bearing witness, but it also exposes the ways in which testimonial narratives "encounter—and make us encounter—*strangeness*."[60] Shohana Felman's notion of testimony as a discursive practice is particularly informative in this context. According to Felman, testimony is "a situation *with no cure.*"[61] In broad strokes, it is an ongoing process of translation that both inscribes and transposes (rather than cures) the estranging effects and affects of memory.

Shalom Auslander's novel, *Hope: A Tragedy*, provides further insight into the challenge of bearing witness in the posthuman age. His novel asks, what is the relationship between memory and humanity? Exploring its fluid topography, Auslander's novel examines the many turns of memorialisation—its narrativization and institutionalization—and its postmemorial manifestations. As Ruth Gilbert writes, Auslander's novel is a "rather serious meditation on the subtle hauntings that infuse post-Holocaust consciousness."[62] And yet it is much more than a novel about haunting. Pondering the transgenerational guilt and its influence on post-Holocaust generations, but also commenting on the globalization of the Holocaust or what Daniel Levy and Natan Sznaider call "the Americanization of the Holocaust,"[63] Auslander's novel probes the cult of tragedy driving contemporary American culture. Engaging with the current adage that "tragedy and suffering sell," Auslander delves into the grotto of the American unconscious, questioning America's "basest form of patriotism" as a series of "threats, dares, provocations."[64] Pervading the novel, however, is the notion of memory and/as forgetting, forgetting and/as memory. In his satirical rendering of America's commodity grief culture as a grotesque tour of postmemory's many (re)turns, *Hope: A Tragedy* is a call to memory that lays bare the ethical challenges of bearing witness in the posthuman age.

THE TOURS OF POSTMEMORY AND THE CHALLENGE OF BEARING WITNESS IN THE POSTHUMAN AGE

Recent studies of post-Holocaust memory have raised concerns about integrative forms of remembrance associated with public memorials and memorial museums. Their highly formulaic, experiential agendas frequently produce the opposite of remembering.[65] As Geoffrey Hartman emphasizes, collective memory is subject to institutionalization; hence, it is important "not to confuse fiction and memory . . . and for history not to succumb to sentimental or mystical ideas about a community's 'world-historical' destiny."[66] Instead, Hartman sees literature and art as a productive "counter-force" that can deautomatize memory and deaestheticize violent politics.[67] In her recent work on testimonial narratives, Marianne Hirsch similarly notes the ways in which "narratives of return"—be they by survivors, their children, or postgenocide generations—present the complex entanglements or turns of memory as resisting closure or recovery.[68] Instead, such narratives present the "impulse to return as a fractured encounter between generations, cultures, and between mutually imbricated histories," to use Hirsch's words.[69] This fracture is, as Felman emphasizes, "a situation with no cure" but also the very medium that transmits the estranging effects and affects of memory.[70] In Auslander's novel, postmemory unfolds as an assembly of fractured events and their (dis)embodied transfigurations that are mirrored by the characters whose stories are as fluid as their identities. Kugel, the main protagonist, mimics his mother's posttraumatic stress and vicarious victimhood through his own preoccupation with death and suffering. Bree, Kugel's wife, is an aspiring writer and an advocate for moving on from the past. Then there is the "hideous, horribly disfigured—terribly old" transfiguration of Anne Frank who sets up her writing residence in his attic.[71] Kugel's son, Jonah, who almost dies from pneumonia, an illness associated with the inhumane conditions of Nazi concentration camps, also figures as an important aspect of Auslander's "narrative of return." As others have acknowledged, while Jonah figures minimally in the novel, his presence is central to Kugel's hope for a better future. Affectively transfigured by the past and its effect on their present, Auslander's characters evoke the many different turns of Holocaust postmemory. They speak to its Americanization and institutionalization as a "universal imperative" and "a product of consumption,"[72] to use Levy and Sznaider's words, but also as a performative and (dis)embodied assembly of fractured history spanning generations and cultures.

As Auslander reveals, one of the dangers of contemporary obsession with the tragic as the new American gothic is the blurring of ethical and consumer agendas that reduces the "never forget" imperative to a tokenized death "tour" and vicarious victimhood. One of the most striking passages in the text is the moment when Kugel's mother takes him on a tour of death camps, only to realise that she is in Germany and the main extermination camps were "far away" in the East.[73] From subjecting photos of Holocaust victims to her "editorial" decoupage to her insistence on being the carrier of traumatic memory by layering Holocaust pictures with her family's photographs, Kugel's mother is the ultimate death tourist. When Kugel "beg[s] Mother not to editorialize," she retorts that "it was just adding context, making history more alive."[74] When she takes Kugel on a tour of Sachsenhausen, she is disturbed by the fact that "all the really famous camps were far away."[75] She chastises the tour guide, complaining, "I don't want to get out there and find some sanitized park grounds."[76] While the guide reassures her that "it's very disturbing,"[77] she is equally chagrined by Kugel's lack of engagement caused by a bout of violent diarrhoea, rebuking him: "You ruined the whole concentration camp for me."[78] Here, Auslander uses irony and satire to problematize death tourism as a performative assembly that is, on the one hand, what Butler calls an "ethical solicitation" to memory,[79] and, on the other hand, an act of populist automatization of "nostalgic propaganda and . . . forgetting."[80]

Deautomatization of perception is an important aspect of art. Or, as Geoffrey Hartman puts it, "Art can and does move away from historical reference by a characteristic distancing."[81] According to the Russian formalist Victor Shklovsky, art has the potential to estrange and defamiliarize "habitual" perception that has turned into a form of amnesia.[82] Such defamiliarizing potential pervades testimonial narratives of return in which the inaccessibility of traumatic events and the challenges of bearing witness are frequently mediated by objects (e.g., photographs, diaries, and other tokens of memory). As Hirsch notes, such objects can "embody memory and thus trigger affect shared across generations."[83] But as Auslander's novel reminds us, while family mementos, passports, and photos are often the only remaining connection survivors and the post-Holocaust generations have to the atrocious past, these objects can be (and often are) abused as tokens or souvenirs sold in museum shops. In the novel, Auslander takes care to counter any form of objectification and instead perpetually humanises objects—be it through his representation of the transfigured, living, albeit disfigured, body of the dead Anne Frank, Mother's anthropomorphizing of objects, or Kugel's own preoccupation with hope as a mark of humanity.

This pursuit of humanization strives to deautomatize, to use Shklovsky's words, any racial, ethnic, or gender objectification. In the novel, the dead come alive and nonhuman objects are humanised. Described as a "relentless anthropomorphizer" who is "concerned for the agony of the logs he condemned to the fireplace,"[84] Kugel has empathy for all forms of life and death: "the heartache and sorrow of the families of those innocent creatures—the grasshoppers, the ants, the frogs—that perished so gruesomely under the blade of his lawn mower. Never again, whispered the spiders. Never again, replied the crickets."[85] In his (ironic) embrace of the complex and interrelated relationship between human and nonhuman forms, Kugel is a true posthumanist. Weary of humanism's darkest otherizing projects—be it colonialism, imperialism, Nazi genocide, or xenophobia—Kugel disrupts the self–other, human and nonhuman binaries through the emphasis on a vibrant "ecological sensibility," to borrow Jane Bennett's words, that acknowledges our coexistence with other social and environmental networks, technologies, or nonhuman environments.[86] In his unique juxtaposition of estranged parallels and related events, Auslander masters the art of satire. For Auslander, everything is, and all are, connected.

Throughout the novel, Auslander establishes the kind of estranging parallelism that Shklovsky associates with the function of art and Holocaust scholars like Hartman, Hirsch, and Felman align with testimonial narratives of return. The grotesque parallelism of nonhuman objects being humanised is clearly a critique of the Nazi marginalization and objectification of Jews and other marginalized groups, but it is also a critique of any supremacist ideology, including humanism's many foibles. By refusing to mediate the trauma of history through objects that are dead, Auslander animates the nonhuman form as a defamiliarizing device that thwarts the clichés of American commodity grief culture and instead encourages new ways of thinking about the ethics of remembering and forgetting. As I have mentioned in my previous work,[87] the transfiguration of Anne Frank embodies the post-Holocaust generation's "transgenerational phantom,"[88] to use Nicolas Abraham and Maria Torok's words, and thus "blur[s] the line between the body historic and [the body] hysteric."[89] Similarly, Ruth Gilbert deploys Anne Frank as a golemic figure that is at once an imaginary "textual creation"[90] and "the return of the repressed"[91] haunting the novel. Furthermore, as an important defamiliarizing device that distances the reader from the now automatic, populist narratives of Anne Frank, the young victim, Anne Frank's imaginary disfigured, aging body also evokes the grotesque of contemporary America's body politic. By refusing to be dead, Anne Frank's transfiguration provides a critique of post-Holocaust and post-9/11 commodification of trauma and its emphasis on healing and recovery through objects and souvenirs.

Like the Bakhtinian grotesque body, Auslander's Anne Frank is a hyperbole that rejects both amnesia and closure. It is a "body in the act of becoming."[92] In Bakhtin's words, "in the grotesque body, . . . death brings nothing to an end, for it does not concern the ancestral body, which is renewed in the next generation."[93] Accordingly, Auslander's Anne Frank is an affirmation of memory that escapes the commodified grief tour through another narrative turn. As she says to Kugel, "Pulitzers, . . . not Oscars. Art is not convenient, Mr. Kugel, art is not safe."[94] Consequently, for Auslander, the future of postmemory and hope for the future lie with art, not a commodified grief tour.

THE POSTHUMANIST FUTURE: FROM WAR TO EMPATHY

While focusing primarily on post-Holocaust memory, Auslander's *Hope: A Tragedy*, is also a novel that inscribes the tragic events of 9/11. As I mentioned earlier in this chapter, Kugel's coping with the "tapping sound of history"[95] is interwoven with the state of contemporary America as "the nation at war."[96] Kugel and his family seek respite from the onslaught of memory, brought on by his mother's posttraumatic stress but also by the challenge of living in post-9/11 New York. The parallels between the ashes of the 9/11 victims covering the city of New York and the atrocities perpetrated in death camps are part of Auslander's unique "rewriting."[97] His critique of contemporary death tourism echoes Torres's dismay at the persistent institutionalization and commodification of grief as a national(ist) and sovereign affect affirming American heroism. Advocating for a posthumanist future, Auslander laments the loss of true American values, "a feeling beyond patriotism—a feeling rather of belonging, of oneness with a nation of strangers."[98] So, to echo Kugel: "[Are] there lessons to be learned?"[99] If so, what is the future of postmemory and humanity in the age of consummate forgetting?

Both Auslander and Torres refrain from providing a definite answer; instead, suspicious of memory's many wondrous and not-so-wondrous tours, their narratives perform a call to an ethical, albeit empathetic treatment of memory. But this call, as their works suggest, must be aware of empathy's own affective challenges and biases, political and personal agendas, and, most importantly, conflicting detours. As Butler cogently reminds us, an "ethical solicitation"[100] must acknowledge that which escapes the "claim to the political"[101] or the claim to never forget. To take this notion further, the future of postmemory as an ethical imperative will depend on the present and future generations' understanding of memory's many turns and unpredictable returns, but also their recognition that its reach expands beyond individuals, nations, cultures, or textual and visual media. As Torres has suggested in her article, "A 9/11 Widow's Advice to the Most Recent Victims of Violence and Terrorism," postmemory's ethical potential lies in our ability to acknowledge that grief is "more complicated and arduous than the pat process of 'coming to terms' with the tragedy as a nation."[102] If postmemory has a future, perhaps hope, taking Auslander's cue, is its only answer.

BIBLIOGRAPHY

9/11 Memorial. National September 11 Memorial Museum. Last modified 2018. http://www.911memorial.org.
Abraham, Nicholas and Maria Torok. *The Shell and the Kernel: Renewals of Psychoanalysis*. Chicago, IL: University of Chicago Press, 1994.
Agamben, Giorgio. *Remnants of Auschwitz: The Witness and the Archive*, translated by Daniel Heller-Roazen. New York: Zone, 2002.
Auslander, Shalom. *Hope: A Tragedy*. New York: Picador, 2012.
Bakhtin, Mikhail. *Rabelais and His World* (1965), translated by Helene Isowlsky. Bloomington: Indiana University Press, 1984.
Bennett, Jane. *Vibrant Matter: A Political Ecology of Things*. Durham, NC: Duke University Press, 2010.
Braidotti, Rosi. *The Posthuman*. Cambridge: Polity, 2013.
Butler, Judith. *Precarious Life: The Powers of Mourning and Violence*. New York: Verso, 2006.
———. *Frames of War: When Life Is Grievable*. London: Verso, 2009.
———. *Notes towards a Performative Theory of Assembly*. Cambridge, MA: Harvard University Press, 2015.
Clark, Laurie B. "Ethical Spaces: Ethics and Propriety in Trauma Tourism." In *Death Tourism: Disaster Sites as Recreational Landscape*, edited by Brigitte Sion, 9–35. London: Seagull, 2014.
Doss, Erica. *Memorial Mania: Public Feeling in America*. Chicago: University of Chicago Press, 2010.
Erll, Astrid. *Memory in Culture*. London: Palgrave, 2011.
Felman, Shoshana. "Education and Crisis, or the Vicissitudes of Teaching." In *Testimony: Crises of Witnessing in Literature, Psychoanalysis, and History*, edited by Shoshana Felman and Dori Laub, 1–56. New York: Routledge, 1992.
Felman, Shoshana, and Dori Laub, eds. *Testimony: Crises of Witnessing in Literature, Psychoanalysis, and History*. New York: Routledge, 1992.
Freeman, Lindsey A. "The Manhattan Project Time Machine: Atomic Tourism in Dave Ridge, Tennessee." In *Death Tourism: Disaster Sites as Recreational Landscape*, edited by Brigitte Sion, 54–74. London: Seagull, 2014.
Gilbert, Ruth. 2018. "Jewish Ghosts: Haunting and Hospitality in Shalom Auslander's *Hope*." *Holocaust Studies* 24 (2): 240–58. doi.org/10.1080/17504902.2017.1411021.
Gourevitch, Philip. "Behold Now Behemoth: The Holocaust Memorial Museum: One More American Theme Park." *Harper's*, July 1993. https://harpers.org/archive/1993/07/behold-now-behemoth/.
Hartman, Geoffrey, ed. *Holocaust Remembrance: The Shapes of Memory*. Oxford, UK: Blackwell, 1994.
Heller, Dana, ed. *Selling 9/11: How a National Tragedy Became a Commodity*. New York: Palgrave Macmillan, 2005.

Hirsch, Marianne. *The Generation of Postmemory: Writing and the Visual Culture after the Holocaust*. New York: Columbia University Press, 2012a.

Hirsch, Marianne. "Object of Return." In *After Testimony: The Ethics and Aesthetics of Holocaust Narrative for the Future*, edited by Jakob Lothe, Susan Rubin Suleiman, and James Phelan, 198–220. Columbus: Ohio State University Press, 2012b.

Levy, Daniel, and Natan Sznaider, eds. *The Holocaust Memory: In the Global Age*, translated by Assenka Oksiloff. Philadelphia: Temple University Press, 2006.

Pendleton, Mark. "Theme Parks and Station Plaques: Memory, Tourism, and Forgetting in Post-Aum Japan." In *Death Tourism: Disaster Sites as Recreational Landscape*, edited by Brigitte Sion, 75–96. London: Seagull, 2014.

Radia, Pavlina. *Ecstatic Consumption: The Spectacle of Global Dystopia in Contemporary American Literature*. Newcastle upon Tyne: Cambridge Scholars Publishing, 2016.

Radia, Pavlina. "Mobilizing Affective Brutality: Death Tourism and the Ecstasy of Postmemory in Contemporary American Culture." In *Mobilities, Literature, Culture* (Palgrave Mobilities, Literature, Culture Series), edited by Lynne Pearce, Charlotte Mathieson, and Marian Aguiar. London, UK: Palgrave, forthcoming.

Sachsenhausen Memorial and Museum. Last modified 2018. https://www.sachsenhausen-sbg.de/en/.

Shaming, Mark. "From Evidence to Relic to Artefact: Curating in the Aftermath of 11 September 2001." In *Death Tourism: Disaster Sites as Recreational Landscape*, edited by Brigitte Sion, 139–66. London: Seagull, 2014.

Shklovsky, Victor. From "Art as Technique" (1917). In *Modernism: An Anthology of Sources and Documents*, edited by Vassiliki Kolocotroni, Jane Goldman, and Olga Taxidou, 217–21. Chicago: University of Chicago Press, 1998.

Sion, Brigitte, editor. *Death Tourism: Disaster Sites as Recreational Landscape*. London: Seagull, 2014.

Sodaro, Amy. *Exhibiting Atrocity: Memorial Museums and the Politics of Past Violence*. New Brunswick, NJ: Rutgers, 2017.

Torres, Alissa. *American Widow*. New York: Villard, 2008.

———. "Widow's Advice to the Most Recent Victims of Terrorism and Violence." *Salon*, 7 December 2015. https://www.salon.com/2015/12/07/a_911_widows_advice_to_the_most_recent_victims_of_terrorism_and_violence/.

———. "Wrath of a Terror Widow." *Salon*, 15 March 2002. https://www.salon.com/2002/03/15/widow_wrath/.

Tripadvisor.ca. Accessed 1 July 2018. http://tripadvisor.ca/.

Viator.com. Accessed 1 July 2018. http://viator.com/.

United States Holocaust Memorial Museum. Museum Press Kit. Accessed 26 March 2018. https://www.ushmm.org/information/press/press-kits/united-states-holocaust-memorial-museum-press-kit/.

NOTES

1. Alissa Torres, *American Widow* (New York: Villard, 2008).
2. Alissa Torres, "Wrath of a Terror Widow," *Salon*, 15 March 2002, https://www.salon.com/2002/03/15/widow_wrath.
3. Brigitte Sion, ed., *Death Tourism: Disaster Sites as Recreational Landscape* (London: Seagull, 2014), 1.
4. Torres, *American Widow*.
5. Shalom Auslander, *Hope: A Tragedy* (New York: Picador, 2012).
6. Marianne Hirsch, *The Generation of Postmemory: Writing and the Visual Culture after the Holocaust* (New York: Columbia University Press, 2012), 33–35.
7. Rosi Braidotti, *The Posthuman* (Cambridge: Polity, 2013), 7.
8. Auslander, *Hope*, 223.
9. Auslander, *Hope*, 222.

10. Judith Butler, *Notes towards a Performative Theory of Assembly* (Cambridge, MA: Harvard University Press, 2015), 18.
11. Butler, *Notes*, 100.
12. Hirsch, *The Generation of Postmemory*, 130.
13. Hirsch, *The Generation of Postmemory*, 33.
14. Hirsch, *The Generation of Postmemory*, 39.
15. Amy Sodaro, *Exhibiting Atrocity: Memorial Museums and the Politics of Past Violence* (New Brunswick, NJ: Rutgers, 2017), 22.
16. Sodar, *Exhibiting Atrocity*, 11.
17. Pavlina Radia, "Mobilizing Affective Brutality: Death Tourism and the Ecstasy of Postmemory in Contemporary American Culture," in *Mobilities, Literature, Culture*, ed. Lynne Pearce, Charlotte Mathieson, and Marian Aguiar (London: Palgrave, forthcoming). Also see Radia, *Ecstatic Consumption: The Spectacle of Global Dystopia in Contemporary American Literature* (Newcastle upon Tyne: Cambridge Scholars Publishing, 2016).
18. Daniel Levy and Natan Sznaider, eds., *The Holocaust Memory: In the Global Age,* trans. Assenka Oksiloff (Philadelphia: Temple University Press, 2006), 132.
19. Erica Doss, *Memorial Mania: Public Feeling in America* (Chicago: University of Chicago Press, 2010), 15.
20. Erica Doss, *Memorial Mania*, 26.
21. Sodaro, *Exhibiting Atrocity*.
22. Mark Pendleton, "Theme Parks and Station Plaques: Memory, Tourism, and Forgetting in Post-Aum Japan," in *Death Tourism: Disaster Sites as Recreational Landscape*, ed. by Brigitte Sion (London: Seagull, 2014), 87.
23. Doss, *Memorial Mania*.
24. Sion, *Death Tourism*.
25. Sodaro, *Exhibiting Atrocity*.
26. Doss, *Memorial Mania*, 130.
27. Sodaro, *Exhibiting Atrocity*, 47.
28. Philip Gourevitch, "Behold Now Behemoth: The Holocaust Memorial Museum: One More American Theme Park," *Harpers,* July 1993, https://harpers.org/archive/1993/07/behold-now-behemoth/.
29. Sodaro, *Exhibiting Atrocity*, 51.
30. Doss, *Memorial Mania*, 143.
31. Sodaro, *Exhibiting Atrocity*, 159.
32. Doss, *Memorial Mania*, 115.
33. Geoffrey Hartman, ed., *Holocaust Remembrance: The Shapes of Memory* (Oxford, UK: Blackwell, 1994), 18.
34. Dana Heller, ed., *Selling 9/11: How a National Tragedy Became a Commodity* (New York: Palgrave Macmillan, 2005), 3.
35. Torres, *American Widow*, 174.
36. Torres, *American Widow*, 174.
37. Torres, *American Widow*, 201.
38. Heller, *Selling 9/11*, 17.
39. Heller, *Selling 9/11*, 16.
40. Judith Butler, *Precarious Life: The Powers of Mourning and Violence* (New York: Verso, 2006), 6.
41. Butler, *Precarious Life*, 6.
42. Heller, *Selling 9/11*, 2.
43. Radia, *Ecstatic Consumption*, 177–98.
44. Hirsch, *The Generation of Postmemory*, 33.
45. Torres, *American Widow*, 132.
46. Torres, *American Widow*, 132.
47. Torres, *American Widow*, 132.
48. Torres, *American Widow*, 132.
49. Torres, *American Widow*, 136.
50. Sodaro, *Exhibiting Atrocity*, 143.

51. Butler, *Notes*, 5.
52. Torres, "Wrath of a Terror Widow."
53. Heller, *Selling 9/11*, 3.
54. Mark Shaming, "From Evidence to Relic to Artefact: Curating in the Aftermath of 11 September 2001," in *Death Tourism: Disaster Sites as Recreational Landscape*, ed. Brigitte Sion (London: Seagull, 2014), 4.
55. Shaming, "From Evidence to Relic to Artefact," 141.
56. Giorgio Agamben, *Remnants of Auschwitz: The Witness and the Archive*, trans. Daniel Heller-Roazen (New York: Zone, 2002), 36.
57. Agamben, *Remnants of Auschwitz*, 34.
58. Torres, *American Widow*, 164.
59. Agamben, *Remnants of Auschwitz*, 39.
60. Felman and Laub, *Testimony*, 7.
61. Felman and Laub, *Testimony*, 5.
62. Ruth Gilbert, "Jewish Ghosts: Haunting and Hospitality in Shalom Auslander's *Hope*," *Holocaust Studies* 24, no. 2 (2018)(2): 253.
63. Levy and Sznaider, *The Holocaust Memory*, 132.
64. Levy and Sznaider, *The Holocaust Memory*, 222.
65. For more detailed studies of memorials, see Sodaro; Doss; Radia, "Mobilizing Affective Brutality."
66. Hartman, *Holocaust Remembrance*, 16.
67. Hartman, *Holocaust Remembrance*, 18.
68. Marianne Hirsch, "Object of Return," in *After Testimony: The Ethics and Aesthetics of Holocaust Narrative for the Future*, ed. Jakob Lothe, Susan Rubin Suleiman, and James Phelan (Columbus: Ohio State University Press, 2012b), 200.
69. Hirsch, "Object of Return," 200.
70. Felman and Laub, *Testimony*, 7.
71. Auslander, *Hope*, 25.
72. Levy and Sznaider, *The Holocaust Memory*, 132.
73. Auslander, *Hope*, 175.
74. Auslander, *Hope*, 106.
75. Auslander, *Hope*, 175.
76. Auslander, *Hope*, 175.
77. Auslander, *Hope*, 175.
78. Auslander, *Hope*, 177.
79. Butler, *Notes*, 100.
80. Lindsey A. Freeman, "The Manhattan Project Time Machine: Atomic Tourism in Dave Ridge, Tennessee," in *Death Tourism: Disaster Sites as Recreational Landscape*, ed. Brigitte Sion (London: Seagull, 2014), 59.
81. Hartman, *Holocaust Remembrance*, 19.
82. Victor Shklovsky, "Art as Technique" (1917), in *Modernism: An Anthology of Sources and Documents*, ed. Vassiliki Kolocotroni, Jane Goldman, and Olga Taxidou (Chicago: University of Chicago Press, 1998), 219.
83. Hirsch, "Object of Return," 200.
84. Auslander, *Hope*, 65.
85. Auslander, *Hope*, 65.
86. Jane Bennet, *Vibrant Matter: A Political Ecology of Things* (Durham, NC: Duke University Press, 2010), xi.
87. Radia, *Ecstatic Consumption*, 149–77.
88. Nicholas Abraham and Maria Torok, *The Shell and the Kernel: Renewals of Psychoanalysis* (Chicago, IL: University of Chicago Press, 1994).
89. Pavlina Radia, *Ecstatic Consumption: The Spectacle of Global Dystopia in Contemporary American Literature* (Newcastle upon Tyne: Cambridge Scholars Publishing, 2016), 164.
90. Gilbert, "Jewish Ghosts," 250.
91. Gilbert, "Jewish Ghosts," 244.

92. Mikhail Bakhtin, *Rabelais and His World* (1965), trans. Helene Isowlsky (Bloomington: Indiana University Press, 1984), 316.
93. Bakhtin, *Rabelais*, 322.
94. Auslander, *Hope*, 183.
95. Auslander, *Hope*, 12.
96. Auslander, *Hope*, 222.
97. Auslander, *Hope*, 106.
98. Auslander, *Hope*, 222.
99. Auslander, *Hope*, 222.
100. Butler, *Notes*, 101.
101. Butler, *Notes*, 18.
102. Torres, "Widow's Advice to the Most Recent Victims of Terrorism and Violence," *Salon*, 7 December 2015, https://www.salon.com/2015/12/07/a_911_widows_advice_to_the_most_recent_victims_of_terrorism_and_violence/.

Chapter Six

Art, Trauma, and History: A Survivor's Story

Aaron Weiss

"The new generation has to hear what the older generation refuses to tell it."[1] This contention by Simon Wiesenthal, in the context of the Holocaust and wartime survivors, brings into focus the paradox that confronts both survivors and their offspring—the need to learn by hearing from those who do not wish to teach through telling their stories. This paradox is complicated by a myriad of factors bound to the issue of inducing trauma through survivor's guilt, the act of recalling memories which may be tantamount to emotional self-mutilation, and parental anxiety surrounding the potential effect on their offspring—exposure to a form of narrative trauma. In addition, the preexisting emotional state of the survivor and his or her offspring must also be considered due to their exposure to trans- and intergenerational traumas.

The material discussed in this chapter is an extension of an artistic documentary, produced by the author, the focus of which was the investigation of expressions of trauma in various art forms, as well as personal interviews conducted with the subject.[2] The documentary examined a child survivor of the Holocaust, whose pseudonym in this chapter is "Rachel," and two subsequent generations. A pseudonym was employed to disguise Rachel's identity because she agreed to participate on condition of anonymity. Rachel had exhibited a penchant for drawing images of the Holocaust, including images with a religious theme. Rachel avoided discussing her experiences with family,[3] but her artwork contained a visual vocabulary: a combination of specific words, pictures, and symbols that encapsulate her history, thoughts, and feelings, revealing some of that of which she could not speak. Drawing on interviews with Rachel and an on examinations of her artwork, this chapter explores the ways in which art, trauma, and history not only intersect in the survivor's drawings, but also create an alternative space for expression that would otherwise be difficult to communicate. This chapter argues that artwork created by the Holocaust survivor represents a fertile ground for self-expression and provides further insight into her wartime experiences, without necessarily triggering additional trauma in the subject. But it also provides an important space where future generations can learn from the past and "never forget." Overall, this chapter seeks to engage with the following questions: Can art serve as a medium to communicate Rachel's wartime experiences while mediating the effect of the trauma associated with discussing the subject? If so, can art operate as an agent to bridge the gap regarding the survivor's experiences—be they related to mother and offspring, or to the survivor and the reception of her artwork?

This chapter offers a close reading of Rachel's artwork, specifically her use of visual vocabulary and her specific themes. For instance, the chapter examines individuals who are presented in the drawings and those who are omitted, inclusion or exclusion of religious symbols and markers, and the specific placement of religious symbols on the page. Furthermore, underpinning this chapter are Rachel's life experiences as shared with me in interviews and her profile speaking in her own words, including a brief discussion of her family's reception of Rachel's art. While not a theoretical or psychological examination of trauma, but rather a close retelling of the survivor's artwork story, my reading is informed by E. A. Brett's (1985) scholarly work in the field of art therapy and trauma which speaks to the role of art as a tool to mediate conditions such as posttraumatic stress disorder (PTSD) and by Zolton Vass's (2013) psychological research on the interpretation of drawings. This chapter draws on my previous work on Holocaust survivors and trauma. It specifically engages with the artwork produced by survivors, to examine the ways in which art can serve as an alternative space for working through traumatic events.

It is important to acknowledge that conducting this study presented ethical issues in terms of data collection methods while raising important questions for both researchers and subjects (survivors and family members), specifically, how to collect data from the subjects while managing the risk profile for the participants. As this chapter suggests, these complexities surrounding the issue of communicating wartime experiences require methods that privilege alternative forms of expression. These complexities require a shift from oral traditions (the traditional concept of the "talking cure") towards the visual arts that may serve as an entry point into understanding the lived experiences of survivors and their direct, as well as transgenerational, influence. As noted by scholars such as Brett, art therapy can be used to offset the effects of traumas like PTSD through the creation of a safe place that provides the survivor with an opportunity to process his or her emotions in alternative ways.[4] Therefore, a survivor's drawings function as a canvas for self-expression that communicates experiences within a safe space, minimizing distress while providing an opportunity to bear witness. In addition to Rachel's drawings, this chapter also includes references to my documentary, which involved an interview with Rachel, as well as material from prerecorded interviews she had done for the Shoah Foundation.[5]

RACHEL'S PROFILE (SURVIVOR)

Rachel was born premature on October 30, 1939, in France during the Holocaust. The first five years of her life were spent hiding from the Nazis. Prior to the war, her English father was employed as an accountant and later joined the Royal Air Force as a pilot. He also had a penchant for gambling and alcohol. Her Parisian mother was a hat designer. Rachel spent the primary phase of her early child development (the first five years) "constantly moving,"[6] hiding in dark unfamiliar environments from the Nazis; it was a time when "nothing made any sense,"[7] thereby disrupting a key stage in the construction of her physiological, psychological, emotional, and intellectual development through a lack of exposure to social experiences and general stimuli for the five senses.

Rachel attributes her discomfort with the light and poor eating and sleeping habits as some of the lingering effects of living in a perpetual state of darkness from infancy to early childhood.[8] She states in relation to her childhood that "the war totally messed me up as a human being . . . it doesn't go away or fade."[9] After the war, Rachel emerged from hiding to be placed in the care of her maternal grandfather who performed the role of primary caregiver. Within a year, Rachel was forcibly removed, without notice, by her parents and taken to England, which she regarded as a horrific event. Consequently, she "hated" her parents, and "did not want them touching her."[10] Rachel stated that her initial feelings of discontent were rooted in a resentment that emerged after her removal from the one and only stabilizing and nurturing figure in her life, her grandfather, or as she called him affectionately, "Grandpa." Rachel was particularly disturbed by not being informed in advance of the move, or provided with the opportunity to say goodbye to him. Exacerbating the trauma of the move was also Rachel's separation from another source of solace and serenity: the frog at the pond near her Grandpa's.

Once in England, her parents' refusal to allow Rachel to maintain contact with her grandparents intensified her trauma. She recalled feelings of extreme distress, aligning with separation anxiety, loneliness, and mourning. Alone, under the supervision of virtual strangers in a new land, and impeded by limited social and communication skills, her troubled state was compounded by almost daily physical abuse administered by her father. Rachel described her mother as a silent bystander, who was thereby complicit in the act.[11] Rachel speculated that the abuse may have been the root cause behind her parents' decision to disconnect her from her Grandpa, as a means to protect this family secret.[12] Rachel felt unwanted by her mother, but did give her credit for sending Rachel to private school, which prevented further abuse.

Prior to adolescence, both Rachel and her sister confessed to having been raped by an uncle.[13] In early adulthood, following her older sister's lead, she emigrated from London to Montreal at age sixteen. Their reunion was short-lived, as the elder sister soon married, leaving Rachel to fend for herself. Rachel enrolled in classes at McGill University but dropped out of school prior to the completion of her first year. Were some of the learning challenges she faced at the university a part of the equation which led to her forsaking her education prematurely? If so, dropping out speaks to one of the residual effects of operating from a deficit of knowledge and experience due to the disruption of the early childhood learning cycle. Another residual effect of early trauma on her inability to complete her higher education could be the mental health challenges arising from her trauma. Her employment prospects were dim based on a dearth of work experience combined with limited education, consequently leaving her to monetize her appearance by working as a "bunny-server" at the Playboy club. In the pursuit of some semblance of 1960s normalcy, Rachel accepted an invitation to a date with a local Jewish boy. A lovely evening on the town concluded with another incident of rape. The repeated incidents of sexual assault exposed Rachel to an additional layer of trauma. At this stage, aside from her Grandpa, men, whether family or friend, could be reduced to fit into two categories: sexual predators or physical abusers. The totality of these incidents spanning from the cradle to early adulthood culminated in Rachel's admittance into a psychiatric ward. Subsequent years included numerous incidents of attempted suicide and extended periods of alcoholism.

With regards to family, Rachel had four children, with four different men. Three of the children were conceived out of wedlock, with one of the children placed for adoption. Rachel's three children moved out by the age of sixteen. Rachel described her parenting style as overprotective and possessive.[14] Rachel sums up her time as a spouse as follows: "I didn't enjoy marriage ... too much work."[15] As her children grew, Rachel sought ways to provide for her family by embarking on a variety of employment endeavours largely dedicated to entrepreneurial ventures. Rachel's gravitation towards self-employment may be accounted for by her lack of higher education and mental health challenges, but it is also worth considering that self-employment provided her with a sense of agency. However, as she herself indicated, anti-Semitism was also at play in her job search, for example, when she was told, "You people take too many holidays."[16] A pattern emerged where she would start a business that would enjoy a degree of short-term success. For example, Rachel created one of the first kosher meats section in a secular grocery store (Loblaws); founded and managed a modelling and talent agency in downtown Toronto; designed a line of popsicle stick lamps and shades along with a "Do It Yourself Kit" which Lewiscraft offered to purchase outright (she declined); and a shavings company, where Rachel, a diminutive figure, drove a pink tractor trailer with her two young daughters seated next to her, with a shotgun for protection. Rachel's work as a truck driver speaks to her ability to adapt and survive within a nontraditional vocation for women in the late 1960s. Her fight to keep herself employed illuminates the fact that survivors are not just victims.

Nonetheless, a variety of factors (partners, personal health issues, family issues) impeded her success, contributing to the suspension of the businesses. Principal among these impediments to success were Rachel's suicide attempts, which were indicators of underlying mental health issues that were subsequently diagnosed. Consequently, commencing in the 1970s to the present day, Rachel has been, partly to exclusively, dependent on one form of social assistance or another (private and public) to subsidise her living expenses. Rachel presently resides in subsidised housing and receives monthly assistance from a Jewish charitable foundation, in addition to her Holocaust reparation payments. Rachel's previously noted history of alcoholism has been largely dormant for over a decade.

Last but not least, it is important to note that Rachel's relationship to her Jewish faith, using the practice of rituals (Shabbat observation—davening) and observance of Jewish High Holidays as the metric to assess outward expression of her religiosity, may be categorised as Reform. Practitioners of Reform Judaism are characterised by a focus on the cultural as opposed to a religious practice of their faith. For those who identify as part of the religion, Reformers privilege a secular and assimilated existence.

THE STORY OF RACHEL'S DRAWINGS

Rachel began drawing in the mid-1990s, coinciding with a period when she was recovering from a serious car accident. Despite multiple surgeries, the incident had left Rachel somewhat debilitated due to extreme pain caused by severed nerves in the brain. To mitigate the pain, Rachel was prescribed a host of drugs, mainly opioids for pain management, thereby providing limited physical mobility. Art may have provided her with an emotional outlet during this period. By 2007, Rachel had amassed a collection exceeding one hundred drawings. However, in 2012, she destroyed all but ten of her drawings. When asked about the reason behind her decision, Rachel replied:

> "I loved my drawings. I got a call one day, from someone I did not know which upset me. They said I should close my business down (a booth at the flea market selling doggie bags and mosquito-resistant clothing) because I wasn't making money. That, along with some other issues, got me very upset, and I destroyed them."[17]

The following pages examine three of her original works, which Rachel shared with me to conduct my research. The first drawing (figure 6.1), created in 2001, is called "Elderly Bearded Man." This drawing features an elderly bearded male.

The man resembles a rabbinical figure. Given Rachel's lack of religious observance, it is a symbolic gesture that requires further examination. When questioned about who this figure was, and what he signified, the survivor confirmed, "They [this and the subsequent picture] were Rabbis" who speak to her feelings of "not being accepted by the Jewish community."[18] Rachel's drawing of a Rabbi reveals what is at stake in the context of her sense of nonbelonging. It portrays a tension between Rachel's deep sense of nonbelonging (feeling unaccepted by her community) and her desire for acceptance and ultimately inclusion. The Rabbi's presence in the picture thus speaks to Rachel's sense of exile—not only from herself, but also from her own community. At the same time, however, the absence of the Rabbi's yarmulke undermines his religious authority, and thereby the legitimacy of his, and by extension, the Jewish community's scorn. The image thus inevitably communicates Rachel's need for a sense of agency, but also a desire for being accepted and understood.

In this context, the subject, who functions as a representative agent of the faith that rejects her, is looking straight ahead, demanding attention. But whose attention—the attention of those contained in the drawing? Facial expressions are an important indicator of mood. The Rabbi, however, appears quiet and serious. His large mass reflects the size and depth of despair this issue casts upon Rachel. Also important is the Rabbi's placement on the page. Placed to the left, the Rabbi's position signifies the past,[19] suggesting that this matter stems from an earlier time, yet remains unresolved, at least until 2001, the date of the work.

In stark contrast to the image of the Rabbi, whose size and placement denote power and status, Rachel presents herself as a small figure who is situated at the bottom of the page. The Rabbi is hovering over her, colonizing her surroundings. These artistic choices connote depression, low self-esteem, intimidation, and withdrawal, all of which correlate with Rachel's real-life experiences and feelings. Overall, Rachel's work mirrors a turbulent emotional state plagued by feelings of insecurity, loneliness, and exclusion. This emotion is, however, counterbalanced with the inclusion of a blanket and a frog. The blanket and the frog signify a sense of comfort, signalling that the

Figure 6.1. Aaron Weiss, "Elderly Bearded Man." *Personal Collection*

"Rachel" in the drawing does not confront this reality alone. The blanket, which she is holding, can be read as a "security blanket," or a comfort object enlisted to protect herself. In this vein, Rachel has placed a frog literally by her side; as noted earlier, a frog was a source of comfort during her post-

Holocaust period. As a child in Paris, one of the few good memories Rachel cherished was playing with a frog outside of her grandfather's residence. The frog in the drawing thus performs the role of a nonthreatening friend and playmate, representing a safe space, but also evoking a sense of familiarity and closeness.

Thus the picture of the Rabbi illustrates Rachel's struggles with the Jewish community and the religion itself, whereas the frog and blanket are symbols of security, protection, and belonging. In addition, the drawing includes the words, "How do we go on." Of note, the question mark was omitted. This omission suggests that this is a statement or a rhetorical question which does not require an answer. In the search for clarity, the artist was asked to answer the question and Rachel stated, "with love, kindness and understanding."[20] Interestingly, these experiences were absent from her childhood. But what does the inclusion of specific words and images offer in terms of understanding Rachel's traumatic topography?

I propose that based on past events in her life, the words speak to her desire to not live with her pain, but also her desire not to die, indicating that her pain has created a type of purgatory. The remaining words are dates: "1939 Paris France" and "2001." The first denotes the date of her birth, and the latter, the completion date of the drawing. Interestingly, she drew herself as a young child; however, in 1939, Rachel was a newborn.

The second drawing, titled "Elderly Man with Hat," was completed in May 2013, approximately twelve years after the previous drawing. Once again, Rachel chose a rabbinical figure as the subject for her drawing, indicating that her previous issues with religious figures were a lingering matter. Juxtaposing figure 6.1 ("Elderly Bearded Man") and figure 6.2 ("Elderly Man with Hat"), I explore this thread of rabbinical figures to draw parallels and to address points of departure through close reading of attire, choice of symbols, and image placement.

In "Elderly Man with Hat," Rachel portrays the Rabbi with a traditional hat, a symbol associated with many members of Orthodox Jewry. Rachel's choice provides this figure with a degree of religious currency not seen in the previous drawing (see figure 6.1). Does this suggest that he is more righteous? If so, why? The answer is located in what the drawing omits: Rachel herself. Rachel's absence, compared to her appearance in figure 6.1 ("Elderly Bearded Man"), suggests that this Rabbi does not stand in judgment of her, which may speak to why he is afforded the hat, which serves the same end as a yarmulke.

Rachel continues her tradition of skewing figures to the left, representing a past traumatic event. However, this drawing was completed several years ago and makes no mention of 1939, nor does it mention her childhood. The Rabbi in figure 6.2 is looking away. His image signals tension, but also intrigue. Regardless, the Rabbi in this drawing presents a departure from the

Figure 6.2. Aaron Weiss, "Elderly Man with Hat." *Personal Collection*

Rabbi in figure 6.1, whose image is confrontational and authoritative. It is important to note that, unlike the Rabbi in figure 6.1, the Rabbi in figure 6.2 is located within the white space, which symbolises purity of the Jewish people. Conversely, the religion itself is articulated through the Star of David, which is in black instead the traditional blue, thereby placing the religion within a state of darkness. Based on Rachel's experience with the Holocaust and other traumatic experiences, it is not surprising that Jewishness is equated with death. Furthermore, this drawing opts out of using language as a means of communicating trauma. The exclusion of words limits the visual vocabulary on display. Instead, Rachel employs a minimalist approach in her message: a combination of white and black space framing the image of the Rabbi.

Figure 6.3 consists of three people (a woman, a boy, and a girl), symbols (candles, a Star of David, a frog, and a blanket), and words that tell another fragmented story of Rachel's traumatic past. Rachel confirmed the identities of the individuals as follows: the woman was her mother; the boy, her son; and the girl in the bottom right of the page is herself. Thematically, figure 6.3 has shifted from figure 6.1 and figure 6.2, in that religion has been removed from the foreground and placed into the background, with family front and centre. Does this indicate that her concerns pertaining to religion have been resolved or lessened? Alternatively, are Rachel's issues with religion still present, but have they been supplanted by anxieties surrounding family? The following reading seeks to explore these questions.

In figure 6.3, "Mother and Son," Rachel situates her son and a book with his name on it in two separate circles. The name has been withheld to protect the family's anonymity. These circles speak to the relationship between mother and son, which, according to Rachel, had begun to drastically deteriorate in 2013. As noted previously, the female figure represents Rachel's mother who died young. In other words, it outlines the lack of resolution between the mother and her daughter. Rachel's mother is placed close to the centre of the page, looking directly at the viewer. Both figures represent family and unresolved, troubled relationships. The third circle contains an open book with "2013" written underneath. This raises questions—with her son's name on the spine, is the book about her son's life or her own life since her son was born? The circle with her son may operate to contain that which appears to be slipping away, her relationship with her son.

The use of additional symbols such as the candle light, as well as the Jewish Star of David, bears further significance. The candle light is placed to Rachel's right, representing the future. Its large size, by comparison with her, provides it with a sense of power. The flame appears somewhat detached from its wick. Is the light heading up towards her son? Is the light of G-d so powerful it cannot be contained? The symbolism offers a palimpsest of possible meanings, highlighting that traumatic experiences must be understood

Figure 6.3. Aaron Weiss, "Mother and Son." *Personal Collection*

in their complexity and diversity. The Star of David appears in the top right of the page, evoking an image, due to its placement and size, of an omnipresent light that shines over all.

Below Rachel and underneath the image of her child, the words "the candle will always give you light amen" and "Paris France Mama 1939" appear. Rachel explained the words' meaning as "giving everyone light that didn't have it during the war." Rachel has placed the image within 1939, yet included her son in it, who was not born at the time. The tendency to blur time and space might signal that the mind of the adult has been trapped within the spirit and sensibilities of a child—a type of arrested development, but also an effect of unresolved trauma. In Rachel's case, art becomes a safe space to process events, where loving people are associated with support and kindness. This is evidenced by the image of Rachel as a child, under a much larger image of her son, suggesting that Rachel sees him as a protector, in addition to the safety blanket and frog. When questioned about whether she considers her son as a protector, Rachel confirmed that, as a single mother, she hoped her son would take care of her.[21] The need for safety, love, and a childlike vulnerability is articulated in the drawings.

Overall, Rachel privileges black pencil as the artistic medium of choice for her artwork. This choice equips Rachel with the flexibility to make changes. However, the darkness and starkness articulated by the black and white scheme could be also read as indicators of the dark and sad nature of her state of mind. The inclusion of people in these works is limited to rabbinical figures and family members. Nonetheless, it is important to note that her daughters are absent from these works. The significance of this is undermined by a lack of context due to the destruction of the majority of her work, to which I did not have access. Therefore, we don't know if her daughters were also omitted from the vast body of her artwork.

BRIDGING THE SILENCE: AUDIENCE (FAMILY) RECEPTION

In one of the interviews that I conducted, Rachel explained that she rarely shared her drawings with friends or family. On the occasions that she did, she had encountered negative feedback, mostly from her family. Her children, on the other hand, labelled them as therapeutic. The survivor objected to such a classification, feeling these works captured her memories through art, as opposed to functioning as some therapeutic apparatus. The two purposes are not mutually exclusive; however, Rachel's defensive posture in response to their judgments compromise her willingness to consider the benefit of drawing as a means to deal with her pain. Further problematizing the therapeutic properties offered to Rachel through her work, other family members, Rachel notes, would refer to them as "depressing".

These responses by her family help elucidate what's at stake for the artist, family, and researchers: can art serve as a medium to communicate Rachel's wartime experiences while mediating the effect of the trauma associated with discussing the subject? If so, can art operate as an important agent that bridges the gap regarding the survivor's experiences? Between mother and offspring? Between survivor and the audience of the artworks? Undoubtedly, the threads displayed in Rachel's art (religion, family, Holocaust, her childhood, and comfort objects) function as a partial roadmap for communicating her experiences during the Holocaust from multiple viewpoints, in terms of age and perspective (child and adult). At the same time, however, art as mediator for trauma is a complicated notion. In comparison to verbalising, the act of drawing can be seen to lessen the effect for Rachel, evidenced by her comfort with the medium as her preferred mode of communication. Conversely, art allows survivors like Rachel to reclaim some of their agency by expressing (nonverbally) the complex topographies of their traumatic experience.

"WHEN IMAGES SPEAK": ART AS A CATALYST

As Rachel's story reveals, art can operate as a valuable means of expressing one's history to his or her offspring while mitigating its effect on the survivor. However, while art can serve as an important medium or bridge whereby traumatic events can be mediated between survivor and offspring, the reception of *what* and *how* these events are communicated through art will elicit varied responses. Based on Rachel's feedback, the post-Holocaust generation, her children, for example, might perceive her drawings as therapeutic (for her) and depressing (for them). On the other hand, Rachel might contest the therapeutic effect these images have for her. The difference in the family members' responses evoke the complex topographies of transgenerational trauma as fractured and not always accessible to memory or reception. These emotional fractures disrupt the transmission of knowledge between generations and widen the gap in knowledge and understanding. Although the opportunity is present, the survivor and her family members have disconnected. Perhaps repressing, dismissing, or disconnecting are defence mechanisms?

Challenging such defence mechanisms, however, are Rachel's drawings as an opportunity to learn about the survivor's challenging experiences. They speak to some of Rachel's pain and her anxiety about not being heard and understood, given the complicated nature of her experience. Beyond the family, and in the broader Jewish community, one of the central barriers that continues to impede the survivor's (and others like her) ability to recover, her drawings suggest, is the judgment that the survivors experience in hiding is somehow devalued as less traumatic than the experience of those who died and suffered in death camps. Therefore her (their) pain, and any expression of it, can be perceived or (mis)interpreted as an affront to those who suffered in death camps. This narrative of rejection appears frequently in the Jewish community and has been accepted by many as truth and coopted by the survivor and members of her family. This rejection acts to undermine, dismiss, and repress the reality of how diverse the experiences of survivors are. In this context, the value of Rachel's drawings as bridges to traumatic experiences that remain silent becomes even more significant as they serve as sites of communication or an attempt at communication, of bearing witness. Providing a safe space for the expression of pain without judgment, Rachel's drawings demonstrate that art can be a powerful mechanism for addressing trauma and anxiety even if the person does not wish to view it as such. There is opportunity for more research in this area by exploring the stories that the drawings of survivors tell and omit as part of the narrative "to never forget."

BIBLIOGRAPHY

Brett, E. A., and R. Ostroff. "Imagery and PTSD: An Overview." *American Journal of Psychiatry*, 142 (1985): 417–24.

Sager, Darren, director. *Survivor Interview*. Toronto, Ontario: Shoah Foundation, 1997. DVD.

Sheridan, M. D. *From Birth to Five Years: Children's Developmental Progress*. Oxford: Routledge, 2008.

Vass, Zoltan. *A Psychological Interpretation of Drawings and Paintings. The SSCA Method: A Systems Analysis Approach*. Pécs, Hungary: Alexandra Kiadó, 2013.

Weiss, Aaron. *The Art of Therapy*. Toronto, Ontario: Aaron Weiss Communication, 2013. DVD.

Wiesenthal, Simon. *The Sunflower: On the Possibilities and Limits of Forgiveness*. New York: Schocken, 1998.

NOTES

1. Simon Wiesenthal, *The Sunflower: On the Possibilities and Limits of Forgiveness* (New York: Schocken, 1998).

2. The documentary, "The Art of Therapy," examined, in part, how art became a mechanism of expressing the subject's experience during the Holocaust while serving to cultivate better understanding between the parent and her children. This chapter operates as a reframing of my previous research on art and trauma. The documentary was never released because it required more interviewing and editing with additional family members, but they were unavailable.

3. This interview was one of those conducted for the documentary "The Art of Therapy." Aaron Weiss, *The Art of Therapy* (Toronto, Ontario: Aaron Weiss Communication, 2013, DVD).

4. E. A. Brett and Robert Ostroff, "Imagery and PTSD: An Overview." *American Journal of Psychiatry*, 142 (1985): 417–24.

5. Darren Sager, director, *Survivor Interview* (Toronto, Ontario: Shoah Foundation, 1997, DVD).

6. Sager, *Survivor Interview*, 9:50.

7. Sager, *Survivor Interview*, 10:39.

8. Sager, *Survivor Interview*, 13:11.

9. Sager, *Survivor Interview*, 10:45.
10. Sager, *Survivor Interview*, 16:52.
11. Sager, *Survivor Interview*, 30:07.
12. Sager, *Survivor Interview*, 37:46.
13. Sager, *Survivor Interview*, 8:37.
14. Sager, *Survivor Interview*, 52:34.
15. Sager, *Survivor Interview*, 53:45.
16. Weiss, *The Art of Therapy*.
17. Weiss, *The Art of Therapy*.
18. Weiss, *The Art of Therapy*.
19. Zoltan Vass, *A Psychological Interpretation of Drawings and Paintings. The SSCA Method: A Systems Analysis Approach* (Pécs, Hungary: Alexandra Kiadó, 2013), 689.
20. Weiss, *The Art of Therapy*.
21. Weiss, *The Art of Therapy*.

III

Doctrines Revisited: Rewriting the Margins

Sarah Fiona Winters

Literature tells stories about the past, present, and future: stories about the past and future in order to understand the present; stories about the past and present in order to guess at the future; and, of course, stories about the future in order to usher in or ward off that future. In this section of the book, Christine Bolus-Reichert analyses stories about the future while Laurie Kruk considers stories about the present, but the stories in both chapters tell of attitudes to the past as well.

Dystopian visions dominate the present fiction about the future. As Kimberly Reynolds has pointed out, "[v]ery few children's books since the 1980s have offered anything other than dystopian visions of the future."[1] The same is true for the stories that adults write for themselves. This grimness about the future to be found in contemporary speculative fiction perhaps reflects to some degree a reaction to the futurism of the early twentieth century, at least as formulated in Filippo Tommaso Marinetti's 1909 "The Foundation and Manifesto of Futurism," which included a contempt for the past expressed in such statements as the following:

> Admiring an old picture is the same as pouring our sensibility into a funerary urn instead of hurling it far off, in violent spasms of action and creation. . . . In truth I tell you that daily visits to museums, libraries, and academies (cemeteries of empty exertion, Calvaries of crucified dreams, registries of aborted beginnings!) are, for artists, as damaging as the prolonged supervision by

parents of certain young people drunk with their talent and their ambitious wills.[2]

G. K. Chesterton responded to the "Manifesto" in 1910 in *Alarms and Discursions* by calling it the work of "feeble megalomaniacs," and pointing out that the celebration of violence and courage that will distinguish the art of the futurists can also be found "in occasional gleams" in the literature of the past, such as *The Iliad*, *The Song of Roland*, and *Henry V*. He also anticipated the eventual evolution of futurism into fascism: "There is a certain solid use in fools. It is not so much that they rush in where angels fear to tread, but rather that they let out what devils intend to do."[3] Indeed, Marinetti moved on from the "Manifesto of Futurism" of 1909 to the "Manifesto of Fascism" of 1919.

As Bolus-Reichert shows, P. D. James and Nalo Hopkinson, writing almost a century after Marinetti, create oppressive political forces in their future worlds that reflect, and challenge the reader to reject, the oppressive political forces of the 1990s. In their case, the systems are closer to capitalism (specifically disaster capitalism as theorised by Naomi Klein) than fascism, but what both systems have in common is a contempt for those vulnerable people who become, in the eyes of "young people drunk with their talent and their ambitious wills," the detritus of the past.

That is not to say that fascism is linked inexorably to futurism, for it is also, of course, a highly reactionary movement, and an example of the dangers of looking to the past as a preventative for the possible evils of the future. In Terry Eagleton's words,

> On the one hand, Nazism marches ecstatically toward a revolutionary future, trundling behind it the latest gleaming technologies of death. On the other hand, it is a question of blood, earth, instinct, mythology, and the dark gods. This combination is one reason for its potent appeal. It would seem that there is nobody fascism cannot seduce, from mystics to mechanical engineers, bright-eyed champions of progress to stuffed-shirt reactionaries.[4]

The conflict between bright-eyed champions of progress and stuffed-shirt reactionaries, between "certain young people" and older people who fear that the future has made them objects for cemeteries or museums, lies not only at the heart of dystopian speculative fiction, but also, in the smaller scale of narrative about the individual human being, at the heart of the short stories of Guy Vanderhaege. As Laurie Kruk makes clear, the value of chivalry, both gendered as masculine and characterised as of the past, haunts the contemporary male characters of Vanderhaege's stories as they seek to negotiate the privileges and perils of being men in the present. Debates around the concept of "toxic masculinity" and the essential or constructed nature of both sex and gender characterise our present moment and invite visions of and possibly even manifestos about the future of men, masculinity, and maleness.

Consequently, distrust of the dark side of masculinity is a theme that connects the dystopias Bolus-Reichert analyses and the stories Kruk examines. As the former writes, one problem with "the apocalyptic paradigm is that it primes us for surrender to whoever is strong enough to manage the shock and awe apocalypse delivers. The strong man (or woman, but usually man) promises survival on his terms," while Kruk responds to Vanderhaege's belief "that the strong should protect the weak" by asking if, for contemporary readers, this sentiment might read as "a remnant of the hegemonic patriarchal privilege." The future for Marinetti was certainly male, and the strength of the male much more about survival than protection of the weak: "We will glorify war—the world's only hygiene—militarism, patriotism, the destructive gesture of freedom-bringers, beautiful ideas worth dying for, and scorn for woman."[5] In *Children of Men* and *Brown Girl in the Ring*, the bringers of a better future are women with babies, characters that embody an ethic of facing the future with hope rather than despair.

The same year Chesterton wrote his satiric attack on Marinetti's Manifesto, he also mused on the popularity of futurist visions in literature:

> The last few decades have been marked by a special cultivation of the romance of the future. We seem to have made up our minds to misunderstand what has happened; and we turn, with a sort of relief, to stating what will happen—which is (apparently) much easier. The modern man no longer preserves the memoirs of his great-grandfather; but he is engaged in writing a detailed and authoritative biography of his great-grandson. Instead of trembling before the specters of the dead, we shudder abjectly under the shadow of the babe unborn. This spirit is apparent everywhere, even to the creation of a form of futurist romance. Sir Walter Scott stands at the dawn of the nineteenth century for the novel of the past; Mr H. G. Wells stands at the dawn of the twentieth century for the novel of the future.[6]

Both dystopian futurism and realistic fiction set in the present outweigh utopian futurism in the century since Chesterton wrote this: more writers use dark visions of the future and conflicted narratives about the present to warn their readers that something is wrong with the world than use shining visions of the future to encourage readers to work towards, rather than against, something. Perhaps the future of literature will show us something different.

BIBLIOGRAPHY

Chesterton, G. K. *Alarms and Discursions*. Alternmunster, Germany: Verlag, 1910.
———. *What's Wrong with the World*. San Francisco: Ignatius Press, (1910) 1991.
Marinetti, Fillipo Tommaso. "The Foundation and Manifesto of Futurism." In *Art in Theory 1900–2000: An Anthology of Changing Ideas*, edited by Charles Harrison and Paul Wood, 146–49. Malden, MA: Blackwell, (1909) 2003.
Eagleton, Terry. *On Evil*. New Haven, CT: Yale University Press, 2010.

Reynolds, Kimberly. *Radical Children's Literature: Future Visions and Aesthetic Transformations in Juvenile Fiction.* New York: Palgrave Macmillan, 2007.

NOTES

1. Kimberley Reynolds, *Radical Children's Literature: Future Visions and Aesthetic Transformations in Juvenile Fiction* (New York: Palgrave MacMillan, 2007), 154.

2. Fillipo Tommaso Marinetti, "The Foundation and Manifesto of Futurism," in *Art Theory 1900–2000: An Anthology of Changing Ideas*, ed. Charles Harrison and Paul Wood (Malden, MA: Blackwell, [1909] 2003), 148–49.

3. G. K. Chesterton, *Alarms and Discursions* (Alternmunster, Germany: Verlag, 1910), 104.

4. Terry Eagleton, *On Evil* (New Haven, CT: Yale University Press, 2010), 72.

5. Marinetti, "The Foundation and Manifesto of Futurism," 148.

6. G. K. Chesterton, *What's Wrong with the World* (San Francisco: Ignatius Press [1910] 1991), 28.

Chapter Seven

The Shock Doctrine in Apocalyptic Fiction

Christine Bolus-Reichert

Naomi Klein's *The Shock Doctrine: The Rise of Disaster Capitalism*, published in 2007, analyses the behaviour of "disaster capitalists" who see crises as opportunities rather than tragedies. She builds the case that for more than thirty years these disaster capitalists have been exploiting the "collective shock" resulting from catastrophic events in order to reorganise the state and redistribute resources. The pattern Klein analyses exists in—and is repeatedly validated by—apocalyptic fiction. Survivors of imagined disasters could choose to rebuild what was lost, since, as Klein points out, "Most people who survive a disaster want the opposite of a clean slate"[1]; but apocalyptic narratives, with their orientation toward the future, are less interested in simple restoration than in what comes next. In most of these stories, the powerful—or newly empowered—erect a new social order on the ruins of the old. In order to understand the degree to which apocalyptic fiction upholds, promotes, or resists the "shock doctrine," I focus on two apocalyptic works from the 1990s: *The Children of Men* by P. D. James, published in 1992, and *Brown Girl in the Ring* by Nalo Hopkinson, published in 1998. Coming after the end of the Cold War, these fictions eschew the scale of destruction offered by, say, nuclear war in favour of disasters that are slow-moving in the case of James (no children have been born in twenty-five years) and highly localised in the case of Hopkinson (the core of Toronto has suffered an economic collapse as a result of international sanctions, and become isolated from the rest of Canada). In James's novel, the government that emerges after the Omega event follows Klein's pattern exactly, and although the conclusion of the novel ought to offer hope for an escape from infertility's repressive regime—a child is born—the main character sees an opportunity to remake the world yet again: "The sense that everything was possible to him, that what he wanted would be done, that what he hated would be abolished, that the world could be fashioned according to his will."[2] Hopkinson, by contrast, imagines a Toronto that recovers only when the disaster capitalist is defeated, and society is reorganised from the ground up, by the people whom the original disaster left behind. *Brown Girl in the Ring* models a response to disaster that acknowledges the vulnerability of those living in a state of shock and the need for citizens to resist having a social order imposed on them, and proposes that we should not regard catastrophe as a blank slate to be written upon, but as a wound on the social body that needs to be healed.

The great literary critic Frank Kermode, writing in 1965, distinguished the role of the critic from that of the poet:

> It is not expected of critics as it is of poets that they should help us to make sense of our lives; they are bound only to attempt the lesser feat of making sense of the ways we try to make sense of our lives . . . ; but I take comfort from the conviction that the topic is infallibly interesting, and especially at a moment in history when it may be harder than ever to accept the precedents of sense-making.[3]

His topic was "The End," the first lecture in a series that would become the book, *The Sense of an Ending*. His topic is also mine, The End—apocalypse—at a moment in history when we are right to be suspicious not only of the making sense of how we make sense of our lives, but of making sense of life in terms of its catastrophic end. Why was his audience suspicious in 1965? Because of the pace of social and technological change and the advent of a new kind of war: the Cold War. And in 2019 why should we be suspicious? Because of the pace of social and technological change and the advent of a new kind of war: the War on Terrorism. *And* because of the work of another critic adept at making sense of how we make sense of things, Naomi Klein. In 2015, when I began developing a course in apocalyptic fiction, I was pursuing an abiding interest of mine, one that I felt was converging with that of my students. But in trying to make sense of so many apocalyptic narratives at once, both literary and visual, my enthusiasm ran aground on Klein's resistance to the "shock doctrine," the idea propagated by economist Milton Friedman and his followers that "[o]nly a crisis, real or perceived, produces real change."[4] Wasn't this what apocalyptic fiction was doing: demonstrating over and over again that disasters produce real change—sometimes good and sometimes bad? Apocalyptic narratives had become a cultural battleground for what kind of change it was going to be, what kind of new beginning would come after The End. But they didn't seem to offer much resistance to the blank slate apocalypse promises to those who can take advantage of it. Still, there were glimmers of such resistance in the speculative mode of these narratives, in their insistence on the value of foreknowledge.

Apocalypse as a genre often aims to wake up the reader; apocalyptic narratives forecast, critique, warn. That's their job: do something now, they scream at us, before it's too late. Even when they don't scream, they are all about waking people up. Take one early example of the genre's flourishing post–World War II: Bill Masen, the hero of John Wyndham's *The Day of the Triffids*, published in 1951, says of the double catastrophe that has destroyed London (a plague of blindness and the subsequent advance of killer plants, the Triffids):

> I suppose that had I had any relatives or close attachments to mourn I should have felt suicidally derelict at that moment.... [W]hat I found that I did feel—with a consciousness that it was against what I ought to be feeling—was release....
> ... I think it may have come from the sense of facing something quite fresh and new to me. All the old problems, the stale ones, both personal and general, had been solved by one mighty slash. Heaven alone knew as yet what others might arise—and it looked as though there would be plenty of them—but they would be *new*. I was emerging as my own master, and no longer a cog. It might well be a world full of horrors and dangers that I should have to face, but I could take my own steps to deal with it—I would no longer be shoved hither and thither by forces and interests that I neither understood nor cared about.[5]

This sounds suspiciously like the shock doctrine—apocalypse as opportunity. Bill Masen was nobody before, but circumstances have made him somebody—a master. The novel tests his conviction, of course, as he is forced to consider how responsible he is for the lives of others—the blind—but the novel's answer tends to be *not much*, that he should focus on the survival of the few over the many. However, Bill's awakening does allow him to resist being coopted into the neofeudalism that one of the other survivors imposes on the mainland.

To move from an early example of the genre to a very recent one: Emily St. John Mandel's 2014 novel *Station Eleven* delivers a paradigmatic opportunist, the Prophet, who terrorises plague survivors all around the Great Lakes on the way to building a new social order; but it also features Clark, a former management coach, who, in the backward and forward movement of the narrative, realises of his past, preapocalypse self that he had been

> moving half-asleep through the motions of his life for a while now, years; not specifically unhappy, but when had he last found real joy in his work? When was the last time he'd been truly moved by anything? When had he last felt awe or inspiration? He wished he could somehow go back and find the iPhone people whom he'd jostled on the sidewalk earlier, apologize to them—I'm

sorry, I've just realized that I'm as minimally present in this world as you are, I had no right to judge.[6]

Clark's awakening comes before the crisis; the crisis gives him the chance to act upon it, to be fully present in the world that remains—to resist the violence of the Prophet and others like him.

The hero of P. D. James's *The Children of Men* is slow to wake. Fifty-year-old Theo Faron is an Oxford historian whose orientation in the first half of the book is decidedly toward the past, both his own and that of England, or more broadly European civilization. The way he locates himself in relation to his cousin Xan Lyppiatt, the Warden of England, is necessary for understanding the second half of the book, and that final scene I have already alluded to in which Theo considers how all things are possible. But it takes him a while to get there, because like most residents of the United Kingdom living through the slow-motion apocalypse of an aging population to which no children have been born in twenty-five years, he has been reduced to an existence of self-maintenance. There's (almost) no one to teach, nothing to look forward to except a slow, entirely predictable decline, a contraction of civilization to an end point of meaninglessness. Theo's orientation only begins to shift toward the future when Julian, a young woman whom he briefly taught, comes back into his life to ask for access to the Warden of England, his cousin Xan. She is a Christian and a social revolutionary, the leader of the Five Fishes—she still believes it's possible to change things. At first, he's entirely dismissive of her project. "There won't be the energy for evil," he tells her, "any more than there will be the energy for good. Think what that England will be like. The great buildings empty and silent, the roads unrepaired, stretching between the overgrown hedges, the remnants of humanity huddling together for comfort and protection, the running-down of services of civilization and then, at the end, the failure of power and light. The hoarded candles will be lit and soon even the last candle will flicker and die. Doesn't that make what's happening on the Isle of Man [which has become a prison] seem unimportant?" She answers, "'If we are dying we can die as human beings, not as devils.'"[7] By this time, Theo has already taken the message to Xan and the Council, who rejected every one of the Five Fishes' demands, and argued that society is exactly the way people want it to be and Theo is now only interested in talking Julian out of becoming a martyr—like her hero, Jesus.

James does not explain the Omega event and she does not explain the Alpha, Julian's pregnancy—Julian may have been chosen by God or merely overlooked by a fertility-testing regime that excludes anyone imperfect (she has a deformed hand). But she alludes to real-world trends as the background for Omega, notably the falling off in the European birthrate. Europe in 1992 seems to be already stuck in place, self-involved, inward-looking, nostalgic.

The novel's real mystery might be love, how we get to the point where we would "die for [someone else's] life,"[8] which is as outward-looking and selfless as one can be. With extinction clearly visible on the horizon, Julian wakes Theo up first with beauty and then with her striving for something beyond mere existence, which is, in the novel, only another kind of beauty. To borrow Mandel's mantra (which she borrowed first from *Star Trek*): survival is insufficient. By the time Theo has an impulse to buy Julian flowers, she has already conceived the miracle baby and he has turned again, after twenty-five years, toward the future, prepared to die so that she can have one.

Nalo Hopkinson's heroine in *Brown Girl in the Ring*, by contrast, is still a teenager and the apocalyptic events that transformed Toronto are barely a decade in the past—and she is already awake, at least compared to Theo. Ti-Jeanne knows it's not all right that Rudy Sheldon rules Toronto with violence and fear (and magic) from his perch atop the CN Tower. He pushes addiction and ensnares the desperate caught behind the barriers. (One of the book's first ironies is that Toronto is being punished for Canada's treatment of the First Nations, but the people who get stuck in the ring are mostly immigrants and the children of immigrants who came long after the First Nations were all pushed out.) Ti-Jeanne is not awake to the part of her that could, to paraphrase Klein, repair what was *not* destroyed in the cataclysm and "reaffirm [her] relatedness to the places that formed [her]."[9] Her problem, in a way, is the opposite of Theo's. He spends all his time thinking about the past—because what else is there? But Ti-Jeanne holds the future right on her hip—the Baby she has not yet named. She needs to look backward, not to what Toronto was before, but to what her ancestors were, when they left the Caribbean, when they left Africa. The past is present for Ti-Jeanne in the visions she has of the spirit world, which will drive her mad if she doesn't heed them, and in Mami, her grandmother, who wants to teach Ti-Jeanne about her spiritual inheritance before it's too late. Ti-Jeanne's mother, Mi-Jeanne, we learn late in the story, tried to run away from her responsibility to the spirits, and became the malevolent spirit, or duppy, that Rudy Sheldon uses to kill anyone who crosses him. But the authoritarian ruler of Toronto is also Ti-Jeanne's grandfather, and he can't be overthrown until she's willing to use her power against him. Mami points the way to a better future not only with the recovery of ancestral traditions, but by teaching Ti-Jeanne to be a healer, using a mixture of herbal lore and nurse's training. In the barter economy that residents of Toronto use to get around Rudy, Ti-Jeanne's family is central. Twice in the novel, at the beginning and at the end, we see Ti-Jeanne walking the streets from downtown to Cabbagetown. Inherent in her motion is the possibility of a multicultural city that is not powered by greed or electricity, and that "reaffirms her relatedness to the places that formed her."

To be sure, within the apocalyptic paradigm "the emergence of a better world"—or a better self—is, as Marlene Goldman has written, "predicated on a passage through an interval of violence and death."[10] Or, as Kermode puts it, "apocalyptic utopianism is [endemic] to political revolution."[11] Change requires crisis, which is why the genre so often prompts readers to remember the transience of our pursuits. John Wyndham does it in *The Day of the Triffids* when he has Bill Masen look at a view of London: "I knew that it was by no means the first time that it had happened. The corpses of other great cities are lying buried in deserts and obliterated by the jungles of Asia."[12] P. D. James does it in *The Children of Men* when she has Theo visit an ethnological museum: "Here was Victorian confidence, Victorian earnestness; the respect for learning, for craftsmanship, for art. . . . In the cluttered show cabinets, model ships, masks, ivory and beadwork, amulets and votive offerings seemed mutely to offer themselves for his attention."[13] Mandel does it in *Station Eleven* when she catalogues what has been lost since the apocalypse: "An Incomplete List: No more diving into pools of chlorinated water lit green from below. No more ball games played out under floodlights. No more porch lights with moths fluttering on summer nights."[14] This particular list lasts for two full pages of her large format paperback to include things as small as pharmaceuticals and as large as cities, countries, borders, flight. It is memento mori amounting almost to *calavera*, a type of poem written about the dead person before death.

Passages like these appear in almost every example of the genre. There's a pause in the action, a panoramic view or a list, and a memory of ages past, an acknowledgement of the fragility of whatever we have built and how easily it can be lost. And it is generally characters, rather than narrators, hitting pause, creating a moment of synchronicity between story and reader as we contemplate our inevitable demise.

There's no doubt that apocalyptic fiction as a genre works as memento mori, a preoccupation for which it has often been criticized. What happens when you turn memento mori—an exhortation to remember that you die—into a form of entertainment? The 2015 film *Tomorrowland*, a rare box office failure for Disney, tries to answer that very question. Late in the film, Hugh Laurie's character, Senator Nix, the apparent villain of the story, delivers a scathing critique of our addiction to apocalyptic narratives, a monologue worth quoting in full:

> Let's imagine, if you glimpsed the future, [and] you were frightened by what you saw, what would you do with that information? You would go to . . . the politicians? Captains of industry? And how would you convince them . . . data? Facts? Good luck. The only facts they won't challenge are the ones that keep the wheels greased and the dollars rolling in. But what if . . . what if there was a way of skipping the middle man and putting the critical news directly into everyone's head? The probability of wide-spread annihilation kept going

up. The only way to stop it was to show it, to scare people straight. Because what reasonable human being wouldn't be galvanized by the potential destruction of everything they've ever known or loved? To save civilization I would show its collapse. How do you think this vision was received? How do you think people responded to the prospect of imminent doom? They gobbled it up like a chocolate éclair. They didn't fear their demise. They repackaged it. It could be enjoyed as video games, as TV shows, books, movies. The entire world wholeheartedly embraced the apocalypse and sprinted towards it with gleeful abandon. Meanwhile, your earth was crumbling all around you. You've got simultaneous epidemics of obesity and starvation. Explain that one! Bees and butterflies start to disappear, the glaciers melt, algae blooms. All around you the coal-mine canaries are dropping dead and you won't take the hint! In every moment there is the possibility of a better future, but you people won't believe it. And because you won't believe it, you won't do what is necessary to make it a reality. So you dwell on this terrible future and you resign yourselves to it for one reason: because that future doesn't ask anything of you today. So yes, we saw the iceberg and warned the Titanic. But you all just steered for it anyway, full steam ahead. Why? Because you want to sink. You gave up.

The abundance of apocalyptic narratives in North American popular culture is pretty clearly related to a moment when we are again becoming conscious of an existential threat—the one posed by climate change. But *Tomorrowland*'s protest against the genre isn't the same as Klein's protest against the shock doctrine: Senator Nix isn't saying that we see disaster as opportunity; just the opposite—we're ready to give up. Things are so bad there's nothing we can possibly do to avert the inevitable—we resign ourselves to a terrible future, which asks nothing of us in the present. In fact, resignation is one of the key elements of the apocalyptic imagination, as Mary Marjikian points out in her 2014 study of the genre: apocalypse differs from mere disaster because it's believed to be unstoppable. The more of these narratives we consume, the more likely we are to believe the apocalyptic paradigm.

In this worldview, whatever we build will inevitably fall. The refrain of our fiction now, and our culture of "prepping" and "survivalism," is "let's be ready"—not to avert what's coming but to endure it. A large part of the appeal of the genre (at least to the eighty-five students in my course) was exactly this—the adventure of survival, the exploration of a world transformed by disaster. But another response occurs just as often in apocalyptic fiction. Suicide, from the start of the modern genre with Nevil Chute's *On the Beach*, published in 1957, has always been on the table. It appears everywhere from almost the first scene of *The Day of the Triffids* to the Bokononists in Kurt Vonnegut's *Cat's Cradle,* published in 1963, to the barren world of *The Children of Men* to, of course, *Station Eleven*—imagined futures that will present us with a choice: suicide, or survival in the new world. The other problem with the apocalyptic paradigm is that it primes us for surrender to whoever is strong enough to manage the shock and awe apocalypse delivers. The strong man (or woman, but usually man) promises survival on his terms, and somewhere down the road, not usually very far, we figure out that "survival is insufficient."

Theo Faron in *The Children of Men* does learn that lesson, and as readers we are comfortable with where his story is going, because it seems to follow the classic structure of apocalyptic narrative, Omega and Alpha, the ending that leads to a new beginning. At least until the end, when James puts a far more pessimistic "Everybody-Wants-to-Rule-the-World" spin on her redemptive tale. Earlier in the novel we learned how Theo's cousin Xan became the Warden of England, what he offered to the people: "protection, comfort, pleasure"[15]; and how he had managed to hold onto power while instituting "reforms" that in normal times would have seemed outrageous: suspending democracy in favour of a ruling council of five; creating a penal colony on the Isle of Man; importing foreign workers called Sojourners and then deporting them when they are too old to work; and promoting the Quietus, ritual suicide for the elderly that isn't quite as voluntary as the government pretends. These are the things the Five Fishes want to fix, and Theo seems to agree. But as all the chapters about the cousins' childhood have been revealing, Theo and Xan are not all that different. When Xan and the council track Julian and Theo to the shed where she has given birth to the first child born on Earth in twenty-five years, Theo kills Xan rather than let him take the baby. At that point, Julian begs Theo to leave Xan's ring, the symbol of his power—"it's not for you," she says. But he picks it up anyway, imagining that all things are now possible. It is not the novel's last scene—that is the sign of the cross Theo makes on the baby's forehead. A sign of hope to be sure, but the implication of Theo's choice to take Xan's ring is surely repetition rather than new beginning, which makes James's novel a cautionary tale for liberals who think they are never the wielders of shock and awe.

The Children of Men and *Brown Girl in the Ring* have a lot in common. They were written in the 1990s, post-Cold War, when people began to imagine apocalyptic events that didn't involve wiping out all life on earth. Both authors consider issues of science within a religious framework. Both foreground motherhood and the importance of generational knowledge. Crucially, however, there's a shift in perspective in the two novels from global to local, from the mastering point of view of Theo Faron to the limited points of view of multiple characters in *Brown Girl*. It's tempting to argue that novelistic perspective has something to do with where the authors started—James in England in 1920 and Hopkinson in Jamaica in 1960—generations, oceans, and historical cataclysms apart. But they both see the pattern in our apocalyptic imaginings and they both, in my view, get it right. James, perhaps because of her longer view of history, or because of her geographical location, cannot quite imagine that Theo's awakening will lead to anything new. Hopkinson does imagine something new for her world and her characters. Ti-Jeanne is one perspective among many in the novel, and is implicated in a community. She can't change the world alone and should not try to—that would make her another Rudy. Hopkinson, by making the apocalypse local, imagines solutions that could work in a particular place at a particular time. There is no blank slate here, but a frayed tapestry, one that needs many hands to give it form and colour.

In March 2016, at the SpecFic Colloquium in Toronto, A. M. Dellamonica, a featured speaker, asked whether writers of science fiction (including Margaret Atwood, the keynote speaker) had already done enough warning. To build the future, Dellamonica said, we have to imagine it in vivid detail and she challenged the writers in the audience to conceive a future worth fighting for—as I think Hopkinson has. Or, as Paul Kingsnorth and Douglas Hine put it in their 2009 manifesto for the Dark Mountain Project, "If we are indeed teetering on the edge of a massive change in how we live, in how human society itself is constructed, and in how we relate to the rest of the world, then we were led to this point by the stories we have told ourselves."[16] Since 2009, Kingsnorth, who is also a novelist, has been working out what kind of stories we need to tell to end up somewhere other than total collapse. Three nodes emerge that are particularly suggestive for my study of apocalyptic fiction. First, in "A Crisis of Bigness" Kingsnorth asks, "what if big ideas are part of the problem? What if, in fact, the problem is bigness itself?"[17] Like Klein, Kingsnorth sees times of crisis as times when people want to wipe the board clean and start over. But it is precisely the ever-increasing scale of our dreams that makes life on earth (especially of nonhuman nature) ever more precarious. Drawing on the work of the little-known economist Leopold Kohr, Kingsnorth imagines the "breakdown of nations," or "division,"[18] as the solution to our present crisis, a reversion to small-scale communities like the one Hopkinson imagines at the end of *Brown Girl in the Ring*. Solutions are developed locally, rather than being imposed from on high. In the 2016 documentary about Jane Jacobs, *Citizen Jane: Battle for the City*, this imposition from above emerges as precisely the problem with all modern urban planning: if the planners do not get out into the streets and see how people live, their grand plans will fail.

Kingsnorth's second major insight has to do with our stance toward nonhuman nature. "In the Black Chamber" describes his visit to the cave paintings in Niaux, France, and his attempt to understand the people who painted animals in the dark. While the essay is primarily about articulating what we lose when we lose nature, it is also a rejection of the idea that science and technology can restore lost nature: "This is a project that sees the world as imperfect and that sees the duty of enlightened human engineers as correcting the imperfections. The end result will be a planned and controlled world of wealth, happiness and peace for all: a rationalist utopia, designed and run by rationalists."[19] Most postapocalyptic improvers—like Xan Lyppiatt in *The Children of Men*—believe they're doing good; but as James and Kingsnorth argue, they leave out what makes life worth living: the holy, which Kingsnorth traces to Old English *halig*, which "has the same root as the word 'whole.'" As Kingsnorth puts it, you either believe in "the Earth as whole, entire of itself, interconnected [and] yourself as part of a wider living thing" or "you see the Earth as a machine and all living things as separate parts."[20] The stance matters, because if we believe the latter, then there's nothing to stop us rearranging it according to our own idea of what is right—for us.

The third insight goes back to stories. Telling different stories about the future, telling stories in which humans are part of something larger than themselves, is the focus of the Dark Mountain Project. In a 2016 essay for the *Guardian*, "Singing to the Forest," Kingsnorth asks what might be the alternative to the narcissism of the novel and poses what might be an answer to Dellamonica's challenge, to write about a future worth fighting for:

> The ecological crisis we have spawned will "unhumanize" our views for us, whether we like it or not. The notions that only humans matter, or that humans are in control, even of themselves, are unlikely to outlast this century. It seems a good time for writers to "become confident as the rock and ocean," and to begin writing about the rock and ocean as if they had a part to play. The novel looks pretty exhausted these days. Could this be its new frontier?[21]

For Kingsnorth, this means making "living landscape not just a backdrop" in a human drama. If we can learn to see the present from down low, rather than up high, then we might be able to imagine local solutions to local crises and to be suspicious of those who would use disasters to remake the world in their own image. For critics—like the contributors to this volume—who want to make sense of how we make sense of things, it is worth critiquing apocalyptic fiction when it seems to be embracing the shock doctrine, and giving authors their due when, like Klein and Kingsnorth, James and Hopkinson, they identify ideologies that we ought to be resisting.

BIBLIOGRAPHY

Goldman, Marlene. *Rewriting Apocalypse in Canadian Fiction*. Montreal: McGill-Queen's University Press, 2005.
Hopkinson, Nalo. *Brown Girl in the Ring*. New York: Warner Books, 1998.
James, P. D. *The Children of Men*. Toronto: Vintage Canada, 1992.
Kermode, Frank. *The Sense of an Ending: Studies in the Theory of Fiction with a New Epilogue*. Oxford: Oxford University Press, 2000.
Kingsnorth, Paul. *Confessions of a Recovering Environmentalist and Other Essays*. Minneapolis: Graywolf Press, 2017.
Klein, Naomi. *The Shock Doctrine: The Rise of Disaster Capitalism*. Toronto: Vintage Canada, 2007.

Mandel, Emily St. John. *Station Eleven*. Toronto: HarperAvenue, 2014.
Manjikian, Mary. *Apocalypse and Post-Politics: The Romance of the End*. Lanham, MD: Lexington Books, 2014.
Tomorrowland. Directed by Brad Bird. [Film] Burbank, CA: Walt Disney Pictures, 2015.
Wyndham, John. *The Day of the Triffids*. New York: The Modern Library, 2003.

NOTES

1. Naomi Klein, *The Shock Doctrine: The Rise of Disaster Capitalism* (Toronto: Vintage Canada, 2007), 9.
2. P. D. James, *The Children of Men* (Toronto: Vintage Canada, 1992), 241.
3. Frank Kermode, *The Sense of an Ending: Studies in the Theory of Fiction with a New Epilogue* (Oxford, UK: Oxford University Press, 2000), 3.
4. Cited in Klein, 7.
5. John Wyndham, *The Day of the Triffids* (New York: The Modern Library, 2003), 46.
6. Emily St. John Mandel, *Station Eleven* (Toronto: HarperAvenue, 2014), 164.
7. James, *The Children of Men*, 109.
8. James, *The Children of Men*, 226.
9. Klein, *The Shock Doctrine*, 9.
10. Marlene Goldman, *Rewriting Apocalypse in Canadian Fiction* (Montreal: McGill-Queen's University Press, 2005), 8.
11. Kermode, *The Sense of an Ending*, 98.
12. Wyndham, *The Day of the Triffids*, 70.
13. James, *The Children of Men*, 106.
14. Mandel, *Station Eleven*, 31.
15. James, *The Children of Men*, 60.
16. Paul Kingsnorth, *Confessions of a Recovering Environmentalist and Other Essays* (Minneapolis: Graywolf Press, 2017), 270.
17. Kingsnorth, *Confessions of a Recovering Environmentalist*, 9.
18. Kingsnorth, *Confessions of a Recovering Environmentalist*, 12.
19. Kingsnorth, *Confessions of a Recovering Environmentalist*, 170.
20. Kingsnorth, *Confessions of a Recovering Environmentalist*, 175.
21. Kingsnorth, *Confessions of a Recovering Environmentalist*, 230.

Chapter Eight

Guy Vanderhaeghe and the Future of the Marginalized Canadian Male

Laurie Kruk

In the context of the future of humanity, what does the future hold, specifically, for men? What fears and desires are found within contemporary Canadian literature addressing the representation of gender? With the 2015 Governor-General's Award for English-Language Fiction going to Guy Vanderhaeghe's *Daddy Lenin and Other Stories*, the topic of male anxiety has resurfaced in Canada. According to R. W. Connell, "hegemonic masculinity" or "the configuration of gender practice which embodies the currently accepted answer to the problem of the legitimacy of patriarchy, which guarantees . . . the dominant position of men and the subordination of women,"[1] may well be in crisis. Vanderhaeghe has long been fascinated by the nature of manhood, and ordinary men's responses to its cultural depiction, making him perhaps "Canada's premier chronicler of masculinity."[2] Within his award-winning body of work we find four titles that point specifically to a recurring concern with the politics and problems of either being male or of occupying traditional masculine roles: his first Governor-General's winning collection *Man Descending* (1982), the historical novels *The Englishman's Boy* (1996) and *A Good Man* (2011), and now *Daddy Lenin* (2015), his fourth story collection. This newest work features nine stories from the male perspective, revealing authorial ambivalence about a posthumanist politics of gender. Although not a short-story cycle, *Daddy Lenin* is unified by a nostalgic, even elegiac, tone, as the protagonists are all middle-aged or older, looking back on misspent youths from the late 1950s to the end of the 1970s.[3] And, to varying degrees, they are mourning the loss of hegemonic masculinity. As Connell admits, when marginalizing identifications of race, class, and sexuality are included, "[t]he number of men rigorously practising the hegemonic pattern in its entirety may be quite small. Yet the majority of men gain from its hegemony, since they benefit from the patriarchal dividend."[4] This "dividend" is defined by Connell in terms of "honour, prestige and the right to command."[5] I would argue that the difference between Vanderhaeghe's latest work and his previous titles lies in the changing politics between men and women. Women are present here, and often central to the men's desires, but they have their own careers, ambitions, and money, appearing "at once wise and unattainable," as Lisa Moore observes.[6] Whitehead and Barrett, in *The Masculinities Reader*, declare "[We] would go so far as to suggest that feminism was the single most powerful political discourse of the twentieth century, shaping up to have an even greater impact in the twenty-first."[7] Is Vanderhaeghe documenting the triumph of the feminist agenda in contemporary Canadian society? Or rather, the men's failure to grow? Socioeconomic disadvantage may fuel a masculine backlash, and, while Vanderhaeghe's men here may be lumped together in the privileged categories of "white" and (mostly) "straight," class remains the invisible divide in his fiction: as he remarked in 1999, "I always think that class is much more important than gender."[8] Meanwhile, the stigma of physical weakness for men—or for lower-class males, contrarily, of intellectual prowess—continues to have a marginalizing effect. Vanderhaeghe's men respond to this paradoxical marginalization with "double-voiced" discourse reflecting self-consciousness about their complex subjectivity: the assumption of presumed centrality undercut by keen awareness of their frequent failure to live up to their gender norms. For instance, the chivalric notion of "honour" lives on, even if it is frequently ironized by narrator or focalizer as just another performance. Explaining the title of his second published story collection, *The Trouble with Heroes* (1983), Vanderhaege observed that "[T]he 'trouble' with 'heroes' is really the notion of what heroism is . . . what constitutes heroism. In my mind, it has more to do with the distance you travel, than with measures of conventional accomplishment."[9] In his dramatization of contemporary Canadian men reflecting on themselves as complex "heroes," Vanderhaeghe "double-voices" masculinity within his short stories, a form which I have argued in my 2016 book, is already open to "double-voicing." In the broadest sense, I see short story "double-voicing" operating on the level of theme, raising questions about dominant values and discourses. This opens up the technical question of "who speaks?" which I term "thematics of focalization." This choice then shapes the literary mode, or style, of the story, including the "double-voicing" created through irony, satire, or parody. Finally, at the discursive or linguistic level, "double-voicing" appears in terms of the border-crossing dialogizing of language itself. In Vanderhaeghe's case, this dialogizing is most commonly found by incorporation of class markers, vernacular and orality effects, as well as his focalizers' creation of "hybridized constructions." According to Bakhtin, such constructions contain "mixed within [them] two utterances, two speech manners, two styles, two 'languages,' two semantic and axiological belief systems."[10] Vanderhaeghe's creation of these stylized passages depends on subtle shifts between linguistic registers and rhetorical values, revealing the fractured identities of seemingly dominant men coping with social, political, and economic marginalization. In fact, "double-voicing" on all four levels is found in the stories I examine here—"Tick Tock," "Live Large," and "Counsellor Sally Brings Me to the Tunnel"—but I will largely confine my analysis to how the men's discursive and social performance, whether externalised or internalised, is riven with contradictions springing from a contemporary crisis in hegemonic masculinity, and the future for men.

"Tick Tock" is focalized through Charley Brewster, a sixty-two-year-old professor of American literature, who, like the hero of Fitzgerald's classic novel, "was staring longingly at the green light beckoning at the end of the dock, which was, in his case, imminent retirement from a career that had proved to be less than stellar."[11] On the surface a figure of authority by profession as well as by his canonical specialty, Brewster is suggestively a "failure," in contrast to his present lover, the younger Professor Eva, who specialises in courses in "representations of masculinities."[12] Practically a parody of the rising feminist superstar, Eva considers Brewster a "a poster boy for the bad hegemonic variety,"[13] making their relationship a short-lived mistake, at best. But it is another relationship that is disturbing Brewster, and awakening age-old pain in his hands. The pain reappears with the arrival of Brewster's new neighbours in his apartment building, young newlyweds Melvyn and Dina Janacek. Disturbing his work, and driving him to the campus doctor for painkillers, these spasms, a visceral reminder of the broken bones sustained after three fistfights during his youth, are seemingly inspired by signs of domestic abuse next door. Awakened by such noises one night, Brewster considers phoning the police. As he ponders "the etiquette of reporting a disturbance after the disturbance has ended," Brewster addresses himself in the following dialogised internal exchange, an example of a hybridised construction challenging hegemonic masculinity:

> How would that fly with the cops? Well, he was pretty sure it wouldn't, as you might say, *soar*. He would be written off as a pesky wing nut, a busybody prosecuting a feud with his neighbours. . . . Maybe what he'd heard was a housewarming fuck. The date of possession carnally celebrated. But no, that yipping had had a fearful, pleading note to it, had sounded just the way that girl's face had looked when her partner had been chewing her out for her lack of oomph with the mattress.[14]

Self-consciously questioning the reception of his complaint by the police, Brewster extends the idiomatic figure of "fly" into "soar," although ironically underlining his professorial distance from it with "as you might say." He then returns to the vernacular with use of the passive verbal "written off," and the labels "pesky wing nut" (continuing the flight metaphor) and "busybody," although he concludes with the formal legalese of "prosecuting a feud with his neighbours." Brewster thus deftly shifts registers, from the everyday to the elevated, coming back down to earth(iness) in the third sentence with the crudity of "fuck" joined with the genteel adjective "housewarming," its sarcastic echo of neighbourly hospitality. The return to legalese in the following fragment—"the date of possession carnally celebrated"—shows his professorial ability to transform anger into wit. However, his final thought is one of concern for "that girl," the young wife, whose puppy-like "yipping," he assumes, is a vocal translation of the facial expression he had witnessed earlier, as the couple were moving in their marriage bed. He immediately identifies with Dina as victim of her abusive "partner," whom he had seen "chewing her out" for her "lack of oomph with the mattress." However, Brewster's compassion is somewhat diluted by his ironic musical linking, through assonance, of "chewing" with the sound-effect word "oomph."

Brewster thus attempts to talk himself out of interfering, although his hybridised construction reveals the repressed anger beneath his linguistic artfulness, an anger which comes from his own history as a victim of bullying.[15] His past anger is demonstrated by the savage beating of his bully, Ronnie Peel, but then extends to a parking lot fight with a man protecting his sports car, and with a university student pretentiously mocking a weary waitress. Styling himself a defender of the working class into which he was born, Brewster received his comeuppance from an outraged social order as he earns a two-year sentence for this last assault, delaying his education. Forty years later, his hands still hide within them a powerful rage as he anticipates a conflict with his new next-door neighbour, Melvyn the "gym ape." Brewster's hands "act up" again, aching in memory of their past breakages. The next night, after unseen violence behind their shared wall dislodges "Brewster's print of Scafell Pike, a souvenir of a walking tour he had taken in the Lake District thirty years ago,"[16] the man who had admired the Romantic poets turns violent, pounding his aching fists into the wall. Earlier advised by the campus doctor to consider the "New Age" approach of "cognitive behavioural therapy, including kundalini yoga classes," Brewster responds, "I'm not a kundalini kind of guy. I guess I'll just bite the bullet and soldier on."[17] In another hybridised construction, the alliterative flair of "*kundalini kind* of guy" is balanced with "*bite* the *bullet*" and the military identification Brewster adopts instead as a kind of "soldier" in the battle of life. Discussing "Tick Tock," Steven W. Beattie wryly notes how "masculinity as an ideal ... has been replaced by a societal outlook steeped in the dubious virtues of postmodernism and therapy."[18] Is this the future of masculinity, we wonder?

The night of what proves to be their last date, Eva and Brewster are interrupted by a visit from a weeping Dina. While Eva capably sweeps Dina away to a woman's shelter, enacting her feminist principles, Brewster is left holding the bag, literally. For Dina has asked Melvyn to return her purse to her through Brewster. The expected confrontation at Brewster's door occurs, and Brewster prepares to perform his own heroic principles by pursuing the younger man to the parking garage in the wake of Melvyn's parting threat to damage her car and "leave [Dina] something to think about!"[19] Speaking with Herb Wyile, Vanderhaeghe observed, "Honour, in my mind, is closely identified with a moral sense. . . . For instance, that the strong should protect the weak is honourable."[20] Is this belief a remnant of the hegemonic patriarchal privilege, or is it something more? As Brewster descends the stairs, he realises he is still wearing his carpet slippers, and in his interior monologue satirically reflects, *"there's footwear designed to strike terror in the heart of Melvyn, overawe him with your avuncular, cozy Je ne sais quoi."*[21] In another instance of linguistic "double-voicing," Brewster performs a self-parody of the heroic avenger, juxtaposing the prosaic compound "footwear" with the hyperbolic heroism of "strike terror in the heart of Melvyn" (itself not the most "heroic" male name). Sing-song sound effects of alliteration ("overawe" and "avuncular"), the code-shifting French phrase that suggests worldliness and creates a bilingual rhyme with "awe" and "quoi"—show Brewster's ability to both perform, and mock, the role of honourable male, "double-voicing" it. As he enters the garage to confront the younger man, he can't help but notice the painterly effect created by an oil puddle on the concrete floor: "Iridescent under the fluorescent lighting, it shimmered a palette of queasy, vividly unnatural colours, a petroleum-based aurora borealis that was a perfect reflection of the fear coiling in his gut. It was the most beautiful thing Brewster had seen in a long time."[22] Using his artistic sense to anesthetise himself against the coming pain, he spies his opponent damaging his wife's car just as Melvyn had earlier accused Brewster of damaging his. With the contemporary weapon of cell phone as eyewitness, Brewster snaps an incriminating photo. Melvyn's outraged question is met with this serene self-description:

> "Just who the fuck do you think you are?"
> "Me? I guess I'm a rusty time bomb. Either that or an old clock running down. Tick tock, tick tock, tick tock."[23]

As Melvyn prepares to attack his older neighbour, Brewster realises his hands are now pain-free, as if in anticipation of a cleansing blow, the real "pain management" he needs. Like the old soldier proud of his "high pain threshold,"[24] he is ready to "bite the bullet" in his willingness to take a beating from the younger man. In fact, it is suggested that he sees it as a kind of "atonement" for the merciless beating he delivered to Ronnie Peel, as his mental clock "ticks" back forty years to that day. Brewster's two impulses—

the artistic and the violent—are joined as we are told that Melvyn's avenging fist "painted" Brewster's stunned brain with "the same weird colours of the northern lights that he had seen trembling on the concrete floor."[25] The story ends with Melvyn's blow dropping him "gratefully" to his knees on the floor of the parking garage. Is Charley Brewster a late-life victim of his own willingness to "settle problems with violence," as Eva would have it? Or is he standing up for the victimised—Janacek's battered wife, Dina, or even his one-time enemy? The story leaves it up to us to decide, but it does force us, men and women, to reflect on the future of masculine heroism.

"Cages," from Vanderhaeghe's first collection, *Man Descending*, is a much-anthologised story. Fast-forward forty years or so, and its protagonist, smart-talking Billy Simpson, could be Bert Molson, a disillusioned history teacher facing disciplinary action for manipulating the truth in the name of a good yarn, in "Counsellor Sally Brings Me to the Tunnel." For, as in "Cages," this first-person narrative is occasioned by misbehaviour that demands social correction. In teenage Billy's case, he is forced to meet with a social worker; in Bert's, he has been ordered to meet with Counsellor Sally for "psychological treatment" while the Teachers' Federation and his principal figure out what to do with him.[26] This "talking cure" provides the narrative situation in which Bert is encouraged, in external dialogue and internal monologue, to consider if he has "abandonment" issues, related to his being raised by his working-class single mother, under the influence of his Uncle Teddy. Teddy is his would-be father, a violent alcoholic and WWII veteran turned dynamiter, who had a history of being at odds with authority figures himself.

Vanderhaeghe has commented that "the biggest advantage of the first person voice is intimacy. Because I'm interested in colloquial language, I'm drawn to the first person."[27] As with "Cages," we have another literate narrator presenting his story to an implied auditor—Sally, and behind her, us—which allows for multiple "orality effects" and rhetorical gestures of spoken intimacy. Such insertions act as guides to the reader-listener, intensifying our ethical connection to the speaker as he "makes his case" for his particular version of family history. This history is Teddy's ambivalent attraction for him, relayed in scenes with Bert, first, as onlooker, then as active participant. Bert's retrospective accounting allows the child's perspective to be filtered through the adult's more mature vocabulary and insight. Vanderhaeghe's hybrid constructions here reflect generational as well as masculine "double-voicing." As a successful and physically imposing dynamiter back in his hometown on a visit, driving an expensive Mercedes Benz, Teddy Aker has a certain claim to patriarchal authority. Connell observes, "It is the successful claim to authority, more than direct violence, that is the mark of hegemony [though violence often underpins or supports authority]."[28] For example, "[Police Chief] Carmen Kostash is walking on eggs because he went to school with my uncle and knew that hearing the name Teddy Aker in conjunction with a complaint call is a bit like hearing the words *blood in your stool* bandied about in the doctor's office."[29] The child's admiring perspective on "my uncle" at the beginning of the sentence, drawing on the homely cliché "walking on eggs," then shifts sardonically into a middle-aged anxiety about colon cancer—blood in your stool as the warning sign—which is used to represent Teddy's threat to the "body politic."[30] During Bert's childhood, Teddy also provides fodder for entertaining family stories, which allow the mature Bert to enthusiastically "double-voice" in terms of class, masculinity, and generational divides. For instance, he says about Teddy's attempt to run a hotel with his wife Evie: "Aside from being an enthusiastic, awe-inspiring bouncer who tossed troublemakers through plate-glass doors and sent them tobogganing down the concrete steps of the bar on their bellies, Ted didn't have the necessary skill set for success in the hospitality industry."[31] The colourful, mythical imaging of Teddy's violent work as a bouncer, with its rhythmical swing of alliteration ("tossed troublemakers . . . tobogganing," "bouncer . . . bar . . . bellies") is stopped short by the professional abstraction of polite phrases like "necessary skill set" and "the hospitality industry." These shifts reflect not just Bert's blend of class identities—working-class kid turned teacher—but his deep ambivalence about his uncle's role in his life as a male role model.

It is an act of near patricide when Bert is a teenager that forces Teddy out of Bert's life for a long time. In a perverse display of familial "love," a drunken Teddy repeatedly forces his way into his sister's rental house to try to draw his nephew to his home, with the promise of "a regular, normal upbringing."[32] Repeated late-night interrogations tolerated by Teddy's sister traumatise and enrage Bert. Violence is the only outcome, as Bert asserts himself (and defends his mother) one night by pushing a loaded dresser down the stairs onto his uncle. Although Teddy survives with broken bones and a concussion, this ends his nocturnal harassment. But family loyalty runs deep in this working-class clan, and after Teddy leaves his wife, only to be put into a seniors' housing facility, Bert is sent by his mother, with home-cooked lasagne, to be the bridge between the estranged siblings. Now described as a "human pretzel"[33] with severe arthritis, Teddy is fighting a war of words with the nurses who come in for his personal care. The nursing supervisor threatens him with a psychiatric assessment. As Bert admits to Sally, he can identify as both he and Teddy fear being labelled "a head case"[34] for using their language as a weapon. Yet Teddy confides in his nephew his personal thoughts about death, and drawing on numerous reports of near-death experiences, muses on the possibility of "the light" waiting after "the tunnel."[35] Teddy rejects orthodox religion and his nurse's Fundamentalist warnings about going to "the Other Place"; instead, he insists he will "run that tunnel full speed" so he'll be able to give "one mighty leap and sail clear over the hole."³⁶ To his nephew's teasing about "the door" to the light then being "locked," he responds with a "stricken dumb" look as his only real weapon, his posture of defiance, is taken from him. But then Teddy recovers it, to insist, in a replay of their old nocturnal clashes, "I'll pound on that door to be let in. I'll kick the son of a bitch down."³⁷ The violence of his previous behaviour, directed towards a teenage boy and his mother, is here redirected in a more forgivable metaphysical context.

Forgiveness is the lesson Bert takes with him after Teddy dies, for the "eulogy" his nephew gives him is not a defence of a man who alienated so many, but rather, a compassionate reminder of the goodness that was perverted—perhaps by war, perhaps by manhood itself.³⁸ As Bert recalls, "So I told the story of Teddy's plan to leap for the light. I thought it was the truest thing I could say about him."³⁹ Downplaying the "door-banging" which recalls his own childhood trauma, Bert focuses instead on his Uncle's determined energy. In the story's closing sentence, as Bert is released from his therapy with Sally to leave his job on his own terms, he envisions his uncle's death as follows: "Now when I imagine the hollow thunder of an old man battering at a *locked* **door** with his arthritic fists, there at the end of the *long* **dark** tunnel of his *life,* I only hope that the **door did** give way and that he stumb*l*ed, **roaring**, into a great *spill* of *light.*"⁴⁰ Rich with sonorous rhythms, this eulogizing conclusion lyrically "double-voices" by blending pathos with dignity, masculine energy with spiritual grace. Bert's uncle and surrogate father's final act may be slightly clumsy (he "stumbled"), and characteristically defiant (while "roaring"), but his efforts end in "a great *spill* of *light*" (emphasis added) and a blurring of earthly contrarieties.

Billy Constable, of "Live Large," is the youngest and least reflective of the three protagonists discussed so far, and his claim to hegemonic masculinity also seems the most tenuous. However, this story turns sport—golf—into a test of manhood for the struggling plumbing contractor. The satirical story voice presents Constable as impulsive, fallible, a mock-chivalric hero. A summer day in June sees him struggling with his last chance to maintain his image of himself as a successful businessman, his newly achieved middle-class dream symbolised by the cottage his wife and sons are presently enjoying, the "sleek powerboat with its triumphal roar,"⁴¹ his luxury Lexus car, and his suburban home. For Constable has gambled his plumbing contracting business, inherited from his father, on a last desperate pitch: "If Billy could land the contract to install plumbing in the condos Jenkins was building, the bank could be held at bay. . . . He just had to think positive . . . and everything would be fine."⁴² As a sleepless Constable watches the sunrise, he flashes back thirty years, to a book read at university, its author forgotten but its cover art recalled, akin to the "strange, bird-shaped cloud, fiery wings uplifted"⁴³ he now observes. Waiting to hear from Jenkins, Constable gets a last-minute invitation to join a golf "foursome" at his former club. He seizes this distraction; however, the game takes on a more agonistic tone when he discovers that Malcolm Forsythe, "the King of the Car Dealers," will be in the group. Forsythe has become Constable's enemy since delivering him the humiliation of offering him an economical Corolla car rather than the luxury Lexus he craved. Stung by Forsythe's emasculating comment that he sells a lot of them "to female schoolteachers," Constable is driven to "make the big, extravagant gesture"[44] and buy the car he truly can't afford.

Constable will make a similar gesture today when he accepts Forsythe's wager on their golf game, and ups the ante, by proposing the winner of each round earn a hundred dollars a hole. The formerly homosocial "friendly outing" becomes a trial of skill and nerve between the deliberate car dealer, an expert at "putting," and the impulsive businessman with his still-athletic "drive." Constable's motto, "Live Large," is thus enacted to his peril, as he over-bids on their golf wager, and over-drinks on the course, risking losing even more money, and more importantly, missing the phone call that might have saved him from economic ruin. Essentially, he enters into a mock-chivalric contest with his rival on the green fields of the Fairview Golf and Country Club, crudely described by him, mingling poetry and profanity, as a "shepherd's wet dream."[45] While the game begins as a physical test of hand-eye coordination and skill, it turns into a psychological war, as the two men, witnessed by their colleagues, insult and goad each other. Constable also flirts with, and over-tips, the mobile barmaid, Joanne, a single mother categorised by Constable as "a trailer tramp"[46] and so safely beneath him. Sexual attraction and capitalist power combine in his interaction with women who, like Joanne, must rely on male patronage to survive. While hiding his real reason for quitting the club, he confides in her that he is losing to Forsythe. Drinking beer at Joanne's cart, struck by the vernal beauty of the trees of the course, Constable remembers his father, and wonders if he ever enjoyed the fruits of his labour. As he tears up, he hides his wet eyes from Joanne, blaming his tears on the very poplars he had been admiring: "Goddamn allergies." To her admonishment, "Whip Forsythe's ass, *Mr. C*" (maintaining the distance between him as a club member and herself as a female employee), he resoundingly replies, "Consider it whipped."[47] From a gender perspective, Constable and Joanne's exchange provides a contemporary parody of a chivalric jousting tournament, with Constable as the knight fighting for the approval and admiration of his lady, who slakes his thirst while praising his valour, thus sending him back on the field restored in his masculine confidence.

The mock-chivalric echoes that work to "double-voice" hegemonic masculinity continue. For instance, after completing a hole ahead of his competitor, Forsythe performs as follows: "Snatching his ball from the hole with a flourish and pretending to sheathe his putter like a rapier, à la Chi Chi Rodriguez in his cocky prime, he strode past Constable chirping, 'Drive for show, putt for dough.'"[48] Miming a successful pro golfer's gesture, with its nod to the chivalric art of fencing, Forsythe adds insult to injury with his condescending couplet. But further on in the game, when Constable doffs his shoes in imitation of *his* golf hero, Sam Snead, he inverts the verse, reciting "Drive for *dough*, putt for *show*," before he makes "the pressure shot of a lifetime."[49] Yet Constable's triumph over Forsythe is short-lived. Earlier, emptying his beer-filled bladder in an outhouse, he shut the door only to notice the digits on his glowing watch-face: 5:05. In his own "dark night of the soul," Constable recalls the missed phone call, envisioning the message awaiting him at home: "That evil little red eye on his answering machine was giving him a mocking wink: Your last hope is gone."[50] As with Constable's (over)reaction to Forsythe's gendering of the Toyota Corolla as feminine, he has balked at being placed in the feminine position of waiting patiently for the promised five o'clock phone "date" with his potential employer.

Suddenly the dawn cloudscape that evoked a lecture on the phoenix, and D. H. Lawrence's association with it, is recalled in its full meaning as Constable sardonically rewrites this image of heroic (and phallic) regeneration: "Well, he was toast now. Burned to a crisp and nothing left for his creditors to do but sift through the blackened crumbs of him. There was no rising from these ashes."[51] Summer has come to a premature end for Billy Constable, the would-be solar god. Constable's only consolation is in completing his barefoot walk across the green, defying etiquette by "tramping right through a fairway bunker.... The powdery white sand seared his feet and then he felt the lush, cool grass caress and soothe *his soles*."[52] The implied pun on *soul* here reminds Constable of his own potential redemption through the pastoral green world, symbolised by the golf club, from which he is exiled, even as he admits he may have won the (mock-chivalric) battle, but lost the war.

In these three stories from *Daddy Lenin*, Vanderhaeghe shows us the surprising vulnerability of men in a changing world in which their presumed power and authority is increasingly undermined. The rage resulting from this marginalization has been the topic of many sociological and psychological studies of random violence, serial killings, even terrorism.[53] Highly conscious of the factors that lead to such ruptures in our social fabric, Vanderhaeghe employs "double-voicing" to create sympathetic, realistic male protagonists living in a century which increasingly challenges hegemonic masculinity. Recently, Vanderhaeghe distinguished between the attractions (and challenges) of short story and novel as follows: "After giving something close to two decades of my life to researching and writing historical novels, I wanted to return to the darting, glimmering light of short fiction and take a break from the high-beam, steady glare of the novel."[54] Sixteen years earlier, he also drew on light imagery—in a subtly violent figure—to describe his writing goals. Referring to the "luminous" quality of the short story, Vanderhaeghe mused, "In the hands of a master, there's a kind of *explosion* of understanding."⁵⁵ There can be no doubt, now, that Guy Vanderhaeghe is one of those "double-voicing" short-story masters—and a creator of literary detonations.

BIBLIOGRAPHY

Bakhtin, M. M. *The Dialogic Imagination: Four Essays.* Edited by Michael Holquist. Translated by Caryl Emerson and Michael Holquist. Austin: University of Texas Press, 1981.

Beattie, Steven W. "New collections by Guy Vanderhaeghe and Heather O'Neill reside at opposite ends of the spectrum." [Review of *Daddy Lenin and Other Stories*, by Guy Vanderhaeghe, and *Daydreams of Angels*, by Heather O'Neill.] *Globe and Mail.* Retrieved 24 April 2015 from https://www.theglobeandmail.com/arts/books-and-media/new-collections-by-guy-vanderhaeghe-and-heather-oneill-reside-at-opposite-ends-of-the-spectrum/article24106957.

Connell, R. W. *Masculinities.* Berkeley: University of California Press, 1995.

Hluchy, Patricia. Review of *Daddy Lenin*, by Guy Vanderhaeghe. *Toronto Star.* Retrieved 2 May 2015 from https://www.thestar.com/entertainment/books/2015/05/02/daddy-lenin-by-guy-vanderhaeghe-review.html.

Kruk, Laurie. *Double-Voicing the Canadian Short Story.* Ottawa: Ottawa University Press, 2016.

———. *The Voice Is the Story: Conversations with Canadian Writers of Short Fiction.* Oakville: Mosaic, 2003.

Moore, Lisa. "Diving In." [Review of *Confidence,* by Russell Smith, *Daydreams of Angels*, by Heather O'Neill, *Specimen*, by Irina Kovalyova, and *Daddy Lenin and Other Stories*, by Guy Vanderhaeghe.] *Antigonish Review* 185: 55–59. Retrieved Spring 2016 from http://antigonishreview.com/index.php?option=com_content&view=article&id=354&catid=2&Itmid=137. Originally published in *The Walrus* (September 2015).

Strauss, Marina. "Guy Vanderhaeghe on Why He Wrote His New Book, Why Which [sic] Character He Wishes He'd Created, and More." *Globe and Mail,* 1 May 2015. https://www.theglobeandmail.com/arts/books-and-media/guy-vanderhaeghe-on-why-he-wrote-his-new-book-why-which-character-he-wishes-hed-created-and-more/article24215538.

Vanderhaeghe, Guy. "Cages." In *Man Descending*, 99–118. Toronto: Stoddart, 1982.

———. "Counsellor Sally Brings Me to the Tunnel." In *Daddy Lenin and Other Stories*, 192–230. Toronto: McClelland and Stewart, 2015.

———. *Daddy Lenin and Other Stories.* Toronto: McClelland and Stewart, 2015.

———. *The Englishman's Boy.* Toronto: McClelland and Stewart, 1996.

———. *A Good Man.* Toronto: McClelland and Stewart, 2011.

———. "Live Large." In *Daddy Lenin and Other Stories*, 114–30. Toronto: McClelland and Stewart, 2015.

———. "Tick Tock." In *Daddy Lenin and Other Stories*, 14–45. Toronto: McClelland and Stewart, 2015.

———. *The Trouble with Heroes.* Ottawa: Borealis, 1983.

Whitehead, Stephen, and Frank J. Barrett. "The Sociology of Masculinity." In *The Masculinities Reader*, 1–26. Edited by Stephen Whitehead and Frank J. Barrett. Cambridge, UK: Polity/Malden, MA: Blackwell, 2001.

Wyile, Herb. "Doing the Honourable Thing: Guy Vanderhaeghe's *The Last Crossing.*" *Canadian Literature* 185 (Summer 2005): 59–74.

———. "Making History: Guy Vanderhaeghe." In *Speaking in the Past Tense: Canadian Novelists on Writing Historical Fiction*, 25–51. Waterloo: Wilfrid Laurier University Press, 2007.

NOTES

1. R. W. Connell, *Masculinities* (Berkeley: University of California Press, 1995), 77.
2. Patricia Hluchy, Review of *Daddy Lenin*, by Guy Vanderhaeghe, *Toronto Star*. See also Herb Wyile, "Doing the Honourable Thing: Guy Vanderhaeghe's *The Last Crossing*," *Canadian Literature* 185 (Summer 2005): 59–74.
3. Vanderhaeghe, himself an early "Baby Boomer," was born in 1951.
4. Connell, "Masculinities," 79.
5. Connell, "Masculinities," 82.
6. Lisa Moore, "Diving In," *Antigonish Review* (185), 59 (online).
7. Stephen Whitehead and Frank J. Barrett, "The Sociology of Masculinity," *The Masculinities Reader* (Cambridge, UK: Polity/Malden, MA: Blackwell, 2001), 3.
8. Laurie Kruk, *The Voice Is the Story: Conversations with Canadian Writers of Short Fiction* (Oakville: Mosaic, 2003), 224.
9. Kruk, *The Voice Is the Story*, 227–28, original ellipsis.
10. M. M. Bakhtin, *The Dialogic Imagination: Four Essays*, ed. Michael Holquist, trans. Caryl Emerson and Michael Holquist (Austin: University of Texas Press, 1981), 304–305.
11. Guy Vanderhaeghe, "Tick Tock," *Daddy Lenin and Other Stories* (Toronto: McClelland and Stewart, 2015), 30–31.
12. Vanderhaeghe, "Tick Tock," 32.
13. Vanderhaeghe, "Tick Tock," 32.
14. Vanderhaeghe, "Tick Tock," 18–19.
15. Vanderhaeghe, "Tick Tock," 35.
16. Vanderhaeghe, "Tick Tock," 22.
17. Vanderhaeghe, "Tick Tock," 29.
18. Steven W. Beattie, "New Collections by Guy Vanderhaeghe and Heather O'Neill Reside at Opposite Ends of the Spectrum" (24 April 2015), online, paragraph 6.
19. Vanderhaeghe, "Tick Tock," 43.
20. Herb Wyile, "Making History: Guy Vanderhaeghe," *Speaking in the Past Tense: Canadian Novelists on Writing Historical Fiction* (Waterloo: Wilfrid Laurier UP), 49.
21. Vanderhaeghe, "Tick Tock," 43; original italics.
22. Vanderhaeghe, "Tick Tock," 45.
23. Vanderhaeghe, "Tick Tock," 44.
24. Vanderhaeghe, "Tick Tock," 21.
25. Vanderhaeghe, "Tick Tock," 45
26. Interestingly, in both stories it is women who are correcting the deviant men. As a sign of greater female empowerment and gender role reversal, it is a female minister who gives Bert's Uncle Teddy counsel at the end—but also provides an opportunity to flirt with her.
27. Kruk, *The Voice Is the Story*, 222.
28. Connell, "Masculinities," 77.
29. Guy Vanderhaeghe, "Counsellor Sally Brings Me to the Tunnel," *Daddy Lenin and Other Stories* (Toronto: McClelland and Stewart, 2015), 199.
30. Later, Teddy will have a colostomy, and be reduced to carrying a "shit purse" under his shirt, causing him to be weakened and thereby effeminized.
31. Vanderhaeghe, "Counsellor Sally," 202.
32. Vanderhaeghe, "Counsellor Sally," 204.
33. Vanderhaeghe, "Counsellor Sally," 215.
34. Vanderhaeghe, "Counsellor Sally," 225.
35. For example, see Chapter 9 in this volume.
36. Vanderhaeghe, "Counsellor Sally," 226, 227.
37. Vanderhaeghe, "Counsellor Sally," 227.
38. Vanderhaeghe remarked, "[M]y notion of heroism comes closer to stoicism than anything else" (Kruk, *The Voice Is the Story*, 228). By this definition, Teddy may be considered heroic.
39. Vanderhaeghe, "Counsellor Sally," 229.
40. Vanderhaeghe, "Counsellor Sally," 230; my emphasis.

41. Guy Vanderhaeghe, "Live Large," in *Daddy Lenin and Other Stories* (Toronto: McClelland and Stewart, 2015), 115.
42. Vanderhaeghe, "Live Large," 116.
43. Vanderhaeghe, "Live Large," 114.
44. Vanderhaeghe, "Live Large," 114.
45. Vanderhaeghe, "Live Large," 118.
46. Vanderhaeghe, "Live Large," 121.
47. Vanderhaeghe, "Live Large," 124; emphasis added.
48. Vanderhaeghe, "Live Large," 125.
49. Vanderhaeghe, "Live Large," 128; emphasis added.
50. Vanderhaeghe, "Live Large," 129.
51. Vanderhaeghe, "Live Large," 130.
52. Vanderhaeghe, "Live Large," 130; emphasis added.
53. See Bert's comment on the television documentary on youthful serial killers that he watches with appreciation long after enduring his uncle's nocturnal visits in "Counsellor Sally Brings Me to the Tunnel": "As Counsellor Sally is surely well aware, all the latest, up-to-date literature confirms that pumping the teenaged male body full of gallons of stress hormones makes for a seething toxic stew" (Vanderhaeghe, "Live Large," 207).
54. Marina Strauss, "Guy Vanderhaeghe on Why He Wrote His New Book, Why Which [*sic*] Character He Wishes He'd Created, and More." *Globe and Mail*, 1 May 2015. https://www.theglobeandmail.com/arts/books-and-media/guy-vanderhaeghe-on-why-he-wrote-his-new-book-why-which-character-he-wishes-hed-created-and-more/article24215538.
55. Kruk, *The Voice Is the Story*, 215; emphasis added.

Part IV

Posthuman Futures

Laurie Kruk

What do we mean by the *posthuman*? Is it a state we desire to attain where we outgrow, give up, leave behind our humanity for some (we hope) brave new world? Or does it represent the joining together of technologies of science and art that may enrich our sense of ourselves while possibly extending our lives and our vaunted consciousness? Is the posthuman the era of the cyborg, postgender and perhaps postrationality, as famously defined by Donna Haraway several decades ago? We face this possibility with desire, fear, and resistance.

On the eve of 1984, that year also made famous by George Orwell's dystopian novel *1984*, science fiction writer Isaac Asimov was asked by *The Toronto Star* to peek ahead thirty-five years—to 2019—and make some predictions about our future. As Asimov wrote, "the mobile computerised object, or robot, is already flooding into industry and will, in the course of the next generation, penetrate the home."[1] In fact, "the growing complexity of society will make it impossible to do without them."[2]

In an eloquent discussion of the posthuman, Catherine Jenkins explores what she sees as our "persistent need . . . to overcome our mortality." Death studies, also called *thanatology*, have been around since the mid-1800s, yet current technological and medical advances have pushed them into the spotlight. Jenkins begins by examining the possibility of "Life Extension towards Immortality." As life expectancy has increased, some scientists ponder breaking the traditional record of a century of life, while others even hope to find ways to halt the aging process itself. The Human Genome Project, completed in 2003, may be a step in this direction, as the secrets of our DNA are further unlocked. But another vision of the posthuman is the privileging of information over embodiment, turning the body itself into a replaceable prosthetic.

This obviously paves the way for the "Computer and Robot Hosts," as Jenkins outlines in her second section. If the human body is no longer necessary, the Cartesian concept of the *res extensa* takes priority over the *res cogitans*. The example of a human cadaver, digitised through functional magnetic resonance imaging (fMRI) and computed tomography, raises questions about new kinds of subjectivity following biological death. As Jenkins observes, with "the development of robots with human and genetic attributes, a cybernetic convergence seems inevitable," leading to what sociologist Simon Williams calls a "moral, spiritual and existential crisis of the corporeal body." Citing Haraway, Jenkins argues that newer and better methods of medical resuscitation have opened up striking areas of inquiry into consciousness itself, turning the temporally brain-dead body into a kind of cyborg while also renewing scientific interest in "near-death experiences" beyond bodily awareness. In the section titled "Achieving Posthuman Longevity via Cyborg Intervention," she argues that these findings seem to endorse "a split between the *res extensa* and *res cogitans*, [but] they support Descartes's contention that the *res cogitans* is the seat of identity." With a conclusion striking a balance between the utopian and the dystopian prospects of the posthuman, Jenkins notes that "humans move through time, sometimes advancing in positive ways, other times verging on self-destruction. . . . This well-worn path seems unlikely to change." Hence, for the future, she suggests, we must confront our past: our historically human fears and desires.

In "'Not Born in a Garden': Donna Haraway, Cyborgs, and Posthuman Contemporary Art," Eric Weichel explores the work of contemporary artists whose work reflects cyborgian themes: Bharti Kher of India, Andrea Crespo of the United States and Sally McKay of Canada, Patricia Piccinini of Australia, and artist-designer duo Michael Burton and Michiko Nitta of the United Kingdom. As Weichel observes, "All of these artists have won major national and international prizes and are well-represented in solo exhibitions at leading galleries, suggesting that their disparate, yet closely parallel, meditations on the theme of the posthuman are indicative of a wider interest in the field." Here, the cyborg is seen as the site of exciting new cross-disciplinary collaborations which provoke meditations on the nature of human identity. Kher's use of the Hindu "bindi" within abstract paintings explores the complex ethical dilemmas presented by India's approach to twenty-first-century fertility technologies. The increasing reliance on computer screens in medical testing, like the magnetic resonance imaging test, is utilised by Andrea Crespo in powerful visual and digital images of a new kind of genderless cyborg.

Adopting "the feminist proposition that all knowledge is partial and situated," McKay extends the examination of fMRI scanner technologies and their popularity within twenty-first-century healthcare, proposing a certain "intense intimacy" between human and machine. A neural scan thus can have, for the viewer who is also the subject, a portrait-like, symbolic importance. Moving from the mechanical–human hybrid to the animalistic, Patricia Piccinini's sculptures offer another look at the cyborg. Her famous creation, "Surrogate," is "an endearing, domestic, nurturing hybrid, who, if s/he suggests the aesthetic of a dystopian Beatrice Potter, is far removed from the hypersexualised, bodily traumatised killing machines or pleasure dolls beloved as tropes by the Hollywood speculative film establishment." Finally, Weichel shifts from the visual and tactile arts to the performance art of Michael Burton and Michiko Nitta. He describes their daring *Algae Opera* as follows: "mezzo-soprano opera singer Louise Ashcroft is fit with an elaborate, intricate and gorgeously-designed bio-suit that, through a complex system of tubes, expresses the carbon dioxide of her breathing during a performance to the algae tanks beneath her[; the performance] has received considerable critical attention for its beautiful synthesis between performing, hearing, and eating." The politics of food, along with environmental concerns about species extinction—also echoed by the use of the Australian wombat by Piccinini—is here married with a new artistic display, highlighting and bringing attention to our casual "consumption" of culture. Unlike Jenkins, with her measured approach to the pros and cons of the cyborgian future, Weichel's conclusion is that these international artists have offered us a glimpse of that future that is "terrifically optimistic . . . where a posthuman life is marked by the carnality of mutually evolving, co-adapted or symbiotic sensualities." Consequently, Weichel challenges us, with a bold valedictory flourish, "what else, for the future of humanity, but the cyborg?"

BIBLIOGRAPHY

Asimov, Isaac. "I, Asimov." *The Toronto Star* (originally published 31 December 1983), 29 December 2018. "Insight" 1N1–1N7.

NOTES

1. Isaac Asimov, "I, Asimov," *Toronto Star*, 31 December 1983, in *Insight*, 29 December 2018, 1N1.
2. Asimov, "I, Asimov," 1N6.

Chapter Nine

Human versus Cyborg Life

Catherine Jenkins

In 1985, sociologist Norbert Elias said, "Death is a problem of the living. Dead people have no problems."[1] The ways the living respond to death are many and varied, depending on age, culture, beliefs, historical period, and the individual. Elias suggests that moving the dying process from family homes into hospitals, the "rational institutionalization of dying,"[2] mystified the dying process. Our desire to avoid grief and painful reminders of our own mortality may lead to shunning the dying. In hospitals, Elias observes:

> The dying person receives the most advanced, scientifically based medical treatment available. But contacts with the people to whom he or she is attached, and whose presence can be of utmost comfort to a person taking leave of life, are frequently thought to inconvenience the rational treatment of the patient and the routine of the personnel.[3]

The patient may become unrecognizable and barely visible through a curtain of tubes, wires, and machines. In this sterile environment we think "we can micromanage death,"[4] but death is not that predictable. While advanced care may be offered to the biological organism, separation from family and friends can be psychologically and emotionally devastating. Our rejection of the *ars moriendi* affects the dying most of all, as they risk being isolated in a high-tech environment that limits human contact, and in which their failure to live may be seen as a failure of science.

The living tend to think that everybody wants to live for as long as possible, even when the body requires the intervention of invasive medical technologies to maintain essential functions. But do we all consistently suffer from what cultural anthropologist Ernest Becker called "death anxiety,"[5] or is that an assumption made by those of us who are relatively young and healthy? Is this persistent desire to live necessarily shared by the aged or ill?

Are we prolonging life or simply extending the dying process? Is the quality of life suffering because of our fixation on the quantity of life? Are we survivors simply seeking to avoid death or grief?

What is this persistent need we have to overcome our mortality? In *The Denial of Death*, cultural anthropologist Ernest Becker's stated thesis was that "the idea of death, the fear of it, haunts the human animal like nothing else; it is a mainspring of human activity—activity designed largely to avoid the fatality of death, to overcome it by denying in some way that it is the final destiny for man."[6] We invent *causa sui*, immortality projects, to repress the knowledge of our mortality. Becker suggests that even scientific advances are delusional immortality projects, arguing that "a project as grand as the scientific-mythical construction of victory over human limitation is not something that can be programmed by science."[7] Or is it?

Although death studies, or *thanatology*, were first discussed medically in the mid-1800s, interdisciplinary death studies sprung up after Paul Ramsey's 1970 publication, *The Patient as Person: Explorations in Medical Ethics*, and the establishment of the Association for Death Education and Counseling in the mid-1970s. Today, death studies are undertaken in both the sciences and humanities, and this chapter explores death through both lenses. The chapter begins by exploring various life-extension technologies, then discusses developments in computer and robot hosts, and ends by considering the cyborg intervention of resuscitation technologies.

LIFE EXTENSION TOWARDS IMMORTALITY

In the twenty-first century, we live in a privileged context—one in which the effects of many diseases have been greatly reduced. The extension of life expectancy over the last few hundred years has relied on optimizing our biology. Our increase in longevity is largely attributed to better public sanitation and improved access to clean water and good food. Scientific developments since the mid-1900s have further extended life expectancy through improved diagnostics and treatment, as well as pharmacological and surgical advances. Physician and statistician Hans Rosling suggests that prior to 1810, global life expectancy was less than forty years. United Nations statistics now show life expectancy surpassing forty years in almost all countries, reaching eighty years in developed nations.[8] Effectively, life expectancy has doubled in the last two centuries.

Gerontologist Roy Walford developed an approach for optimizing human biology through a calorie-restricted, high-nutrition diet. In a 1996 interview, when asked what he thought the maximum human life expectancy was, he responded, "between 110 and 120," but added, "If you started calorie restriction early in life, I think the survival curve could be greatly extended to 140,

150, 160."[9] Walford was *only* talking about optimizing our given biological potential; more recently, however, leading biologists have taken several different experimental approaches to further enhancing human life expectancy.

Biogerontologist Aubrey de Grey heads the Strategies for Engineered Negligible Senescence (SENS) Project, focusing on regenerative medicine. Recognizing that aging is the result of increasing molecular and cellular damage over time, de Gray has identified seven specific types of metabolic damage: (1) cell loss and tissue atrophy, (2) cancerous cells, (3) mitochondrial mutations, (4) death-resistant cells (which cause inflammation, degrade protein, and may increase cancer risk), (5) extracellular matrix stiffening, (6) extracellular aggregates, and (7) intracellular aggregates.[10] He and his researchers are developing ways to intervene and periodically repair this damage to alleviate systemic health issues. Eventually, he hopes to halt the aging process and prevent age-related death.

Marine biologist Shin Kubota's research focuses on the tiny *turritopsis dohrnii*, the "immortal jellyfish." As humans, we perceive life travelling only in one direction: we are born, we live, and we die. The same cannot be said of the "immortal jellyfish." If the adult jellyfish is physically stressed, perhaps through aging or disease, it retracts into a seemingly dead mass, from which it then rejuvenates to begin life anew. While previous researchers into the related *turritopsis nutricula* jellyfish saw no human application for these unique traits, Kubota sees possibilities; "My opinion is that we will evolve and become immortal ourselves."[11].

Completed in 2003, the Human Genome Project's (HGP) stated goals included identifying the genes in human DNA (commonly called the "book of life" "code of codes" or "blueprint for life"[12]), determining DNA sequences, and addressing "the ethical, legal, and social issues . . . that may arise from the project."[13] The HGP has now moved into "Functional Genomics," analysing and experimenting with "this vast reservoir of data to explore how DNA and proteins work with each other and the environment to create complex, dynamic living systems."[14] As well as locating genes or sequences associated with specific disorders to develop new therapies, some leading geneticists are using the HGP to research life extension or create new life forms.

Molecular biologist John Tower examines the aging process using a population of rapidly generating fruit flies. In most biological organisms, genetic programming determines life span. Tower has found that increasing the amount of superoxide dismutase, a naturally occurring antioxidant also present in humans, overrides the genetic determination of death. His treated fruit flies have a dramatically increasing life expectancy of 40 percent over untreated fruit flies.[15]

At the forefront of functional genomics, Craig Venter announced the creation of a synthetic bacterium in 2010, and the construction of a synthetically sequenced yeast genome in 2014.[16] Amassing over fifty thousand changes in a genome 14 percent shorter than natural yeast, the sequence is based on the known yeast DNA sequence, with researchers selectively deleting what they perceive to be dispensable DNA, and splicing in new DNA. Venter admits, however, that "[t]here is an enormous gap between our ability to build DNA and our understanding of the instructions it encodes."[17]

As sociologist Nikolas Rose asserts, while nineteenth-century biology attempted to discover deep organic information at the bigger-picture molar corporeal level, today's biology has shifted to the microscopic molecular level and technologies like the HGP accumulate flattened data that bear little resemblance to the human body. This shift means that:

> [T]issues, cells, and DNA fragments can be rendered visible, isolated, decomposed, stabilized, stored in "biobanks," commoditized, transported between laboratories and factories, re-engineered by molecular manipulation, their properties transformed, their ties to a particular individual living organism, type, or species suppressed or removed.[18]

Similarly, Katherine N. Hayles calls DNA "bodiless information,"[19] building blocks that can be manipulated at the whim of scientists to create new life forms. The posthuman, as defined by Hayles, has four components: (1) privileging information over physical embodiment; (2) citing that human consciousness is an accident, rather than the seat of our identity; (3) recognizing that the human body is a replaceable prosthesis; and (4) defining humans as information processors that "can be seamlessly articulated with intelligent machines."[20] This model assumes that humans are defined by data fully encoded in their DNA, rather than the embodiment of that information or a nonphysical consciousness. Such a model requires a substantial ontological shift away from the familiar biological human being.

A dualistic mindset of the Cartesian clockwork man is necessary for the mechanistic separation of genetic data from bodies; however, as Rose and science fiction researcher Sherryl Vint suggest, the reductive HGP announces the biological *res extensa* as the central focus of the human project, rather than Descartes's preferred seat of identity, the *res cogitans*, noted in his famous *cogito ergo sum* (I think, therefore I am). Advances in these biological areas suggest that we are becoming more biological, but even within the biological realm, Rose acknowledges that "the vitality of the body has become increasingly open to machination."[21] Medical historian Roy Porter suggests that:

> The emergence of this high-tech scientific medicine may be a prime example of what William Blake denounced as "single vision," the kind of myopia which (literally and metaphorically) comes from looking doggedly down a

microscope. Single vision has its limitations in explaining the human condition.[22]

Theologian Elaine Graham states that "the Human Genome Project does not give a definitive account of what it means to be human; not even to provide final answers on the nature of morbidity and health."[23] Although the HGP has produced an epistemological shift, what does it really reveal about being human? Can we declare that we have overcome death because we can now code an individual's DNA? This concept seems to lack the lively glow of the Fountain of Youth; however, as work by researchers like Tower and Venter indicate, perhaps through DNA, life extension, or even immortality, can be achieved.

Jerry Lemler, CEO of cryonics company Alcor Life Extension Foundation, states: "The aging process is a disease like any other; eventually it will be arrested and then reversed," adding, "In the next generation, or two at the latest, people will not have to die anymore."[24] Death has been medicalised into an illness to be conquered; we seek to cure death. In this medicalised context, death becomes the ultimate failure.[25]

COMPUTER AND ROBOT HOSTS

In 1987, the US National Library of Medicine (NLM) began planning a project to create a definitive anatomical library called the Visible Human Project (VHP), with the stated goal "to create a digital image dataset of complete human male and female cadavers in MRI [magnetic resonance imaging], CT [computed tomography] and anatomical modes."[26] Thirty-eight-year-old convicted murderer Joseph Paul Jernigan was selected to become the first fully digitized human, carrying on the long tradition of performing anatomical dissection on executed criminals. Death by lethal injection and freezing can cause deterioration, so detailed full-body MRI and CT scans were done while the cadaver was still fresh. Because the cadaver was too large to fit into the bespoke cryomacrotome, a device for first freezing and then cutting thin slices from organic matter for examination, it was cut into quarters. Over the next two-and-a-half months, Jernigan's body was ground down one millimetre at a time to facilitate digital photography.[27] After data from each image type was combined, the resulting 1,871 pictures, fifteen gigabytes of information, went online in November 1994, creating the digital archive of human anatomy desired by the NLM.

The VHP provides accurate, interactive data without any mess, stench, or unpleasantness. Several free VHP viewers and video "fly throughs" exist online, but these images have also transitioned into educational and commercial purposes in their afterlife. Because VHP data was gathered using CT and MRI scans, formats commonly used for patient diagnostic imaging, data from living patients can readily be mapped onto the VHP. For instance, Voxel-Man's surgical simulator can interface with CT scan data from living patients to accommodate surgical practice runs, complete with appropriate sound effects and simulated bleeding, quite literally creating Catherine Waldby's "operative images"[28] upon which decisions are made that transform living bodies. For Waldby, the coproduction of images between the VHP and living patients creates a "digital uncanny,"[29] a haunting by data ghosts.

A secondary result of the creation of the VHP was the eradication of Jernigan's physical body and its resurrection as a digital doppelganger. While the NLM sought a neutral "everyman," Jernigan was a unique individual with physical anomalies; by rendering a complete data set from a single cadaver, the VHP has no appendix and only one testicle, because these were peculiarities of Jernigan's body. Jernigan's tattoos are also clearly visible on the reconstruction, creating a unique identity, rather than anonymity.[30] In the ethical controversy surrounding the VHP launch, Jernigan regained his subjective identity. Does his online resurrection form a new type of subjectivity? Corpses no longer possess memories; their consciousness is in a state of death and rebirth, or unconsciousness.[31] Is the digital doppelganger an object or an unconscious subject? Can Jernigan as the VHP be considered a cyborg that upholds the *res extensa* over the *res cogitans*?

Computer researcher Jong-Hwan Kim has taken reductive genetic engineering beyond the biological and into the digital realm. Based on a single strand of human DNA with 14 "artificial chromosomes"[32] creating digital DNA encoded for different states (e.g., curiosity, intimacy, happiness, desire to control), Kim created Rity, a virtual reality dog-like creature, publishing the results in an article titled The Origin of Artificial Species: Genetic Robot. When perceiving the outside world through its sensors, computerized DNA allow Rity to access human emotions, responses, and behaviours and thereby to evolve.[33] Kim also implanted digital DNA into a version of HanSaRam, his humanoid robot, to "imbue the robot with life."[34] HanSaRam VII can play complex games like soccer and basketball.

Car maker Toyota is at the forefront of humanoid robot designs. Their focus is on Human Support Robots for elder care, suggesting that this line has "human characteristics," that they are "agile, warm, kind and also intelligent enough to think for themselves."[35] The units are compact, lightweight, feature articulated arms for fetching small payloads, and are controlled by voice command or through digital interfaces. Competitors in humanoid robot technologies include Toronto's Le Trung, whose Aiko was "the first android to react to physical stimuli,"[36] and Blue Frog's[37] cute Companion Robot Buddy, whose tablet face can exhibit a variety of human emotions.

Although robots have been replacing humans in factory and menial jobs for decades, the United Nations estimated that in 2007, 4.1 million nonhumanoid robots were in our homes performing routine chores like vacuuming.[38] As robots are programmed with more human characteristics, through design (like Toyota), or artificial intelligence that can emulate human emotion and learn from experience (like Aiko or Buddy), or by implanting artificial chromosomes (like Rity or HanSaRam), they become more able to simulate human behaviours and emotions, and the line between humans and robots begins to blur. Computer and robot specialist David Levy suggests that our relationships to domestic robots is similar to our relationships with pets, and potentially superior to our relationships with other people. Levy predicts that by 2050, "Robots will be hugely attractive to humans as companions because of their many talents, senses, and capabilities. They will have the capacity to fall in love with humans and to make themselves romantically attractive and sexually desirable to humans."[39]

The term *robot* was coined by Karel Čapek in his play *R.U.R. (Rossum's Universal Robots)* in 1921. The word derives from the Czech *robota*, meaning "drudgery" or "forced labour." Čapek's robots were biological, rather than mechanical, creations. While most robotic development has relied on electronics, developers like Kim are introducing a biological component into the technology, and genetic researchers like Venter are manufacturing components that could conceivably be incorporated into future robots.

With increasing technological exploration into human behaviour and genetics, and the development of robots with human and genetic attributes, a cybernetic convergence seems inevitable. Such a convergence may lead to what sociologist Simon Williams calls a "moral, spiritual and existential crisis" of the corporeal body.[40] Because our bodies are increasingly plastic, can be rationalized and reconfigured almost at will, and are perceived as constantly at risk, the notion of the physical body becomes "ever more elusive and problematic," straining to find meaning.

ACHIEVING POSTHUMAN LONGEVITY VIA CYBORG INTERVENTION

The beginnings of a cybernetic convergence, what Donna Haraway defined as "the offspring of implosions of subjects and objects and of the natural and the artificial,"[41] are already notable in medical technologies that interface with the body. Since the 1960s, life support systems have been used to maintain bodily functions even after brain death, prompting ethical debates around the value of forcibly keeping a biological entity alive when the consciousness, the *res cogitans*, has deserted. Palliative specialist Diane Meier suggests that when life support is poorly considered, it can lead to a "well-intentioned but harmful intervention."[42] An urge to prolong life at all costs can translate into a potentially cruel prolongation of the dying process, rather than a meaningful extension of life.

Other times, however, mechanical life support is a useful temporary measure towards resuscitation. In the last ten years, resuscitation techniques have improved through new technologies, allowing some patients to effectively return from the dead. Resuscitation specialist Sam Parnia suggests that death is not necessarily a one-way, on-off event, but rather a gradual process in which cell death can take up to twenty-five hours,[43] and that given appropriate medical intervention at the right time, death is reversible. This is another way of exploring what Eric Weichel suggests in his chapter is a nonbinary potential for corporeal extension.

Building on cases of hypothermia with body temperatures as low as 20°C (37°C is normal) in which patients were successfully revived with little or no damage even three-and-a-half hours after medically pronounced death, the Arctic Sun 5000 creates therapeutic hypothermia, supporting a carefully controlled decrease in the patient's body temperature, and then a gradual rewarming.[44] Cooling reduces the cellular metabolic rate, decreasing damage from both death and resuscitation and, when used in conjunction with other resuscitation therapies, improves a patient's chances of full recovery. Manual cardiopulmonary resuscitation (CPR) is exhausting, and difficult to maintain consistently over time. The ZOLL AutoPulse mechanically provides more consistent and forceful chest squeezing than can a human. In hospital contexts, the combination of therapeutic hypothermia, mechanical CPR, and oxygen can yield a 60 percent resuscitation success rate from cardiac arrest, about triple that of conventional CPR in a hospital setting.[45] These and similar technologies merge with the human body, and could be perceived as forming a cyborg, even if only temporarily.

His resuscitation experiences caused Parnia to wonder, "Since there is a way back from death, we must now ask what happens to a person's mind and consciousness—that very essence of who the individual is—during the period when the person enters that unknown territory,"[46] what he also calls the "gray zone"[47] of reversible medical death. Although "near-death experiences"[48] (NDEs) have been recorded since Plato told the story of Er in *The Republic*, most have been dismissed as mystical visions. After experiencing an NDE, Swiss geologist Albert Heim collected thirty other experiences into a volume published in 1892; psychiatrist Raymond Moody published *Life After Life* in 1975 based on interviews with one hundred and fifty people who had experienced NDEs. In spite of these attempted scientific surveys, and a 1982 Gallup poll suggesting that 15 percent of Americans had experienced an NDE, most scientists scoff at the notion, suggesting that chemicals in the dying brain create hallucinations.[49]

In *Erasing Death*, Parnia systematically considers and dismisses medical explanations for NDEs, and then states: "By far the most controversial and difficult explanation to analyze was the idea that what people claimed regarding theirs NDEs might actually be real."[50] The commonalities between experiences and cultures are striking; what varies is their interpretation.[51] NDE survivors often speak of a sense of separation from their physical bodies: looking down upon a hospital scene, they sometimes report on activities that took place while they were clinically dead. Many experience a tunnel, a white light, light beings, or meeting deceased loved ones. The experience is usually one of joy and peace. Although the bodily return is often described as a jolt, upon reflection, most have no fear of death, and a reinvigorated sense of life.[52]

Although Parnia's findings still seem to support Descartes's dualistic ontology, a split between the *res extensa* and *res cogitans*, they support Descartes's contention that the *res cogitans* is the seat of identity. Physician-philosopher Drew Leder asserts that, although a mechanistic model remains dominant in biomedicine, "The full significance of human disease and health necessarily eludes the model of body-as-machine."[53]

Parnia reflects that, although we tend to think of the biological brain as the seat of consciousness, NDEs undermine this conviction. When someone dies, brain function, necessary for consciousness, personality and encoding new memories, ceases within seconds. So how can someone remember an NDE when the brain's circuits are down?[54] Parnia's research suggests that a conscious mind continues, at least for some hours, postmortem.

These findings are significant for our cyborg or posthuman or transhuman conceptions, as many ideas around such hybrids assume that an existing human consciousness, in the biophysical form of the brain or DNA, will be placed into a less fragile vessel like a computer or robot. Parnia's research, however, suggests that such a transfer may miss the most vital part of our being: the *res cogitans*, something far less tangible, and thereby harder to locate and transfer.

Where does the posthuman entity fit into this nature that is not quite natural, this culture that is mired in technoscience? Graham defines the posthuman as "denoting a world in which humans are mixtures of machines and organism, where nature has been modified (enculturated) by technologies, which in turn have become assimilated into 'nature' as a functioning component of organic bodies."[55] But is the cyborg-styled posthuman the only ontological direction the HGP opens? Rejecting this model, Vint calls for an "embodied notion of posthumanism,"[56] but how can that be accommodated, given the technoscientific directions we seem to be heading? Rather than incorporating the clumsy prostheses of cyberpunk science fiction, Rose and Vint both perceive that directions in biological sciences actually render us *more* biological, *more* embodied, by manipulating human Being at the organic level:

> [T]he risky, damaged, defective, or afflicted individual, once identified and assessed, may be treated or transformed by medical intervention at the molecular level. This does not so much imply that we now think of the body as a machine, but rather that humans have become even more biological, at the same time as the vitality of the body has become increasingly open to machination.[57]

Through research, analysis, and the ongoing accumulation of information, humans have increased lifespans, extended reproductive capacity and increased cognitive self-awareness. These innovations have, however, been incremental over time; consequently, any ontological changes they required evolved slowly. How can we interpret the changes wrought by the sudden introduction of the HGP and rapid growth of other biotechnologies? Rose suggests that "we are inhabiting an 'emergent form of life,'"[58] one in which genetic augmentation and transformation will allow us to produce better children, improve sports performance, acquire ageless bodies and have "happy souls."[59] What kind of ontological shift is required of an emerging life form? Hayles asserts, "the prospect of becoming posthuman both evokes terror and excites pleasure"[60]; her posthuman is a new conception of human, rather than the end of us—an emergent being, similar to Rose's and Vint's.

CONCLUSION

Is the posthuman cyborg the immortal human? Does our knowledge and experimentation in advanced biomedical research spell the end of humanity as we know it, or has it simply introduced an ontological shift into the continuum of being human? While Becker cried out against "Manipulative, utopian science," declaring, "It means an end to the distinctively human—or even, we must say, the distinctively organismic,"[61] his voice seems to have been dismissed in the ensuing decades of medical advancement intent on reprogramming our animal nature. We strive to create a Utopia without pain or suffering, where we, and those we love, will be immortal. Reflecting on the influence of medicoscientific advances and their potential for changing humanity as we know it, Rose asserts:

> [A]s with our present, our future will emerge from the intersection of a number of contingent pathways that, as they intertwine, might create something new. This, I suspect, will be no radical transformation, no shift into a world "after nature" or a "posthuman future." Perhaps it will not even constitute an "event." But I think, in a manner of small ways, most of which will soon be routinized and taken for granted, things will not be quite the same again.[62]

Humans move through time, sometimes advancing in positive ways, other times verging on self-destruction, sometimes using our intelligence creatively, other times behaving with brutal violence. This well-worn path seems unlikely to change. We may scoff when today's scientists predict the possibility of doubling our life span or even immortality, but if people living in 1810 had been told that their descendants would routinely live to twice their age, they probably would have reacted with similar disbelief. The ultimate question becomes, is the quality of life suffering because of our fixation on the quantity of life? Our pain upon the loss of a close connection is, of course, twofold: first, we are faced with the permanent and irreversible loss of that person from our lives, and second, we are forced to uncomfortably confront our own mortality.

BIBLIOGRAPHY

Association for Death Education and Counseling. "History of ADEC." Accessed 8 October 2018. https://www.adec.org/Main/ADEC_Main/Discover-ADEC/ADEC_History/ADEC_History.aspx.

Becker, Ernest. *The Denial of Death*. New York: Macmillan, 1973.

Bergson, Henri. *The Creative Mind: An Introduction to Metaphysics*. New York: Kensington, 1946.

Blue Frog Robotics. "Buddy, the First Emotional Companion Robot." Accessed 15 August 2018. https://buddytherobot.com/en/buddy-the-emotional-robot/

Byock, Ira. *Dying Well: The Prospect for Growth at the End of Life*. New York: Riverhead Books, 1997.

Čapek, Karel. *R.U.R. (Rossum's Universal Robots): A Fantastic Melodrama*. Garden City, NY: Doubleday, 1923.

De Grey, Aubrey, and Michael Rae. *Ending Aging: The Rejuvenation Breakthroughs That Could Reverse Human Aging in Our Lifetime*. New York: St. Martin's, 2007.

Elias, Norbert. *The Loneliness of the Dying*. Oxford: Basil Blackwell, 1985.

Gallup Jr., George, and William Proctor, "Have You, Yourself, Ever Been on the Verge of Death or Had a 'Close Call' Which Involved Any Unusual Experience at That Time? Nationally 15% Responded 'Yes.'" In *Adventures in Immortality: A Look Beyond the Threshold of Death*, 198–200. New York: McGraw-Hill, 1982.

Gibson, Daniel G., and J. Craig Venter. "Synthetic Biology: Construction of a Yeast Chromosome." *Nature* 509 (May 2014): 168–69. 8 doi:10.1038/509168a.

Graham, Elaine L. *Representations of the Post/Human: Monsters, Aliens and Others in Popular Culture*. New Brunswick, NJ: Rutgers University Press, 2002.

Haraway, Donna. *Modest_Witness@Second_Millennium: FemaleMan_Meets_OncoMouse*. Oxford: Routledge, 1997.

Hayles, Katherine N. *How We Became Posthuman: Virtual Bodies in Cybernetics, Literature, and Informatics*. Chicago: University of Chicago Press, 1999.

Kim, Jong-Hwan, Kang-Hee Lee, and Yong-Duk Kim. "The Origin of Artificial Species: Genetic Robot." *International Journal of Control, Automation, and Systems* 3, no. 4 (December 2001): 564–70.

Leder, Drew. "A Tale of Two Bodies: The Cartesian Corpse and the Lived Body." In *The Body in Medical Thought and Practice*, edited by Drew Leder, 17–35. Boston: Kluwer Academic Publishers, 1992.

Lemler, Jerry. Interview from *Medical Strategies: Flight from Death, Deleted Scenes*. Accessed 14 August 2018. http://www.youtube.com/watch?v=2g9q2wFvB80.

Levy, David. *Love+Sex with Robots: The Evolution of Human–Robot Relationships*. New York: Harper, 2008.

Marantz Henig, Robin. "Will We Ever Arrive at the Good Death?" *New York Times Magazine*, 7 August 2005. Accessed 15 August 2018. http://www.nytimes.com/2005/08/07/magazine/will-we-ever-arrive-at-the-good-death.html?mcubz=0.
National Human Genome Research Institute. "An Overview of the Human Genome Project." Accessed 15 August 2018 https://www.genome.gov/12011238/an-overview-of-the-human-genome-project/.
Parnia, Sam. *Erasing Death: The Science That Is Rewriting the Boundaries between Life and Death.* New York: HarperCollins, 2013.
Penson, Richard T., Rosamund A. Partidge, Muhammad A. Shah, David Giansiracusa, Bruce A. Chabner, and Thomas J Lynch Jr. "Fear of Death." *The Oncologist*, December 1, 2004. Accessed August 15, 2018. http://theoncologist.alphamedpress.org/content/10/2/160.long.
Porter, Roy. *The Greatest Benefit to Mankind: A Medical History of Humanity*. New York: W. W. Norton & Company, 1997.
Ramsey, Paul. *The Patient as Person: Explorations in Medical Ethics*. New Haven, CT: Yale University Press, 1970.
Richnov, Nathaniel. "Can a Jellyfish Unlock the Secret of Immortality?" *New York Times*, 20 November 2012. Accessed August 15, 2018. http://www.nytimes.com/2012/12/02/magazine/can-a-jellyfish-unlock-the-secret-of-immortality.html?_r=0.
Robertson, Ann. "Biotechnology and the Governance of Life: The Case of Pre-implantation Genetic Diagnosis." In *Critical Interventions in the Ethics of Healthcare: Challenging the Principles of Autonomy in Bioethics*. Edited by Stuart J. Murray and Dave Holmes, 61–80. Farnham, Surrey, UK: Ashgate, 2009.
Rose, Nikolas S. *The Politics of Life Itself: Biomedicine, Power, and Subjectivity in the Twenty-first Century*. Princeton, NJ: Princeton University Press, 2007.
Rosling, Hans. "200 Countries, 200 Years, 4 Minutes." Accessed 15 August 2018. https://www.gapminder.org/videos/200-years-that-changed-the-world-bbc/.
SENS Research Foundation. "A Reimagined Research Strategy for Aging." Accessed 15 August 2018. http://www.sens.org/research/introduction-to-sens-research.
Spitzer, Victor, Michael J. Ackerman, Ann L. Scherzinger, and David Whitlock. "The Visible Human Male: A Technical Report." *Journal of the American Medical Informatics Association* 3 (1996): 118–130.
Tower, John. "Tower Lab." Accessed February 13 2011. http://towerlab.usc.edu/abstract.htm.
Toyota. "Partner Robot Family." 1995–2016. Accessed 15 August 2018. https://www.toyota-global.com/innovation/partner_robot/robot/.
Treung, Le. "Project Aiko," 2007–2013. Accessed 15 August 2018. www.projectaiko.com.
United Nations. "Table A.17 Life Expectancy at Birth, Both Sexes Combined, by Country for Selected Periods." In *World Population Prospects: The 2006 Revision*. New York, 2007. Accessed 15 August 2018. http://www.un.org/esa/population/publications/wpp2006/WPP2006_Highlights_rev.pdf.
US National Library of Medicine. "The Visible Human Project" (2015). Accessed 15 August 2018. https://www.nlm.nih.gov/research/visible/visible_human.html.
Vint, Sherryl. *Bodies of Tomorrow: Technology, Subjectivity, Science Fiction*. Toronto: University of Toronto Press, 2007.
Voxel-Man. Accessed 15 August 2018. https://www.voxel-man.com/.
Waldby, Catherine. *The Visible Human Project: Informatic Bodies and Posthuman Medicine*. New York: Routledge, 2000.
Walford, Roy. *Life Extension Magazine*, June 1996. Accessed 13 February 2011. http://www.walford.com/lifextin.htm.
Williams, Simon J. "Modern Medicine and the 'Uncertain Body': From Corporeality to Hyperreality?" *Social Science and Medicine* 45, no. 7 (October 1997): 1041–49. Accessed 15 August 2018. https://doi.org/10.1016/S0277-9536(97)00031-2.
ZOLL. (2016). Accessed 20 July 2016 from http://www.zoll.com/medical-products/cardiac-support-pump/autopulse/clinical-studies/.

NOTES

1. Norbert Elias, *The Loneliness of the Dying* (Oxford: Basil Blackwell, 1985), 3.
2. Elias, *The Loneliness of the Dying*, 86.
3. Elias, *The Loneliness of the Dying*, 86.
4. Robin Marantz Henig, "Will We Ever Arrive at the Good Death?" *New York Times Magazine*, 7 August 2005.
5. Ernest Becker, *The Denial of Death* (New York: Macmillan, 1973), 22.
6. Becker, *The Denial of Death*, xi.
7. Becker, *The Denial of Death*, 285.
8. United Nations, "Table A.17 Life Expectancy at Birth, Both Sexes Combined, by Country for Selected Periods," in *World Population Prospects: The 2006 Revision* (New York, 2007), 80.
9. Walford, *Life Extension Magazine*, June 1996.
10. SENS Research Foundation, "A Reimagined Research Strategy for Aging."
11. Nathaniel Richnov, "Can a Jellyfish Unlock the Secret of Immortality?" *New York Times*, 20 November 2012, http://www.nytimes.com/2012/12/02/magazine/can-a-jellyfish-unlock-the-secret-of-immortality.html?_r=0
12. Ann Robertson, "Biotechnology and the Governance of Life: The Case of Pre-implantation Genetic Diagnosis," in *Critical Interventions in the Ethics of Healthcare: Challenging the Principles of autonomy in Bioethics,* ed. Stuart J. Murray and Dave Holmes (Farnham, Surrey, UK: Ashgate, 2009), 64.
13. National Human Genome Research Institute, "An Overview of the Human Genome Project," https://www.genome.gov/12011238/an-overview-of-the-human-genome-project/.
14. National Human Genome Research Institute, "An Overview."
15. John Tower, "Tower Lab," http://towerlab.usc.edu/abstract.htm.
16. Daniel G. Gibson and J. Craig Venter, "Synthetic Biology: Construction of a Yeast Chromosome," *Nature* 509 (May 2014), 168.
17. Gibson and Venter, "Synthetic Biology," 168.
18. Nikolas S. Rose, *The Politics of Life Itself: Biomedicine, Power, and Subjectivity in the Twenty-First Century* (Princeton, NJ: Princeton University Press), 14.
19. Katherine N. Hayles, *How We Became Posthuman: Virtual Bodies in Cybernetics, Literature, and Informatics* (Chicago: University of Chicago Press, 1999), 22.
20. Hayles, *How We Became Posthuman*, 2–3.
21. Rose, *The Politics of Life Itself*, 254.
22. Roy Porter, *The Greatest Benefit to Mankind: A Medical History of Humanity* (New York: W. W. Norton, 1997), 8.
23. Elaine L. Graham, *Representations of the Post/Human: Monsters, Aliens and Others in Popular Culture* (New Brunswick, NJ: Rutgers University Press), 120.
24. Jerry Lemler, Interview from *Medical Strategies: Flight from Death, Deleted Scenes*, http://www.youtube.com/watch?v=2g9q2wFvB80.
25. Richard T. Penson et al., "Fear of Death," *The Oncologist*, 1 December 2004.
26. US National Library of Medicine, "The Visible Human Project," https://www.nlm.nih.gov/research/visible/visible_human.html.
27. Victor Spitzer et al., "The Visible Human Male: A Technical Report," *Journal of the American Medical Informatics Association* 3 (1996).
28. Catherine Waldby, *The Visible Human Project: Informatic Bodies and Posthuman Medicine* (New York: Routledge), 27.
29. Waldby, *The Visible Human Project*, 136.
30. Spitzer et al., "The Visible Human Male."
31. Henri Bergson, *The Creative Mind: An Introduction to Metaphysics* (New York: Kensington), 164–65.
32. Jong-Hwan Kim, Kang-Hee Lee, and Yong-Duk Kim, "The Origin of Artificial Species: Genetic Robot," *International Journal of Control, Automation, and Systems* 3, no. 4 (December 2001), 564–570.
33. Kim, Lee, and Kim, "The Origin of Artificial Species," 568.

34. Kim, Lee, and Kim, "The Origin of Artificial Species," 570.
35. Toyota, "Partner Robot Family."
36. Le Treung, "Project Aiko," http://www.projectaiko.com.
37. Blue Frog Robotics, "Buddy, the First Emotional Companion Robot," https://buddytherobot.com/en/buddy-the-emotional-robot/.
38. David Levy, *Love+Sex with Robots: The Evolution of Human-Robot Relationships* (New York: Harper), 297.
39. Levy, *Love+Sex*, 22.
40. Simon J. Williams, "Modern Medicine and the 'Uncertain Body': From Corporeality to Hyperreality?" *Social Science and Medicine* 45, no. 7 (October 1997), 1047.
41. Donna Haraway, *Modest_Witness@Second_Millennium: FemaleMan_Meets_Onco Mouse* (Oxford: Routledge, 1997), 12.
42. Marantz Henig, "Will We Ever Arrive at the Good Death."
43. Sam Parnia, *Erasing Death: The Science That Is Rewriting the Boundaries between Life and Death* (New York: HarperCollins, 2013), 21, 25.
44. Parnia, *Erasing Death*, 50.
45. ZOLL.
46. Parnia, *Erasing Death*, 22.
47. Parnia, *Erasing Death*, 22.
48. Parnia, *Erasing Death*, 150.
49. Parnia, *Erasing Death*, 157.
50. Parnia, *Erasing Death*, 166.
51. Parnia, *Erasing Death*, 153–54.
52. Parnia, *Erasing Death*.
53. Drew Leder, "A Tale of Two Bodies: The Cartesian Corpse and the Lived Body," in *The Body in Medical Thought and Practice*, ed. Drew Leder (Boston: Kluwer Academic), 31.
54. Parnia, *Erasing Death*, 141–217.
55. Graham, *Representation of the Post/Human*, 10.
56. Sherryl Vint, *Bodies of Tomorrow: Technology, Subjectivity, Science Fiction* (Toronto: University of Toronto Press), 16.
57. Rose, *The Politics of Life Itself*, 254.
58. Rose, *The Politics of Life Itself*, 80.
59. Rose, *The Politics of Life Itself*, 77.
60. Hayles, *How We Became Posthuman*, 283.
61. Becker, *The Denial of Death*, 283–84.
62. Rose, *The Politics of Life Itself*, 5.

Chapter Ten

"Not Born in a Garden"

Donna Haraway, Cyborgs, and Posthuman Contemporary Art

Eric Weichel

"The cyborg would not recognize the Garden of Eden; it is not made of mud and cannot dream of returning to dust."[1]

Cyborgs, anthropomorphic entities whose nature is both biological and mechanical, are of much contemporary cultural relevance in a wide variety of media, and in any speculation about the future of humanity's relationship with the arts.[2] The concept of the cyborg is much-articulated within popular culture, where it remains a major and oft-occurring motif in speculative literature and cinema. The artificial, unexpected blending of human and robotic bodies is reiterated in everything from cyborgian anime's rapidly proliferating host of subgenres to recent films that provide thoughtful, poignant, haunting social commentary on the moral vagaries of twenty-first-century capitalist-bourgeois life. As a philosophical construct, the cyborg is also important in contemporary academic life, where, via one celebrated feminist-Marxist meditation on humanity's possible future, the cyborg is a potent theoretical vehicle for deconstructing normative notions of gender identity, sexual expression, and the body's place within its wider world. Donna Haraway's essay "The Cyborg Manifesto," first published in 1984, is a particularly crucial text for researchers seeking to situate their work in dialogue with interdisciplinary methodologies that bridge gaps between disparate fields of study. Haraway's provocative essay cleared a working foundation that the author herself has continued to build upon via a series of later volumes and essays, and her wider work continues to be influential for how a succession of contemporary artists and thinkers have dreamt of the cyborg. As one critic notes, "according to Haraway, the construction of the cyborg, being post-gender, operates both beyond the sex binary and the social realities that accompany it. This positions the cyborg as a possible metaphor for standing outside phallocentric, rational thought."[3] In this chapter, I explore a series of case studies of contemporary artists whose work has been informed by cyborgian themes: Bharti Kher (India), Andrea Crespo (United States) and Sally McKay (Canada), Patricia Piccinini (Australia), and Burton Nitta (UK). All of these artists have won major national and international prizes and are well-represented in solo exhibitions at leading galleries, suggesting that their disparate, yet closely parallel meditations on the theme of the posthuman are indicative of a wider interest in the field. Through the juxtaposition of a discussion of work from Kher, Crespo, Piccinini, and Burton Nitta with the analysis of relevant quotes from Donna Haraway, I explore how one author's ideas have discursively shaped how humanity uses visual art as a crucial tool to forecast its future.

BHARTI KHER: BIOPOLITICS AS HARAWAYAN DIFFERENCE

The futurist potentiality of the Harawayan Cyborg, and the subsequent exploration of these possibilities across a variety of media, is a strategy excitingly employed by artists, poets, cultural historians, and theorists of diverse interests and backgrounds. This diversity of approaches to the cyborgian future was reiterated during a panel I chaired in October of 2016, at the Universities Art Association of Canada Conference in Montreal, Quebec. Under the theme of "Cyborgs: Humanity's Future and Interdisciplinary Contemporary Art," participants Dr. Sally McKay (McMaster) and Dr. Sarah Evans (Northern Illinois University) reflected on their long-running academic engagement with Haraway's work, showcasing how new and innovative approaches to an understanding of the cyborg were contributing the production of new and collaboratively enacted, interdisciplinary relationships between such previously binarised categories as "the body" and "the machine."

In her paper "This Way and Never Another: Biopolitics as Difference Reproduced in Bharti Kher's Art," Evans highlighted the problematic juxtaposition of the emergence of new reproductive technologies with the colonizing exploitation of subaltern Asian women, especially in India, where widespread abuses of the global surrogacy trade led to the outright banning of commercial surrogacy in 2017 (homosexual couples were already banned from participating in India's reproductive industry of commercial surrogacy as early as 2012).[4] In their response to the Surrogacy Regulation Bill, representatives of women's health group Sama ask the state not to ban commercial surrogacy but to regulate it, along with the rest of the assisted reproductive technology sector.[5] Evans points out that the "western-backed sterilization of low-caste women, employment of docile surrogates, and bulk harvests of eggs for stem cell research heighten the country's global profile as a corporate-funded biotechnology hub as well as a stage for the profitable instrumentalisation of women's reproductive capacities."[6]

Artistic work that responds to the complex ethical dilemmas presented by India's turbulent regulatory approach to twenty-first-century fertility technologies include the award-winning sculptures, paintings, and drawings by the Indian artist Bharti Kher, whose "grotesque" sculptures, as Evans notes, can be read as "non-Western cyborgs melding female, divine, animal and alien elements."[7] Kher also "produces harmonious 'abstract paintings' from boards encrusted with felt bindi. Most of the bindi take the traditional circular form signifying happiness in marital fertility; but others are leftovers from a fashion for sperm-shaped stick-ons."[8] Just as collected human sperm is manually observed and tested through the laboratory's microscope, so computer-assisted sperm analysis software and its visual imaging capabilities (as of 2014, "strobe-like images of 500 to >2000 sperm, at 50 or 60 frames per second") allows for newly integrated biotechnological relationships of profound import for the future of humanity.[9] As Evans notes, "the sperm never penetrate the egg-like bindi. They flow past or spiral in on themselves. 'Natural' heterosexual reproduction looks unlikely."[10]

Kher's deployment of the visual language of the microscope in her aesthetically and theoretically provocative body of work is of great interest to Evans, who points out that for Haraway "the regenerative cyborg promised escape from the gender binary of the reproductive family."[11] If, for Haraway, the cyborg's very identity is a futurist alternative to the monolithic compulsory heteronormativity of femininity as exploited as labour by the Judeo-Christian, bourgeois-capitalist nuclear family unit, for Evans, "Kher's cyborgs may represent a postgender, post-race and post-human assemblage ... her bindi 'paintings' vividly juxtapose rivers of sperm with what look like vast stockpiles of eggs, evoking persistent gender and racial differentiation in Indian biopolitics."[12] Many Indian cultural discourses ostensibly take the nuclear family unit as a central tenant of identity: the heterosexual marriage as a *de facto* priority in Bollywood film, to take one egregiously omnipresent example.[13]

India's highly publicised regulatory struggle with the realities of commercial surrogacy on a global world market, including the deliberate exclusion of access to reproductive technology by gay couples, involves an attempt to limit the potentialities of a cyborgian reality beyond the traditional structure of heterosexual family life: in and of itself, the very existence of commercial surrogacy hints at a new cyborgian realities that transcend traditional taboos about sex, family, and society. Kher's work engages with these and other social and sexual anxieties. In *Dark Matter MM* (2015), Kher's large-scale bindi paintings create a sense of vivaciously coloured monumentality that Evans notes carries all the connotations of a microscopic photograph of zygotisation at embryogenesis: the moment of fusion between the sperm and egg, resulting in new life.[14]

With its fusion of traditional and contemporary, mythology and science, microscopic and universal, Bharti's Kher's art is a powerfully meditative tool with which to view these ongoing debates about humanity's cyborgian future.[15] The notion of being inexplicably joined, of mergings that destabilise abject or subject notions of bodily integrity-identity, is also a major component of Kher's artistic output. As the Vancouver Art Gallery notes in its analysis of her 2016 exhibition *Matter*, "In Kher's early photographic images and sculptures, it is ideas of hybridity that feature prominently.... Male and female are blurred, the sacred and profane are fused, and human and animal merge."[16] The blurring of boundaries between machine and human, human and animal, and animal and deity are similarly long-running motifs in Haraway's writing.

ANDREA CRESPO: SCREEN, SCANNER, AND SIGNAL

Hybridity is as central to Haraway's later meditations on a wide variety of subjects as it was when she defiantly argued, of the cyborg, that "biological organisms have become biotic systems, communications devices like others. There is no fundamental, ontological separation in our formal knowledge of machine and organism, of technical and organic."[17] Like Kher's fusions of traditional and medical imagery, and similarly in tandem with Haraway's conceptual focus on the category of the hybrid, a variety of emerging feminist artists take hybridity as their visual and theoretical focus, creating works that deploy transient, liminal concepts of the body, the subject-object, and the relationships between human, animal, and machine. One of them is Andrea Crespo, who creates videos, installations and drawings heavily inspired by bodily hybrids: two-headed, multilimbed beings culled from the vast corpus of images created by fans and fetishists and uploaded to popular internet galleries such as Deviantart. For Crespo, as for Haraway, body and machine have already merged.[18]

Crespo's video *Parabiosis: Neurolibidinal Induction Complex* suggests something of their representation of the machine-body cyborgian present, where the computer screen—or the scanner, or the photocopier—is "related to with intense intimacy" by the human user. In a conversation with curator Stella Botai, Crespo suggests that "Screens and scannerbeds readily accumulate dust, hair, condensation, bodily residues, etc. They seem prone to static clinging. They act like slices or slides, capturing a particular material history."[19] For Crespo, "this tells us less of the utility and usage of screens than of tactile relationality and coupling with and/or through machines." *Parabiosis* explores these extant couplings, underscoring our twenty-first-century reality of body/screen assemblages by showing video of the scanner light itself: the rhythmic movements of the scanner, and the high-pitched humming of disembodied, machine-produced white noise, are juxtaposed with fetishistic images of multilimbed manga characters from the online fan community and with "minimal diagrams of mitochondrial reproduction, suggestive of the biological processes within technology."[20]

These hybrid, mitotically derived visual images are combined with medical terms relating to autism, pluralism, and a pathologised understanding of the human body. Such images and medical, or moral, terms are combined with more poetic explorations of language that dance beautifully across a Stygian screen: "you are becoming lighter"; "you are a signal." The result, as Crepo's collaborator Jack Kahn points out, is a "chimeric composition of data and flesh that flows between the sensual and the machinic."[21] How apt that "our best machines are made of sunshine," wrote Haraway, "they are all light and clean because they are nothing but signals, electromagnetic waves, a section of a spectrum. . . . Cyborgs are ether, quintessence."[22] Crespo's light in *Parabiosis* might not be made of sunshine, but in the work's assemblage of internet images, scanner lights, machine whirring, and nervous keystrokes, the ethereal newness or *presentality* of our contemporary cyborgian collectivity is made tangible.

Like Bher's work, which subverts or expands the bindi's place in traditional Indian iconography, thus destabilizing neat, binary, or heteronormative understandings of human sexuality and reproduction, Crespo's deployment of assembled, hybrid, monstrous, screen-fused bodies has a dangerously subversive social potential, one the artist seems well aware of. In dialogue with Crespo, Kahn writes of *Parabiosis* that "consumer electronics function as a prosthetic to the neurodivergent body," and the new relationships of the postmodern visual economy "function not by quarantining those deemed pathological by the immunization efforts of modernity, but by harnessing their affects, their capacity or tendency to relate, within virtual space structured by data."[23] In this present, user-generated fetishes of many-limbed manga women with conjoined bodies, or two-headed digital avatars that embark on sequential adventures (Crespo's *A day in the lives of*, from 2016, for example), are representative of cyborgs that transcend modern identity definition, and are difficult to encompass within a morality system informed by compulsory heteronormativity.[24]

The "monstrous" social and personal potential of a world without gender can be difficult for any artist, including Crespo, to grapple with. As Haraway suggests, "The regrown limb can be monstrous, duplicated, potent. We have all been injured, profoundly. We require regeneration, not rebirth, and the possibilities for our reconstitution include the utopian dream of the hope for a monstrous world without gender."[25] In a recent artist statement about their latest work (is it a performance?), Crespo seems to renege on the postgendered cyborgian possibility of *Parabiosis* and its successor, *A day in the lives of*, which has been removed from view. Writing of her earlier video work, Crespo suggests it represents "an unnatural convergence of internalised body-image issues and externally directed obsessions toward the image of dicephalic conjoined twins seen on television at an early-age." Troublingly, instead of celebrating the liberatory potential of the cyborg that was at the centre of much of Parabiosis' critical acclaim, Crespo seems now to have taken refuge back within Eden, thus explicitly rejecting the liminal, alterior, or queer possibilities inherent in their earlier work. "Having experienced all this, I can only say: God works in mysterious ways," Crespo writes, apparently retreating into Merleau-Ponty's "malaise" of Judeo-Christian ontology that situates the divine as extra-natural.[26] "The silver-lining to this unusual story lies in how it eventually 'broke' and liberated me from my transgender identity, opening my eyes to the apparent incommensurabilities inherent to trans narratives, of wanting to be what the Lord has not created one to be," writes Crespo, in reductive and fundamentalist language that simultaneously denies the rights of transgendered people to self-determination and respect, the growing body of scientific literature that reiterates transgendered identity as a biological reality, and, of course, any potential for transgendered spirituality in a Judeo-Christian context itself.[27] Liberation, in this new discourse by Crespo, is a concept inherently offensive to an already vulnerable transgender population.

The daringly simultaneous irreconcilabilities, syntheses, syncretisms, and liminal, malleable, permeable contexts of the machine-mediated body are, I believe, the most interesting facets of Crespo's early work, well-showcased by the clinical, medicalised context of how the work was shown in the exhibition "Polymorphoses" at Hester gallery in New York in 2015. "I pray for the deliverance of recent generations coming of age by the screen," reads Crespo's final artist statement footnote, "of outcasts who take refuge in the darkest corners of computer networks, the wounded who struggle with unspeakable traumas, and those who are taught to worship the self and its insatiable lusts." I suggest that Crespo might well also pray for the postgendered world of the cyborg, which, as Haraway's manifesto suggests, in its liberatory innovation, "is a world without genesis, but also a world without end."

SCANNERS AND SENSATION: SALLY MCKAY

While Crespo's scanner in *Parabiosis* suggests the "static clinging" of a conjoined screen-body hybrid, thus suggesting the transmitotic potentiality of a Harawayan Cyborg, scanners are also the focus of a Sally McKay's research, where collaborative projects between students from diverse departmental backgrounds suggest "the scanner itself as an active (and mythic) agent in the construction of post-human subjectivity."[28] Blending approaches from biology, healthcare, literature, the visual arts, and community outreach, McKay's team takes the functional magnetic resonance imaging (fMRI) scan as a potent cultural and critical signifier. Adopting "the feminist proposition that all knowledge is partial and situated," McKay's work involves a "subjective address to the scanner as a social agent speaks to the urgency, articulated in *The Cyborg Manifesto*, for critical understandings of the role of technology in embodied experience."[29] The cultural role of fMRI scanner technologies, their ubiquity within twenty-first-century healthcare, and a certain "intense intimacy" between human and machine, well-documented in the varying responses of the team to the experience of an fMRI scan, suggest the potentially portraitistic, symbolic image-value of a neural scan, or the value of collapsing a simple subject-object divide when thinking of how bodies and machines interact.

For McKay, in two specific contexts, "inside the art gallery and inside the MRI scanner . . . embodied knowledge emerges, in part, through the situated standpoint of participants and observers." This makes Crespo's deployment of the almost unspoken iconographic potential of the scanner, and the contextual circumstances of her work's exhibition and display, key attributes in the creation of a cyborgian assemblage. As McKay notes, "despite the seeming passivity of art audiences and scientific subjects, one does not perform either role as a blank slate or empty vessel, but as an alert and active entity primed and conditioned by personal past experience and collective cultural knowledge," and the art gallery, the clinical laboratory, and the university classroom certainly offer three different radically contextual encounters with the scanner.[30] These multiplicities are present in Crespo's video work. For example, when responding to an exam question dealing with *Parabiosis*, one of my own students noted how the scanner seems to scan the theatre audience itself, encompassing viewers within an assemblage vision; others merely noted the "anime" aesthetic of the represented conjoined bodies, or the abject detritus, suggested by the imprints of bodily residues briefly flashed on screen. Haraway's insistence on situated knowledges is of much value to McKay's parallel understanding of how each viewer brings a cultural dimension to their diverse experiences with a range of imaging devices and scanners, be it a printer's scanner bed or the fMRI scanner. In her work's methodological fusion between the practical application of neuroscience, aesthetic theory, and art history, McKay allows for valuable insights of what needs a future humanity might have.

PATRICIA PICCININI: POSTHUMAN EMBRACES OF THE SHELTERING WOMBAT

One striking need of any future humanity is likely to be innovative solutions to environmental problems, including species extinction, where human causes (either intentional or inadvertent) of species eradication result in the terrifyingly sudden collapse of biodiversity across the planet. Artistic responses to this grim reality have taken many forms, but one of the most "Harawayan," in its beautifully representative, sensually evocative cyborgian corporeality, is the work of Australian sculptor Patricia Piccinini, whose human–animal hybrids suggest the bodily inextricability of human, animal, and machine. For example, *Meet Graham*, a hyper-"realistic" sculpture of a future humanoid, is Piccinini's "cyborg prototype of hypothetical anatomy, designed to mitigate the physical trauma experienced by the human body in high-speed collisions."[31] Commissioned by the Australian Transport Accident Commission and designed in consultation with a surgeon and a crash investigator, Piccinini's silicon-and-human-hair creation is a taciturn and recalcitrant cyborg. Significantly, "he" is gendered, with chest fuzz, a sparse goatee, and axillary hair, as well as the generic masculinity of his moniker "Graham." *Meet Graham*, Piccinini insists, is a figure whose stance, clothing (blue shorts), and confident gaze proclaim masculinity, albeit one penetrated as much by the adjacent iPods running augmented-reality videos of "his" hypothetical organs as by biomedical intervention (the feet and lower legs are extended, as a kangaroo's are, allowing for the cyborg to leap from danger). As artist and writer Sophie Knezic points out, in its plethora of citations from the structural language of machinery and from the visual language of animality, Piccinini's *Meet Graham* destabilises "the clear delineations of human and machine, human and animal, echoing Haraway's call to take pleasure in the confusion of boundaries."[32] As such, in *Meet Graham*, as well as in much of Piccinini's other work, the "ontological ambiguity of her sculptures makes them perfect embodiments of the cyborg with its permanently contradictory identity status."[33]

Piccinini's work often uses the subject of the child to suggest innocence, youth, family love and cohesion, hope, and the excitement of a new beginning, but such optimism is often tempered with a (highly) contradictory unease at what innovations or improvements in genetic engineering, reproductive technology and human–animal hybridization might entail in humanity's (near) future. In *Still Life with Stem Cells* (2002), a hyperrealistic sculpture of a child grasps nebulous balls of wrinkled flesh, some segmented in a manner simultaneously suggestive of testicles, tumours, or toy terriers. Haraway is delighted by the piece, mentioning that "the cell-blob/human-girl playgroup in *Still Life with Stem Cells* is neither utopian nor dystopian; it is seriously playful and so curious, inquisitive and risky," while in commenting on this work, Piccinini noted the "nowness" of cyborgian hybridity, saying of genetic engineering that "the question of whether this is a good or a bad thing is both too simplistic and a little academic. As with so much of this biotechnology, the extraordinary has already become the ordinary."[34] For the artist, "the real question is 'what are we going to do with it?'"[35] *Still Life with Stem Cells* is certainly "one kind of answer," and one certainly taken even further in *Meet Graham*, where the ethical and commercial dimensions of genetic manipulation and corporal modification are rendered more forcibly noticeable by Piccinini. And yet, Piccinini's sculptural hybridizations can sometimes suggest unthought hopes or miraculous solutions, albeit at the cost of a comfortable psychological reliance on a Cartesian dichotomy between body and mind, or self and other.

In *Undivided*, Piccinini famously creates a human–animal hybrid that, through its conjoined, merged, liminal, or machine-blended qualities, allowed for the conceptualization of species recovery through a loss of special purity. As environmental activist and educator Affrica Taylor writes, Piccinini's provocative piece forced her "to think hard about the connections between wombat-settler relations, settler children and the ethics and politics of common worlds [of] inheritance, kinship and cohabitation" that are at the heart of this author's practice.[36] The work shows a small settler-descendant child clad in indigo pyjamas sparkled with starbursts, sleeping peacefully on little trundle bed wrapped in comfortable cerulean sheets. A teddy bear lies akimbo on a soft rug underneath. In its vision of comfortable middle-class domesticity and family nurture, the work hits at the social, and the economic, values underpinning the very familiarity of much bourgeois-capitalist society. The child, however, is snuggled next to an "older sci-fi, non-human, but strangely humanoid creature," spooned next to the bare-skinned being in an attitude of tranquillity and peace.[37] The creature itself is *Surrogate*, a reoccuring character in Piccinini's *Nature's Little Helper's* series of 2004–2005.

Surrogate is an unexpected cyborg, an endearing, domestic, nurturing hybrid who, if s/he suggests the aesthetic of a dystopian Beatrix Potter, is far removed from the hypersexualised, bodily traumatised killing machines or pleasure dolls beloved as tropes by the Hollywood speculative film establishment. Instead, Surrogate literally carries on and within her the potential for ecological recovery, as marching down the spine of this extraordinary creature are six marsupial pouches, grafted onto her plump, motherly body in elegant cohesion. From the bottom two of Surrogate's inexplicable orifices emerge her charges: the hirsute visages of a pair of almost-grown Northern Hairy-Nosed Wombats, one of Australia's most cherished, and most threatened, endemic species. When Piccinini first envisioned Surrogate, this charming marsupial was reduced to a population of just over twenty-five breeding females, confined to a heavily monitored reserve in Epping Forest National Park and protected, if limited, by a two-meter-high fence that acts as a predator deterrent. As Taylor reminds us, "Undivided not only alerts its audiences to the plight of the Northern Hairy-Nosed Wombat, but it confronts us with the ways in which techno-cultural and ecological dilemmas, or sticky knots, become inseparably entwined."[38] Piccinini's installation, like the work of Bharti Kher, both reflects on the phenomenon of surrogacy and does so through cyborgian methods that hybridise, "stitch together," or otherwise meld discrete objective identities to present alternatives.

Piccinini's work is also a useful counterpart with which to make visible the assemblages of discourses, scientific and cultural, that are brought to bear on the conservation of a highly endangered species. As two conservation agencies report, the Epping Forest population has been "monitored via remote sampling and genetic techniques since 2000, thus avoiding the detrimental effects on the animals of trapping and increasing the precision of abundance estimates."[39] Their own study reports on new methods of making "non-invasively collected" DNA analysis "that will reduce the time and cost of future northern hairy-nosed wombat hair censuses."[40] Man, machine, and animal biology are already inextricably linked, certainly in this specific species' instance, and Piccinini's sculpture allows for a vision of a future humanity that is increasingly aware of its undivided affinities with other, non-human subjects.

BURTON NITTA: CYBORGIAN OPERA

Unexpected affinities between the human body and specific species of plants and animals are of central concern to the artist-designer duo of Michael Burton and Michiko Nitta, who as Burton Nitta have collaborated with a wide variety of scientists on innovative projects that fuse science, visual art, dance, dining, and music. Burton Nitta's *Algae Opera*, where the mezzo-soprano opera singer Louise Ashcroft is fit with an elaborate, intricate, and gorgeously designed bio-suit that, through a complex system of tubes, expresses the carbon dioxide of her breathing during a performance to the algae tanks beneath her, has received considerable critical attention for its beautiful synthesis between performing, hearing, and eating.[41] Burton Nitta note that algae, due to its potential for radically exponential growth, is likely to become increasingly in demand as a food source in humanity's immediate future. Some forms of algae, such as the blue-green cynobacteria *Spirulina*, are already a significant part of dining within a variety of cultures, while others have as-yet untapped commercial or cultural potential. The singer's bio-suit is thus part of an emerging technocultural experiment that sees increased attention, and respect, paid to the way in which algae might be grown, eaten, or even worn. In the sartorial "cyanosplendour" of Burton Nitta's operatic bio-suit, the embodied or even transcorporeal cyborgian possibilities of the future of humanity are made not only visible, but wearable, leading to new and stunningly collaborative liminalities between human, plant, animal, machine, and the wider environment.

Burton Nitta are specifically inspired by the syncretic ideas of Debora Mackenzie and Michael Lepage, who, in a 2010 article titled "Eat Light: Dawn of the Plantimals," pointed out the photosynthetic capabilities of certain species of fish and marine organisms, including lichen, sea slugs, and salamanders, all of whom, through symbiosis, "wear" algae in their very bodies.[42] The potential for future agricultural animals, or even humans, to use some sort of similar biology via genetic engineering is a fascinating one made all the more concrete, visible, and even auditory through Burton Nitta's *Algae Opera*, which first premiered during 2012 Design Week at the Victoria and Albert Museum. Working in close collaboration with the composer Gameshow Outpatient, both singer and musician reworked the conventional vocal techniques of classical opera to "sonically enhance" the algae itself. Two years later, such technocultural enhancements were further expanded in a 2014 performance called the "Algae Opera House" for the Beyond Biennial at EYE in Amsterdam, where diners were encouraged to take seats beside a riverine pool deftly manipulated by a bejewelled hostess equipped with a prosthetic flipper: song-infused algae prepared and presented by a chef floated past in colour-coded combinations, infusing the diner's palette with a new sensory collaboration between music and machine, plant life and artistic expression.[43]

Such a future suggests cyborgian experiences that are terrifically optimistic: in their invocation of unexpected assemblages or heightened sensory realities, where a posthuman life is marked by the carnality of mutually evolving, coadapted, or symbiotic sensualities, Burton Nitta's *Algae Opera* and *Algae Opera House* expands Haraway's notion of the feminist-Marxist cyborg into new conceptual territory. Like Burton Nitta, Patricia Piccinini's disturbingly hyperrealistic sculptures, troubling in their intimacy, construct a vision of a not-so-distant future peopled by genetic chimaeras, fusions between the animal and the human that somehow express, despite the collapse of bodily boundaries, a surprising sense of peace. *Meet Graham*, iconographic meaning riddled with the daily trauma of a life reliant on the car, is not a reassuring vision of humanity's future, but it is one that uses all the canonical stillness and materiality of representational sculpture to ground a viewing experience somewhat closer to the future: if "he" lounges on his concrete sofa with a fixed stare and stretched-out arm deliberately evocative of a man watching television, might "they" not also take pleasure in the savoury delights of sonically enhanced operatic algae? Would such an embodied cyborg experience yet another layer of technocultural situation through the wearing of the Burton Nitta biosuit, and what kinds of knowledges might such a posthuman sensory apparatus deploy? Crespo's technological assemblages of computer, videogame, and video parts and projections conjure the twinned horrors of the surgery theatre and the interrogation room in a less optimistic way, but they still playfully link ephemera from digital comics and manga with the emerging sentience of our everyday machines. In a similar fashion, McKay's pedagogy foregrounds a collaborative aestheticized response to both the medicalised body and its collective response to a medical scanner. And Kher's bindi paintings, swarming with sperm and dominated by the spherical monumentality of the ova as glimpsed through the microscope, are, as Evans reminds us, potent reminders of the conjoined pitfalls of commercial surrogacy and social eugenics, where fraught ideas about class structure, national citizenship, and sexual identity condition access to new reproductive technologies. Each of these artists reminds us, after their own fashion, that Haraway's radical ideas about the cyborg continue to be of much relevance for contemporary life. The cyborg might not be born in a garden, but syncretic ecosystems bedazzle its assembled body, writhing between contours in unexpectedly musical salaciousness. In many ways, we are all already cyborgs, tested and observed long before birth, the "biofog" of our messy, dripping, shedding bodies stretched out over a multitude of observant machines, linked to each other with an immediacy our ancestors can hardly have dreamt of, when they mused on what the future might bring for their descendants. What else, for the future of humanity, but the cyborg?

BIBLIOGRAPHY

Amann, R. P., and D. Waberski. "Computer-Assisted Sperm Analysis (CASA): Capabilities and Potential Developments." *Theriogenology* 81, no. 1 (2014): 5–17. doi: 10.1016/j.theriogenology.2013.09.004.

Burton, Michael, and Michiko Nitta. "Algae Opera." Accessed 14 June 2018. http://www.burtonnitta.co.uk/AlgaeOpera.html.

Campbell, Robert A. "Cyborg Salvation History: Donna Haraway and the Future of Religion." *Humboldt Journal of Social Relations* 26.5 (2001): 154–73.

Cornell, Lauren. "Andrea Crespo—A Day in the Lives of (2016)," *Rhizome* (21 September 2016). Accessed 31 May 2018. https://rhizome.org/editorial/2016/sep/21/a-day-in-the-lives-of/.

Crespo, Andrea. "Joined for Life: 2017." Accessed 31 May 2018. http://andreacrespo.com/.

Crespo, Andrea, and Stella Bottai. "virocrypsis." *Vdrome.org* (25 November–8 December 2015). Accessed 31 May 2018. http://www.vdrome.org/andrea-crespo-virocrypsis/.

Crespo, Andrea (video), and Jack Kahn (text). "Parabiosis: Neurolibidinal Induction Complex." *DIS Magazine*. Accessed 31 May 2018. http://dismagazine.com/dystopia/72978/andrea-crespo-sis-parabiosis/.

Dunlevy, T'cha. "DHC/ART: Bharti Kher's Bindis Are Watching You Watching Them." *Montreal Gazette* (4 May 2018). Accessed 31 May 2018, http://montrealgazette.com/entertainment/arts/dhc-art-bharti-khers-bindis-are-watching-you-watching-them.

Evans, Sarah. *This Way and Never Another: Biopolitics as Difference Reproduced in Bharti Kher's Art*. Montreal: Universities Art Association Conference, October 2016.

Evans, Sarah, and Bharti Kher. "Matter, Vancouver Art Gallery, 2016." *ASAP* (27 November 2017). Accessed 15 June 2018. http://asapjournal.com/bharti-kher-matter/.

Folch, Christine. "Why the West Loves Sci-Fi and Fantasy: A Cultural Explanation." *The Atlantic* (23 June 2013). Accessed 31 May, 2018. https://www.theatlantic.com/entertainment/archive/2013/06/why-the-west-loves-sci-fi-and-fantasy-a-cultural-explanation/276816/.

Gruss, Susanne. *The Pleasure of the Feminist Text: Reading Michèle Roberts and Angela Carter*. Amsterdam: Rodopi, 2009.

Haraway, Donna. "A Cyborg Manifesto: Science, Technology, and Socialist-Feminism in the Late Twentieth Century." In *Simians, Cyborgs and Women: The Reinvention of Nature*. New York: Routledge, 1991.

Haraway, Donna. "Situated Knowledges: The Science Question in Feminism and the Privilege of Partial Perspective." *Feminist Studies* 14, no. 3 (Fall 1988).

Haraway, Donna. "Speculative Fabulations for Technoculture's Generations: Taking Care of Unexpected Country." *Australian Humanities Review* 50 (2011): 102.

Haugen, Anton. "A Scanner, Darkly: On Andrea Crespo's 'polymorphoses.'" *Rhizome* (26 August 2015). Accessed 13 September 2018. http://rhizome.org/editorial/2015/aug/26/crespo-review/.

Kearny, Richard. "Sacramental Imagination and Eschatology." In *Phenomenology and Eschatology: Not Yet in the Now*, edited by John Panteleimon Manoussakis. London: Routledge for Taylor and Francis, 2009–2016.

Knezic, Sophie. "Review, Patricia Piccinini: Meet Graham." *Artlink* (23 September 2016). Accessed 1 June 2018. https://www.artlink.com.au/articles/4533/patricia-piccinini-meet-graham/.

Mackenzie, Debora, and Michael LePage. "Eat Light: Dawn of the Plantimals." *New Scientist* 208, no. 2790 (11 December 2010): 32–35.

McKay, Sally. *The Haunted Scanner*. Montreal: Universities Art Association Conference, October 2016.

McKay, Sally. *Repositioning Neuroaesthetics through Contemporary Art*. PhD Dissertation. Ontario: York University, 2014.

Merleau-Ponty, Maurice, and Dominique Segland, composer. *Maurice Nature: Course Notes from the College de France*. Evanston, IL: Northwestern University Press, 1995.

Murray, Soraya. "Cybernated Aesthetics: Lee Bul and the Body Transformed." *PAJ: A Journal of Performance and Art* 89 (2008): 39.

Nadimpally, Sarojini, Sneha Banerjee, and Deepa Venkatachalam, Sama Resource Group for Women and Health. *Commercial Surrogacy: A Contested Terrain in the Realm of Rights and Justice*. Kuala Lumpur: Asian-Pacific Resource and Research Centre for Women (ARROW), 2016.

Piccinini, Patricia. *Still Life with Stem Cells*. Biennale of Sydney (2002). Accessed 15 June 2018. http://www.patriciapiccinini.net/writing/24/117/64.

Rajadhyaksha, Madhavi. "No Surrogacy Visa for Gay Foreigners." *Times of India*, 18 January 2013. Accessed 31 May 2018. https://timesofindia.indiatimes.com/india/No-surrogacy-visa-for-gay-foreigners/articleshow/18066771.cms.

Rudrappa, Sharmila. "India Outlawed Commercial Surrogacy—Clinics Are Finding Loopholes." *The Conversation* (23 October 2017). Accessed 31 May 2018. https://theconversation.com/india-outlawed-commercial-surrogacy-clinics-are-finding-loopholes-81784.

Russo, Francine. "Is There Something Unique about the Transgender Brain?" *Scientific American* (1 January 2016). Accessed 31 May 2018. https://www.scientificamerican.com/article/is-there-something-unique-about-the-transgender-brain/.

Taylor, Affrica. *Reconfiguring the Natures of Childhood*. London: Routledge, 2013.

Tieu, Matthew. "Oh Baby Baby: The Problem of Surrogacy." *Bioethics Research Notes* 19, no. 1 (March 2007). Accessed 31 May 2018. http://www.bioethics.org.au/Resources/Online%20Articles/Opinion%20Pieces/1901%20Oh%20Baby%20Baby%20The%20Problem%20with%20Surrogacy%20MT.pdf.

Vancouver Art Gallery. "Bharti Kher: Matter." *Past Exhibitions* (9 July to 10 October 2016).

Whatmore, Sarah. "Hybrid Cartographies for a Relational Ethics." In *Architectural Theories of the Environment: Posthuman Territory*, edited by Ariane Lourie Harrison, 249–257. New York: Routledge for Taylor and Francis, 2013.

White, Lauren C. Alan Horsup, Andrea C. Taylor, and Jeremy J. Austin. "Improving Genetic Monitoring of the Northern Hairy-Nosed Wombat (Lasiorhinus Krefftii)." *Australian Journal of Zoology* 62, no. 3 (2014): 246–50. doi:10.1071/zo14031.

NOTES

1. Donna Haraway, "A Cyborg Manifesto: Science, Technology, and Socialist-Feminism in the Late Twentieth Century," in *Simians, Cyborgs and Women: The Reinvention of Nature* (New York: Routledge, 1991), 151.

2. Using Haraway's notion of an "implosion of the natural and artificial," Catherine Jenkins, another author in this volume, suggests the poignancy of posthumanist endeavours to prolong life, stressing a cyborgian link between grieving, death, and the sciences of resuscitation.

3. Soraya Murray, "Cybernated Aesthetics: Lee Bul and the Body Transformed," *PAJ: A Journal of Performance and Art* 89 (2008): 39.

4. Madhavi Rajadhyaksha, "No Surrogacy Visa for Gay Foreigners," *The Times of India* (18 January 2013), accessed 31 May 2018, https://timesofindia.indiatimes.com/india/No-surrogacy-visa-for-gay-foreigners/articleshow/18066771.cms.

5. "As a policy response, a ban runs the risk of creating black markets and further exacerbating the vulnerabilities of women who act as surrogates. In patriarchal societies, families can also be exploitative towards women who may be coerced to become surrogates for close relatives. Thus, the argument that commercial surrogacy is an exploitative arrangement, while altruistic surrogacy is not, does not stand on firm ground." Sarojini Nadimpally, Sneha Banerjee, and Deepa Venkatachalam, Sama Resource Group for Women and Health, *Commercial Surrogacy: A Contested Terrain in the Realm of Rights and Justice* (Kuala Lumpur: Asian-Pacific Resource and Research Centre for Women [ARROW]), 2016. See also Matthew Tieu, "Oh Baby Baby: The Problem of Surrogacy," *Bioethics Research Notes* 19, no.1 (March 2007), accessed 31 May 2018, http://www.bioethics.org.au/Resources/Online%20Articles/Opinion%20Pieces/1901%20Oh%20Baby%20Baby%20The%20Problem%20with%20Surrogacy%20MT.pdf. See also Sharmila Rudrappa, "India Outlawed Commercial Surrogacy—Clinics Are Finding Loopholes," *The Conversation* (23 October 2017), accessed 31 May 2018, https://theconversation.com/india-outlawed-commercial-surrogacy-clinics-are-finding-loopholes-81784.

6. Sarah Evans, *This Way and Never Another: Biopolitics as Difference Reproduced in Bharti Kher's Art* (Universities Art Association Conference, Montreal, October 2016).

7. Sarah Evans, Bharti Kher. "Matter, Vancouver Art Gallery, 2016," ASAP (27 November 2017), Accessed 15 June, 2018, http://asapjournal.com/bharti-kher-matter/.

8. T'cha Dunlevy, "DHC/ART: Bharti Kher's Bindis Are Watching You Watching Them," *Montreal Gazette* (4 May 2018), accessed 31 May 2018, http://montrealgazette.com/entertainment/arts/dhc-art-bharti-khers-bindis-are-watching-you-watching-them.

9. R. P. Amann and D. Waberski, "Computer-Assisted Sperm Analysis (CASA): Capabilities and Potential Developments," *Theriogenology* 81, no. 1 (2014): 5–17. doi: 10.1016/j.theriogenology.2013.09.004. "Modern CASA systems can automatically view multiple fields in a shallow specimen chamber to capture strobe-like images of 500 to > 2000 sperm, at 50 or 60 frames per second, in clear or complex extenders, and in < 2 minutes, store information for ≥ 30 frames and provide summary data for each spermatozoon and the population."

10. Sarah Evans, Personal Communication of 14 June 2018.

11. Evans, *This Way*, 2016. See also Susanne Gruss, *The Pleasure of the Feminist Text: Reading Michèle Roberts and Angela Carter* (Amsterdam: Rodopi, 2009), 70.

12. Evans, *This Way*, 2016.

13. Christine Folch, "Why the West Loves Sci-Fi and Fantasy: A Cultural Explanation," *The Atlantic* (23 June 2013), accessed 31 May 2018, https://www.theatlantic.com/

entertainment/archive/2013/06/why-the-west-loves-sci-fi-and-fantasy-a-cultural-explanation/276816/.

14. Evans, *This Way*, 2016.

15. Sarah Whatmore, "Hybrid Cartographies for a Relational Ethics," in *Architectural Theories of the Environment: Posthuman Territory*, ed. Ariane Lourie Harrison (New York: Routledge for Taylor and Francis, 2013), 250.

16. Vancouver Art Gallery, "Bharti Kher: Matter," *Past Exhibitions* (9 July to 10 October 2016).

17. Haraway, "A Cyborg Manifesto," 178.

18. Andrea Crespo, "Joined for Life: 2017," accessed 31 May 2018, http://andreacrespo.com/.

19. Andrea Crespo and Stella Bottai, "virocrypsis," *Vdrome.org* (25 November–8 December 2015), accessed 31 May 2018, http://www.vdrome.org/andrea-crespo-virocrypsis/.

20. Anton Haugen, "A Scanner, Darkly: On Andrea Crespo's 'polymorphoses,'" *Rhizome* (26 August 2015), par. 3, accessed 13 September 2018, http://rhizome.org/editorial/2015/aug/26/crespo-review/

21. Andrea Crespo (video) and Jack Kahn (text), "Parabiosis: Neurolibidinal Induction Complex," *DIS Magazine* (New York), par. 1, accessed 31 May 2018, http://dismagazine.com/dystopia/72978/andrea-crespo-sis-parabiosis/.

22. Haraway, "A Cyborg Manifesto," 183.

23. Crespo and Kahn, "Parabiosis," par. 4.

24. Lauren Cornell, "Andrea Crespo—A Day in the Lives of (2016)," *Rhizome* (21 September 2016), accessed 31 May, 2018, https://rhizome.org/editorial/2016/sep/21/a-day-in-the-lives-of/.

25. Haraway, "A Cyborg Manifesto," 181.

26. See Richard Kearny, "Sacramental Imagination and Eschatology," in *Phenomenology and Eschatology: Not Yet in the Now*, ed. by John Panteleimon Manoussakis (London: Routledge for Taylor and Francis, 2009–2016), 62; and Maurice Merleau-Ponty and Dominique Segland, comp. *Maurice Nature: Course Notes from the College de France* (Evanston, IL: Northwestern University Press, 1995), 133.

27. Francine Russo, "Is There Something Unique about the Transgender Brain?" *Scientific American*, 1 January 2016, accessed 31 May 2018, https://www.scientificamerican.com/article/is-there-something-unique-about-the-transgender-brain/; see also Robert A. Campbell, "Cyborg Salvation History: Donna Haraway and the Future of Religion," *Humboldt Journal of Social Relations* 26.5 (2001), 154–73; and Anton Haugen, "A Scanner, Darkly: On Andrea Crespo's 'Polymorphoses,'" *Rhizome* (26 August 2015), accessed 31 May 2018, http://rhizome.org/editorial/2015/aug/26/crespo-review/.

28. Sally McKay, *The Haunted Scanner* (Universities Art Association Conference, Montreal, October 2016).

29. McKay, *The Haunted Scanner*. See also Donna Haraway, "Situated Knowledges: The Science Question in Feminism and the Privilege of Partial Perspective," *Feminist Studies* 14, no. 3 (Fall 1988): 579.

30. Sally McKay, *Repositioning Neuroaesthetics through Contemporary Art* (PhD Diss., Ontario, Canada: York University, 2014), 3.

31. Sophie Knezic, "Review, Patricia Piccinini: Meet Graham," *Artlink* (23 September 2016), accessed 1 June 2018, https://www.artlink.com.au/articles/4533/patricia-piccinini-meet-graham/.

32. Knezic, "Review."

33. Knezic, "Review."

34. Donna Haraway, "Speculative Fabulations for Technoculture's Generations: Taking Care of Unexpected Country," *Australian Humanities Review* 50 (2011), 102; and Patricia Piccinini, *Still Life with Stem Cells*, Biennale of Sydney (2002), accessed 15 June 2018 http://www.patriciapiccinini.net/writing/24/117/64

35. Piccinini, *Still Life with Stem Cells.*

36. Affrica Taylor, *Reconfiguring the Natures of Childhood* (London: Routlege, 2013), 111.

37. Taylor, *Reconfiguring the Natures of Childhood*, 111.

38. Taylor, *Reconfiguring the Natures of Childhood*, 111.
39. Lauren C. White, Alan Horsup, Andrea C. Taylor, and Jeremy J. Austin, "Improving Genetic Monitoring of the Northern Hairy-Nosed Wombat (Lasiorhinus Krefftii)," *Australian Journal of Zoology* 62, no. 3 (2014): 246–50. doi:10.1071/zo14031.
40. White et al., "Improving Genetic Monitoring," 250.
41. Michael Burton and Michiko Nitta, "Algae Opera," accessed 14 June 2018, http://www.burtonnitta.co.uk/AlgaeOpera.html.
42. Debora Mackenzie and Michael LePage, "Eat Light: Dawn of the Plantimals," *New Scientist* 208, no. 2790 (11 December 2010): 32–35.
43. Burton and Nitta, "Algae Opera."

V

Humanity in the Digital Era

Pavlina Radia

When, in 1997, Peter Weir's film *The Truman Show* introduced audiences to the concept of humanity reduced to a petri dish of Baudrillard's simulacra and reality television, the effects of virtual reality and the possibilities of the digital realm generated trepidation among many. What will be the future of humanity in the wake of ever-evolving digital technology? If artificial intelligence is the new paradigm of human connectivity and capability, what implications do these connections have for the future? In the 1990s, films like *The Truman Show* (1997) or *Bicentennial Man* (1999), a film based on Isaac Asimov's 1976 novelette of the same title, explored some of these questions. On the one hand, these films challenged the humanist ideology of human supremacy, and, on the other hand, they launched an important conversation about the ever-increasing dependence on and relationship with the digital. In 2019, a complex blurring between the human and the digital is our day-to-day *virtuality*. Glued to our iPhones, Facebook, or Twitter accounts, we have morphed into virtual environments ourselves. As the line between the human and the non/post/human digit is increasingly disappearing, questions about humanity's *future* continue to proliferate.

In his recent work, *On the Future: Prospects of Humanity*, the well-known astronomer Martin Rees (2018) argues that the future of humanity very much depends on its ethical and sustainable deployment of science and technology. The influence of artificial intelligence (AI) technologies on the future of humanity will continue to expand. As Rees emphasizes, "already our smartphones substitute for routine memory storage and give near-instant access to the world's information. Soon, translation between languages will be routine. The next step could be to 'plug in' extra memory or acquire language skills by direct input into the brain."[1] Ontologically, human bodies are carriers of information (similar to computers): they are machine-like environments with complex structures powered by interrelated bionetworks. To use Rees's words, "cells, viruses, and other biological microstructures are essentially 'machines.'"[2] With the increasing capability of AI technology, human information (behaviour patterns, speech acts, facial ticks, and so on) will be integrated through machine learning, inviting perhaps a very different notion of futurity as the past and the present become integrated through artificial neural networks and new technologies. As Rees cautions, how we deploy their potential is one of the central questions for the "future" or the concept of the future as we know it.

The two final chapters of our book, *The Future of Humanity: Revisioning the Human in the Posthuman Age*, provide further insight into this challenging, yet potentially exciting future as they ponder the very notion of the human and its (post)humanist foibles in the light of the ever-increasing capability and potential of the digital.

In "Radical Post-Cartesianism: Or, the Post-human Potentials of Artificial Neural Networks in Our Hyperconnected Age," Chris Vitale echoes Rees's fascination with the great potential of computational technologies such as artificial neural networks (ANNs). As Vitale reminds us, these highly adaptive technologies underpin platforms like Facebook, Siri, or DeepDream. According to Vitale, within a very short period, ANNs have acquired human capabilities that challenge our perception of the human–machine relationship and its integrative and adaptive potentialities. Learning from human behaviour and integrating various patterns, ANNs challenge the Cartesian divide between mind and matter, pushing the very boundary of what it means to be human. As Vitale emphasizes, the definition of human and human consciousness requires serious reconsideration. According to Vitale, "we live in an age of networks" where, with "computers behaving in ever more organic ways," it is equally important to acknowledge that the human mind is like a network. ANNs rely on simulation of behavioural and neural processes. As a result, they can outperform a human at a video game and continue finding better, more effective strategies to score higher than expected. While the social advantages of ANNs are impressive and ever-increasing, Vitale warns against the potential abuse of their power. Echoing Rosi Braidotti's concern of advanced capitalism's abuses of bio- and AI technologies and their increasing "modes of appropriation,"[3] Vitale warns of the dangerous military deployment of ANNs in drone strikes, for example. Such deployment relies on permeating violence through "surveillance, data mining, and military motobotics." In his chapter, Vitale calls for an ethical use of ANNs, critiquing what Braidotti (2013) calls "necro-technologies,"[4] technologies that are driven by capitalist and colonizing ideologies.

Countering such ideologies, however, can be a more productive deployment of ANNs as networks that challenge our limited world view of human consciousness, but also as mechanisms that provide us with alternative ways of thinking about humanity and its future. Understanding futurity from a hybrid and interrelational, adaptive, ever-emergent, "networkology" perspective is what Vitale's chapter proposes. It is a fascinating proposition, a proposition worth considering. There are two important messages to take away from Vitale's chapter. Echoing Braidotti's notion of the posthuman as an intra- and interrelational becoming, Vitale declares, "We need posthuman worldviews for the posthuman times to come." Furthermore, both human brains and computers can be considered information networks or hybrid, interrelated "networkologies" that redefine and will further change our perspective of not only humanity but perhaps the cosmos at large.

In "Actual Fantasy, Modulation Chains, and Swarms of Thought-Controlled Babel Drones: Art and Digital Ontology in the Posthuman Era," Adam Nash also ponders the future of humanity from the perspective of the digital era and its relationship to the posthuman. What is the future of artificial intelligence and what role can it play in live performance? What is the relationship between art and virtual reality? Between robots and love? As a digital virtual artist, Nash sets out to reexamine the complex relationship between humans and the digital world—be it virtual reality, robots, or artificial intelligence. Challenging the humanist notion of the nonhuman *other*, Nash's work encourages us to see beyond biological essentialism into a world where art and virtual reality, artificial intelligence, and robotics can teach us about human emotion, affect, and individuation. Drawing on the works of Rosi Braidotti (2013) and Gilbert Simondon (2009), Nash argues for a more nuanced and modular understanding of the posthuman as a "new individuating entity" that challenges the human-machine/animate-inanimate boundary through digital art.

As Nash emphasizes, whether viewed as extensions of the human as argued by Marshall McLuhan (1964) in the early 1960s or Braidotti's (2013) posthumanist theory, the posthuman era marks a new zeitgeist where human behaviour can be recorded and modulated through drone software. Referring to the Arizona State University's *Human-Oriented Robotics and Control Lab* project, spearheaded by Panagiotis Artemiadis, Nash notes the sophistication of the "swarm of thought-controlled drones" or Silicon Valley's increasing production of the digital *cool*. Arguing against the persistent tendency to delineate individuation processes as us versus them, the human and the other, Nash's chapter takes a nonanthropocentric approach that allows for a broader world view, a world view that highlights multiplicity, reciprocity, and process to examine our relationship to the digital world. Drawing parallels between the subject as a Deleuzian multiplicity of becomings and information and data, for example, Nash argues that humans are an amalgamation of modular data, individuation processes, social networks, and affect. As such, they can be considered to be "transindividuals," in Simondon's (1980) terms. However, since "Big Data" and global data networks rely on human input that is then "captured" within and as data, they do not eliminate the centuries-old anxiety about the influence of the digital world on the future of humanity, specifically as it relates to the question of ethics.

Art, on the other hand, can provide some respite from this anxiety, but can also generate intriguing insights into what Nash calls "new concepts of affective relations that operate beyond the human." Nash's own digital art highlights digital ontology as diverse and hybrid. In collaboration with John McCormick, Nash, for instance, encourages audiences to interact with a robot in their installation titled *Child in the Wild* (2016–2018). This installation is a perfect example of Braidotti's posthuman at work. Through an engagement with a robot, audiences create authentic and affective relationships with a digital machine, thus challenging their own preconceptions of what it means to interact with a robot. The work relies on robotics, artificial intelligence, and human and machine learning.

In addition to his recent virtual artwork, Nash also speaks to his other collaborative installations, including his work with Christopher Dodds and Justin Clemens: *Babelswarm* (2007) and *Autoscopia* (2009–2016), both using 3D technology and the virtual environment *Second Life* to explore virtual–human interactions and their modulations. Digital art, as Nash emphasizes, can provide an ethical and much needed sociophilosophical alternative to the anxiety surrounding "Big Data" by encouraging a constant play on interactive processes and their meanings. While the global economy's increasing reliance on Big Data and social media tends to replicate the power asymmetries that have plagued human history, digital art can provide a way to dissect and expose some of these asymmetries by drawing attention to the interrelational and transindividual quality of our (post)human environment.

Both Vitale and Nash emphasize that humanity has always been (in some ways) posthuman. Historically, humanity has depended on its "definition" by distinguishing itself from the rest—frequently, at least in the western world, humanity has been defined against the nonhuman other. Since the late 1980s, however, scholars and theorists like Felix Guattari (1986) or Bruno LaTour (1996) have been asking for a diverse, more sustainable (post)human ecology of seeing and representing our so-called *future*.

BIBLIOGRAPHY

Braidotti, Rosi. *The Posthuman*. Cambridge: Polity Press, 2013.
Rees, Martin. *On the Future: Prospects for Humanity*. Princeton, NJ: Princeton University Press, 2018.
Guattari, Felix. *The Three Ecologies*. Translated by Ian Pindar and Paul Sutton. London: Athlone, 1986.

LaTour, Bruno. *Aramis; or, The Love of Technology*. Translated by Catherine Porter. Cambridge: Harvard University Press, 1996.
Simondon, Gilbert. *On the Mode of Existence of Technical Objects*. Trans. Ninian Mellamphy. London: University of Ontario Press, 1980.

NOTES

1. Martin Rees, *On the Future: Prospect for Humanity* (Princeton, NJ: Princeton University Press, 2018), 105.
2. Rees, On the Future, 83.
3. Rosi Braidotti, *The Posthuman* (Cambridge: Polity Press, 2013), 7.
4. Braidotti, *The Posthuman*, 9.

Chapter Eleven

Radical Post-Cartesianism

Or the Posthuman Potentials of Artificial Neural Networks in Our Hyperconnected Age

Christopher Vitale

Artificial neural networks (ANNs), the technology behind Apple's *Siri*, Facebook's *Deep Face* facial recognition algorithm, and Google's *Deep Dream* ("Inceptionism"), are likely to become what Bower and Christensen (1995) famously called a "disruptive innovation"[1]: a technology which, like the Internet or the printing press, redefines a wide variety of paradigms in its wake. Unlike traditional forms of machine learning, ANNs use parallel and distributed forms of processing which resemble those at work in the brains of living organisms, and as a result, such networks give rise to results which are often uncannily organic and even "human-like" (Markoff 2012; Clark 2001). While ANNs have already begun to impact a wide variety of cultural domains, now that the rudiments of the field are in place, there seems every reason to think that the development of this field, and the changes it could unleash upon the cultural domain, have only just begun.

Such artificial intelligence (AI) not only has radical potential implications for how we live our everyday lives in relation to changing technology, but could even give rise to shifts in how we understand our very selves. For as machines seem increasingly able to behave in animalian and even "human-like" ways, they may very well lead us to question what we take to be at stake with traditional notions of what it means to "think," and with this, the ways in which notions of what it might means to be a "self" understood as "living" or "human" form of "subjectivity" have often been framed in relation to this.

ARTIFICIAL NEURAL NETWORKING, OR THE RADICAL POTENTIALS OF LEARNING MACHINES

ANNs are quite different from the forms of computation which brought about the first computer revolutions of the twentieth century. In particular, ANNs are not programmed with code. Rather, they learn from the feedback, whether from humans, more traditional computers, or conditions within their environments. While they are "wired" in a series of architectures which predispose them to particular forms of adaptive learning, the strength of the connections between aspects of their networks begin with random settings. They are then presented with a set of "training data," and when even the slightest of their settings lead to an output which their trainer, human or otherwise, deems a success, a message is sent backwards through the network to strengthen the connection which gave rise to it (Bechtel and Abrahamson 2002). Such "back-propagation" leads to "long-term potentiation," and such "reinforcement learning" is how the network rewires itself in regard to responses from its environments.[2] In many senses, such networks "program" themselves, if in relation to their environments, but the only code at work is that on which the virtual simulation of these neural processes run.

From there, ANNs, like children, learn from their environments, including teachers and trainers, and their method of doing so, namely, back-propagation, is precisely that at work in living animalian brains (LeDoux 2003). In this, they differ substantially from more traditional forms of AI, often now disparagingly referred to by ANN researchers as *GOFAI* ("Good Old-Fashioned Artificial Intelligence"). Such older models are most often forms of "expert systems," traditional forms of computer programs produced by coders who fill them with executable trees of "if . . . then" rules which determine how the program is to behave in particular circumstances (Haugeland 1985). Expert systems of this sort are notoriously rigid and brittle, able to be frustrated whenever they encounter circumstances which differ even in small ways from those it has been programmed to expect (Clark 2001). But as ANNs are trained rather than coded, adaptation is essentially what they do. And since they are trained by reinforcing not only complete "successful" responses but partial ones as well, even down to successes in responding to microfeatures, ANNs excel at completing patterns based on incomplete data, and "guessing" about which pattern to apply to circumstances which at least partially resemble those on which they were trained (Clark 2001).

In this, they are able to extrapolate to new conditions based on analogy. What's more, ANNs do not crash if overloaded; rather, their memory gets "fuzzy" until they "forget," and they can repair damaged connections in a manner similar to stroke patients by training around the damage (Spitzer 2000). ANNs are excellent at guessing by filling in incomplete patterns, and are able to extrapolate from known patterns with similarities to situations in remarkably flexible ways (Spitzer 2000). ANNs can extract patterns and concepts from data simply by looking for regularities, are able to associate in a human-like manner (e.g., "Hillary . . . and Bill," "peanut butter . . . and jelly"), can synthesize processes over time and map fuzzy collections of data with ease, and even seem to possess abilities analogous to human forms of dreaming, fantasizing, projecting, and imagining (Bechtel and Abrahamson 2002; Mordvintsev et al. 2015).

Beyond this, ANNs even share some of the drawbacks of living neural networks, namely, those in animal and human brains, in that they perform poorly on long strings of computations, even as they do well with the sorts of naturalistic and fuzzy situations which are simple for children but tend to frustrate even the most highly developed forms of traditional computers. ANNs are relatively slow compared to serial computers because they are full of lateral connections which slow down individual steps, but, like living brains, they make up for having to deal with all these extra pathways with a massive increase in flexibility (Clark 2001).

If traditional computers are extremely fast calculators, ANNs are virtual mini brain-lets. They are not full brains, of course, in that they are usually designed to perform specific tasks, such as facial recognition or language processing. And they are often functionally linked to more traditional computing systems, either to take care of the more tedious early training stages, or to accomplish hybrid tasks which make use of the potential synergies between traditional and more neural forms of processing, leaving more tedious computations, for example, to more traditional forms of computing.

ANNs also differ from living brains, of course, in that, as very few of them are attached to complex webs of feedback with bodies, robotic or otherwise, they generally are disembodied in a quite radical sense.[3] For unlike neural networks in living organisms, or even early experiments in this field, which created artificial neurons by means of electrical circuits and wires, today's ANNs are virtual simulations of neurons and their networks. As with many virtual realities, however, from human fantasies to anticipations, the virtual realities at work within ANNs are able to produce novel forms of feedback between inputs and outputs which, like those at work within living brains, and in ways evidence by the increasing successes produced by this field, can give rise to highly concrete physical results. While some ANNs have begun to be more integrated into bodies in the form of "mobots" (such as the terrifying general dynamics mobot "Big Dog"), these are the exception rather than the rule today (Bongard and Pfiefer 2006).

Despite these differences from living brains, the capabilities of ANNs, even at this early stage in their development have often exceeded even the most optimistic predictions. While it was once thought that facial identification was decades of research away, Google was able to jumpstart the field nearly overnight simply by providing a huge increase in server power to the task (Le et al. 2012). Facebook soon thereafter developed facial recognition ANNs which now rival human levels of accuracy, and which, once trained, now run quickly and seamlessly on basic desktop computers (Taigman et al. 2014). Apple's *Siri* personal assistant uses ANNs to help process human "natural" language, and Google has recently announced that it has taught an ANN not only how to play video games, but how to learn to increase its score over time (MacMillan 2014).

ANNs can now study the works of an artist, abstract away their brush stroke and overall style, and apply this to any photo you feed them (Culpin 2016). ANNs even seem to be able to "project" what they "want" to see into what they are shown in the world in a sort of network "imagining" or "dreaming" (Mordvintsev et al. 2015). Such networks are now even able to compose works of new prose fiction in the "style" of a given author based on only a few sentences of sample text (Jones 2019). That said, the US military apparatus is now using ANNs to process satellite data to devise targets for remote drone strikes, and so ANNs have also already been used to kill, including most likely completely innocent civilians (Pasquinelli 2016). The potentials for violence by means of surveillance, data mining, and military mobotics are profound, which is to say, we ignore ANNs at our peril.

ANNs are able to do what they do largely by modulating the types of feedback at work within them and between them and their environments. Doing this in various ways, researchers have found, in a process of trial-and-error which is uncannily not radically dissimilar to that whereby evolution seems to have given rise to living brains, that they have been able to simulate various sorts of cognitive functions. For example, by means of nearly fully connected networks of virtual neurons which are able to amplify or inhibit each other's firing patterns, a network will tend to memorize what it is shown. Such networks do not crash when overloaded, but rather seem to get fuzzy and confused in a more holistic way, differing from more traditional forms of machine learning in ways which recall forgetful humans.[4] While tight feedback tends to produce recognition and recall memory, loose connections between such networks tend to give rise to associations between these not unlike those seen in free-association tests.[5] Feedback which progressively increases with each new stage of networks tends to produce something like an ability to layer past and future states over time, such as is needed to plan multistage actions or understand the meaning of a sentence with its multiple words.[6]

What's more, when there are bottlenecks or pinches in the back-propagating feedback, such that a large number of inputs is fed into a small number of neurons, then expanded back out, the result is conceptual abstraction. That is, present such a network with a group of animals, and by means of such pinches, it will abstract general categories at work within the data set and use these categorize new inputs by means of these. Thus, once such a network is trained, when "concept" neurons are stimulated, they will in turn stimulate the input and output neurons whose generalizations they describe, not in words, but in the form of their connections. In this way, such networks perform the induction of generalizations from data sets. These pinches or bottlenecks are the "hidden" or "deep" layers which give "deep learning" its name, the discovery of which potentiated the birth of this entire field (Bechtel and Abrahamson 2002).

When several of these logics are combined, the results are "self-assorting feature maps" which not only learn to recognize patterns, but sort them into maps according to various forms of similarities and differences between the outputs, with more frequent inputs having larger swaths of space on the maps.[7] When these maps are layered with a matching algorithm, similar to that at work in human cortical columns,[8] the layers of networks abstract patterns from each other's maps at micro- and macro-levels of scale. Facebook's facial recognition algorithm, for example, uses such a structure (Taigman et al. 2014). "Lower-level" maps closer to inputs recognize micro-features, such as edges, mid-level maps recognize shapes and assemblages of shapes, and the more abstract meta-maps near the "top" of the network compare assemblages of shapes to groupings of these, in particular faces, and eventually links these to names. All this happens in maps and meta-maps, with feedback between the layers at multiple levels of scale, but with results which now seem to exceed that of humans in accuracy (Taigman et al. 2014).

As a result, some researchers now view the study of neural networks as simply one field with two branches, namely, the study of living neural networks, and the study of simulated virtual ones (Cotterill 1998). For while brains and ANNs have many differences, the basic ideas at work within these are more similar than different, as artificial neural networks are essentially attempts to produce abstract mini-brains. While so far these are mostly aimed at specific purposes, the brains of living organisms also evolved from ganglia, small nodules of interconnected nerves which only later began to coordinate to give rise to the more general purpose brains of animals (Martin and Hine 2008), a fact attested to in the modularity of the more basic aspects of the brain, even if the cortex largely wires itself, like neural networks, more generally based on incoming data provided to its inputs.

While these revolutionary new technologies have already begun to affect everyday life, seeping into the applications so many use on a regular basis on their smartphones, laptops, and tablet computers, the fact that this approach to computing is radically different from prior forms seems to have gone largely unnoticed by the Western-dominated technocultures which have increasingly colonized the globe. Nevertheless, ANNs epitomize a shift already begun in a variety of aspects of contemporary culture, a shift in popular conceptions of what it means to think, from one dominated by notions of the brain conceived, on the model of computers of generations past, as a very fast set of binary switches, to a far more networked conception thereof which is already dominant in many fields of science and technology (Vlasits 2017), and with some radical potentials.

NEURAL NETWORKING AS A NEW "IMAGE OF THOUGHT"

While ANNs are remarkable in many ways, there is clearly more at stake here than new appliances. For there are many reasons to think that technologies form us as much as the reverse. Terrence Deacon (1998), for example, indicates how language not only sculpts each brain upon being learned, but according to archaeological evidence, seems to have influenced the evolution of human brains and even nonneural anatomy (Deacon 1998). Donna Haraway (1991) has likewise argued that humans have always already been cyborgs, in that our tools helped shape our differentiation from other species (Haraway 1991). Bernard Stiegler (1998) has argued that our tools mirror aspects of our bodies they were designed to extend, and, as with human caretakers, our webs of tools, including screens and other interactive forms of media, can be understood as parts of the ways in which the networks of the world "call" us to take up places as we do within them (Stiegler 1998). For Stielger, human selves are the result of the networking of such multiplex mirrorings. That is, Stiegler sees humans as projecting aspects of themselves into their environments, in ways which give rise to powerful feedback effects, such that young children see a world partially in waiting for them, as if calling them to form themselves at least partially in the molds provided by the past, whether these take the form of words, images, material artefacts, buildings, or social structures of various sorts.

Stiegler builds on prior such notions, one of the more influential of which, particularly in regard to thinking, is that of an "image of thought" as proposed by Gilles Deleuze.[9] Deleuze (1968) argues that "images of thought" tend to frame for cultures what they imagine thinking to be, and in ways which tend to not only describe thinking as it currently is, but also shape what we understand as our horizons for what thinking is and could become, and with this the shapes of the thinkable. In this, images of thought tend to become self-fulfilling prophecies of a sort, as they are imaginations of what we take to be at stake with thinking in a general sense (Deleuze and Guattari 1996).

Images of thought tend to derive from notions of what is understood as giving rise to thinking, often the brain, but as the brain has until quite recently been seen as so unimaginably complex to be largely a mystery, there is a long history of using images abstracted from technologies to imagine what the brain does, giving rise to images of thought thereby, often with powerful ramifications on what we take thinking to mean. And as the very notion of the "human" has so often been defined as a "rational animal" in regard to a sense of what it means to think (Osbourne 2007), images of thought derived from technologies have a tendency to become strange mirrors for human cultures which have had a tendency to frame their essential differences from others by means of these.

For from seventeenth-century clockwork fantasies of the brain to Sigmund Freud's electrical and hydraulic metaphors, from the electrical relays of Claude Shannon to the digital dreams of GOFAI, there is a long history of cognitive imaginaries modelling themselves on the most advanced machines of the times (Lister 2009). Despite the clearly more adaptable and fluid forms of animalian ways of relating to the world, the speed, power, and precision of machines and then computers have captivated imaginations and provided ideals for emulation for many. And so, during the heyday of binary, serial, traditional computers, it was the digital computer, composed of binary switches and a central processing unit, which provided the hope for a "universal machine" which, at least in theory, would be capable of thinking anything computable (Turing 1950). By means of such a dream, images of thinking were often reduced to images of computation (Vlatsis 2017).

Today, however, all this seems to be changing. We now live in an age of networks (Castells 1996). The Internet and its virtual double, the Web, have now captured popular imagination as the image of what it means to be a cutting-edge machine, and the structure of the Internet and Web are hardly like the insides of traditional computers, with their rigid lines of silicon hierarchically and centrally arranged. The networking of the Internet and its virtual realities, however they are mapped, are, on the contrary, radically decentralized and dynamic, often morphing and growing like organisms, or even swarms of them, even as a map of the Internet resembles little more than a giant brain.[10]

From such a perspective, it perhaps should not surprise us that the image of the brain as a hardware computer has begun losing its hold on dominant images of thinking. Scientists are increasingly describing the ways in which the brain is unlike traditional binary computers (Cotterill 1998), while researchers are defining ever more of the world, from markets to ecosystems to organisms and languages, in terms of networks (Lázsló-Barbási 2002). As wider swaths of the world learn about the structure of ANNs, most likely in the wake of the shock of finding computers behaving in ever more organic ways, it is likely that images of thought based on traditional computing will likely fade even more dramatically, with new images of computation giving rise to new images of thinking and thought.

PERFORMATIVELY DECONSTRUCTING THE LEGACIES OF CARTESIANISM

While the brain was often understood on the model of physical machines, and thinking understood in relation to these, running parallel to this is a long history of seeing something like the capacity to think, awareness, or "mind," as something metaphysical, something so special and beyond explanation as to be an exception to the rules of physical matter, and in fact, beyond matter itself. Even during times of the most mechanistic worldviews, the mind was often described as something like an otherwordly nucleus, as a barely secularized inheritor of religious notions of a soul or spirit, somehow seated in the physical world like a nut within a shell (Markie 1992). But today we find ourselves in the strange situation, a moment of "coming full-circle," to so speak. That is, the brain is starting to be taken, if mediately by means of artificial neural networks and an increasingly brain-like Web, as a model for itself.

And with this, perhaps we have a chance to liberate thinking from some of the fetters within which it has been kept of old. For in their potent new abilities, ANNs provide a radical challenge to many of the dualist assumptions which have been foundational to many Euro-American scientific and philosophical ways of thinking since the highly influential work of René Descartes. For ANNs show that it is possible for nonliving matters to be woven together in ways which give rise to behaviours which would, up until quite recently, been deemed all but impossible, and the preserve only of human-style thinking. If human-style thinking can be produced by weaving together aspects of the world created by humans, aspects which seem to have no evidence of anything such as "mind" before this, then perhaps the very notion of "mind," at least in its otherwordly, Cartesian sense, needs to change.

For according to Descartes (1637), the world is radically split in two between extended matter and mind which thinks (Markie 1992). There is no middle ground. But if silicon and energy can be networked in ways which, despite the relative binary and serial nature of the chips involved, make it possible to behave in ways which, from the outside, certainly seem like thinking, or at least aspects of this, then perhaps it is possible to see precisely how something like thinking "mind" could emerge from extended matter, thereby jumping the Cartesian gap within the stuff of the world.

In this sense, rather than see thinking as bound to a particular sort of stuff, such as carbon-based life, or as many in the past had asserted, a God-given soul, thinking can instead be understood as having the form of particular types of complex networking. That is, perhaps thinking in a human-style sense would arise in any sort of material system which is able to dynamically network in such a manner. Just as computation, as argued by Turing (1950), can be seen as a sort of abstract processes which can be instantiation in many forms, electronic or otherwise, perhaps the same could be said in regard to neural forms of networking (Turing 1950).

For if matter can be networked with itself to give rise to what seems to be human-style thinking, then what need is there for a hypothesis of the radical disjunction between matter and mind, along with all the dreams of human cognitive or mental "exceptionalism" which this brings? In this sense, as they complexify, ANNs perhaps may give rise to something like what Jürgen Habermas famously referred to as a *performative contradiction*, but of a different sort than he intended (Habermas 1985). That is, the very existence of ANNs, their ability to do what they do, could come to function, for our increasingly global culture as a whole, as a reason to question the need to any longer see thinking and matter as necessarily disjunct and distinct. And with this, an entire set of barely implicit cultural baggage which has been epitomized and reinforced by centuries of Cartesianism, including the dualist and binary exclusionary thinking which goes along with this, can perhaps begin to lose some of its hold on our contemporary cultures.

It is true, of course, that there are currently no ANNs that are even remotely of the same scale of a human brain. But if, as Stiegler argues (1998), mirroring is multiple and distributed, perhaps what is needed is what technologists tend to call "proof of concept," which is to say, a new image of thought and thinking which, even if in its infancy, is having ever more powerful effects in the world beyond images and concepts by the day. While some could argue, however, that the silicon processors on which such simulations run remain serial and binary, with the networking only manifested in virtual simulation, in some sense, the results are quite actual, and hence, the "proof is in the pudding," so to speak. That is, even if the means are virtual, the results are anything but.

All of which can perhaps also cast new light on what it means in this sense to be virtual. For what is organic life itself, if not the ways in which the digital code of the genome, a language composed of discrete tokens which are used to represent others, is woven together by less rigid processes beyond them, in chains of feedback massive and multiplex, and in ways which have given rise to the most supple, robust, and creative forms of living and thinking that we know? Digital has produced the analogue and organic before, for the digital is merely a cut within the continuity of the analogue, but one which can then be reapplied back to it. Languages digitize sound, and yet the sonorities of poetry and song testify to the fact that new forms of beauty and subtly can arise thereby. It is only when the digital becomes an end in itself, when it is not rewoven and renetworked, that it tends to lead to rigid ends.

BEYOND DUALISM: FROM ANNS TO NEUROSCIENCE

A nondualist approach to the question of what it means to think is also supported by contemporary neuroscience which, to a large degree, is starting to shed its Cartesian heritage and presuppositions. Antonio Damasio, in highly influential texts such as *Descartes' Error: Emotion, Reason, and the Human Brain* (1994), has argued that Cartesian dualism has in fact hindered our ability to see the ways in which the brain and its functions provide little evidence for anything like a dualist worldview which sees matter and mind as distinct (Damasio 1994). While Damasio is one of the most explicit proponents of such an approach, he is hardly alone (Baum 2004; Cotterill 2000; Edelman and Tononi 2000; Llinás 2001).

For look as one may, scientists have yet to find anything like a single place or seat of consciousness, awareness, the soul, mind, or related such notions, and with this, no ability to determine in any firm, definite, or localizable sense where matter ends, and mind begins, or vice-versa. Even the thalamus, an organ which seems to partake of nearly all cortical higher brain functions, seems to be more something like the amplifier of items in need of attention than anything like a "seat" for consciousness (Koch 2004). And if one looks in the thalamus, there is nothing unusual there, simply weavings of neural fibres, which is to say, bits of organic matter, but matter nevertheless. Many researchers now believe that there is something like a "vital triangle" in which something like awareness occurs, from thalamus to prefrontal cortex and the rest of the brain, and yet it is continually dancing around patterns of activation which explore the brain in wide and distributed ways.[11] Whatever core there is, it is a dynamic and distributed one.[12]

Memory seems likewise distributed in form. Neuroscience researchers have long known that memories are not located in distinct parts of the brain like items stored in small boxes. Rather, they are widely distributed. Many researchers believe that if one were to think, for example, of a notion such as a "dog," that one would draw the colour from colour maps, textures from texture maps, create associations from metamaps, and otherwise weave together a wide variety of the brain's maps and metamaps of feature from macro to micro and in between the process.[13] One may picture even a single dog in one's memory, but doing so draws widely from a wide variety of the brain's mapping and metamappings, and re-creates what it remembers each time on the fly.[14]

Where does "thinking" seem to happen within this? The maps and metamaps are simply weavings of neurons, pulsing living wires. Individual neurons cannot be said to "think" either, for all they "know" how to do is pulse faster when they receive a burst of incoming pulses.[15] Each of such cells is composed of even less seemingly "intelligent" cellular organelles, such as chromosomes and mitochondria. None of these "think," nor can they.

Thinking, on the contrary, seems to be what happens between (Malabou 2008), as a dynamic sort of relational networking in process."

According to many contemporary researchers, thinking is likely the result of shifting of the dynamic patterns of sync and lack thereof between the pulses within these wires, the ways various patterns of sync form "ideas" in relations to the patterns of feedback amplification and inhibition which the patterns of strength and pathway provided by the wires privilege over others, and how flows of these shift, balance, combine, and intertwine over time.[16] As many researchers now argue, consciousness is likely the largest pattern of sync at any given moment, the so-called "dynamic core," and those patterns of activation which are not currently in sync provide a sort of unconscious within which all swims (Edelman and Tononi 2000). The patterns of the living wires make this possible, but it is the patterns of dynamic sync between the pulsations that comprise the distributed dynamic of thinking.

From such a perspective, thinking can be understood as a particularly complex form of feeling, if feeling is relationally understood. From such a perspective, feeling is a betweening and beyonding. For what is feeling, after all, if not feeling what is beyond that which does the feeling? When I run my fingers over a bit of fabric, the fabric is felt as much within me as my feeling is within the fabric. Feeling is between, excessive to the fabric and the fingers seen as atomized, discrete entities. At lower levels of scale, the pressure sensors in my fingers, themselves composed of molecules, are affected by the molecular forces of the molecules within the fabric, and I see that I feel the fabric. There is an interaction of the intermolecular pushes and pulls within my body, whose knottings are the molecules in my finger, with those in the fabric, pushing and pulling between these molecules, and I read the patterns within how the fabric affects me as my fingers affect it in turn. At lower levels of scale, while we are in contact, my fingers are networking with the fabric, and my feeling is the result of my reading of this networking, an emergence produced by the intermodulation of network interactions at lower levels of scale.

Brains do this in more highly complex ways. Each nerve cell feels the effect of the impulses it receives, and this leads it to pulse faster. Our thinking is the global feeling state produced by the interfeeling of the sync between all of these, and how this leads to ripplings of sync up and down our brains and bodies. Such a form of interfeeling is more complex than those in physical forms of networking of course, even if, like life, they grow from these, even as life too is a form of interfeeling. Life can be seen as a form of interweaving feedback which takes the knotted forces of molecules of oxygen, hydrogen, carbon, nitrogen, and so on, one which grounds that at work in brains, which goes beyond the limitations within each of these by means of how they intertwine. Brains have always done this, of course, even if it likely took the rise of the Internet and the networkings in our world to help bring this about for many to see.

From such a perspective, there is no need to separate out thinking and matter. Rather, thinking can be seen as a particularly complex form of feeling, and feeling something that all matter can do, and in fact, that all matter *is*. Electrons *are* how they feel attraction to protons and repulsion from each other, in this sense, even if they cannot feel themselves feeling this. Only living systems seems to have this sort of metafeeling recursion at work within them, thanks to the complex genetic networks within them. Thinking can in this sense be seen as a highly complex form of metafeeling. And in this sense, there seems little reason to think that any dynamic systems of complexity such as that in brains might not feelingly think in their ways, even if differently than humans, or even the limited notions thereof imagined by Descartes in regard to his binarized "thinking things."

THE POST-CARTESIANISM OF COMPLEX SYSTEMS SCIENCE AS PARADIGM FOR AN INCREASINGLY NEURALIZING WORLD

The study of networks, including neural networks, is often described as a part of complex systems science, a field which has much to offer in terms of providing new paradigms for a more networked view of the world. Complex systems science tracks the permutations whereby various structures emerge into greater forms of self-potentiating order relatively spontaneously in the presence of particular conditions, which, while often categorized in varying ways, are generally seen as including diversity, distributedness, metastability, and feedback.[17] When these conditions are met, complex adaptive systems seem to arise semispontaneously.

Complex systems science does not only, however, study conscious or even living phenomenon. Rather, it also studies less developed forms of complexity, such as vortexes (whirlpools), molecular patterns, or hybridly complex formations which arise between living organisms (such as food-webs, the Internet, economies, and languages). These are all complex adaptive systems which, whether living or otherwise, are in the aforementioned conditions able to potentiate greater emergence of more robustly complex potential emergence in the future. Such systems differ from the complicated systems, machines such as automobiles and traditional forms of computing, which lack the sort of complex forms of feedback and metastable conditions needed to adapt to changes within and without in ways which can potentiate emergence on their own (Holland 2014).

Unlike merely complicated systems, neural networks, living and otherwise, can be understood as giving rise to that which is "more than the mere sum of their parts" (Mitchell 2009), with thought as a phenomena which emerges from such dynamic networking, much like a whirlpool from flows of water, flocking of birds, or schooling of fish, the sort of distributed sync which emerges relatively spontaneously when the right conditions are met (Strogatz 2004). Such conditions are those between excess order and destructive disorder, and, rather, come to be at a maximum sustainable differencing which, as complex systems scientists rarely seem to tire of saying, can be understood as existing "at the edge of chaos" (Waldrop 1993).

Such a perspective is one which sees emergence, which is to say, complex networking, as that which gives rise to the sort of sustainable creative development in the world which has given rise to life, evolution, culture, and thinking, along with the potentials for their further creative development beyond the reductions and limitations of prior forms thereof. As has likely become clear, beyond the immediate implications for science and technology, complex systems science has an implicit yet inherent ethics to it. There is a worldview which goes along with the complex systems approach to the world, one which values the sustainable emergence of complexity, often described as robustness, as that which has given rise to life, its development, evolution, and growth, culture, and all which, in a sense, makes life worth living (Wagner 2007).

As is hopefully evident, there is in fact an overall antiatomizing, antireifying approach within complex systems science, and researchers in this field often describe their approach to science as antireductionist (Mitchell 2011). Rather than place the human at the centre of all values, such a perspective argues that we should not value characteristics we see as belonging to the human, but rather, those we feel give rise to the best we see in the world around us, regardless of whether they arise from systems which are human or otherwise. From the perspective of complex systems science, this would be any system which fosters the sustainable emergence of complexity in itself and its surroundings, aspects of each other once one takes a more relational view of things, and in regard to the qualities which seem to foster sustainable emergence in this fashion, including diversity, distributedness, metastability, and feedback (Vitale 2014).

From such a perspective there is no need to see thinking as either "merely" physical, nor of a "transcendent" origin which is an exception to the rules of the rest of the world. Rather, thinking can be understood as the sort of interfeeling which comes to be when particularly complex forms of networking arise. Thinking in this sense perhaps is simply what it feels like from within to be a neural form of networking feeling itself feeling its body feeling its world. This is not to say that ANNs or humans necessarily do so the same way, of course, any more than it is to say that any two humans do so in the same way.

Nevertheless, such a perspective is one from which there is no need to imagine that what makes life, thinking, love, or anything that we value as special is what it is due to arising from something disjunct from the more material aspects of the world. Rather, the potential for everything we have ever known or dreamed or hoped for can be seen as being here and now, even if it can only be unleashed by networking. Learning more about what this could mean, and the potentials it holds for our world, would be the task of an attempt to think networkedly about our world in relation to the science of networking, and the new potentials for a potentially less rigid, exclusionary, reifying, atomizing, and centralizing way of relating to our worlds which this could bring.

The legacies of binary and dualist thinking are long, and it is easy for such forms of thinking about thinking and the human to come into resonance with other forms of dualist and strict binary thinking. From mind-versus-matter to human-versus-nonhuman, from me-versus-the-world to us-versus-them, there is a slippery slope and formal resemblance between binary thinking in its various forms. Moving beyond binary thinking does not mean we will be less violent, of course: surely capitalism is a networked phenomenon. That said, both traditional conservatisms, with their paranoid forms of centralization, as well as cancerous hybrid formations which use distributed means for centralizing ends in ways which are open in terms of content but closed in form (Deleuze and Guattari 1987), can nevertheless both be seen as reductions and limitations of the more radical forms of networking, artificial or otherwise. Network thinking can in this manner help loosen the hold of some of the more centralizingly conservative forms of networking, as well as their cancerous mutations, at work in our world today.

Complex networking can in these senses provide an image of thought for our networked age, one extracted from the rise of the Internet and artificial neural networking as much as the form of living brains, but one which can perhaps point towards forms of thinking beyond those inherited from Descartes, and perhaps able to open up what thinking and humanity could become. Such a new image of thought is also, in its way, an opening to a new imaging of the world as the world of emergence, a world that could be more emergent if it learned to network more emergently, to value the robust emergence of the world for any and all rather than any privileged or exceptional few, with complex systems science and neural networking providing two prime areas of research which could help us learn about such potentials. Our age of networks is in many senses a radical opportunity.

BIBLIOGRAPHY

Ball, Philip. *Critical Mass: How One Thing Leads to Another*. London: Farrar, Strauss, and Giroux, 2004.
Baum, Eric B. *What Is Thought?* Cambridge: MIT Press, 2004.
Bechtel, William, and Adele Abrahamson. *Connectionism and the Mind: Parallel Processing, Dynamics and Evolution in Networks*, 2nd edition. London: Wiley-Blackwell, 2002.

Bongard, Joshua, and Rolf Pfeifer. *How the Body Shapes the Way We Think: A New View of Intelligence.* Cambridge: MIT Press, 2006.
Bower, Joseph L., and Clayton Christensen. "Disruptive Technologies: Catching the Wave." *Harvard Business Review* (January–February 1995): 43–53.
Castells, Manuel. *The Rise of the Network Society: The Information Age—Economy, Society, and Culture*, Volume I. London: Blackwell, 1996.
Clark, Andy. *Mindware: An Introduction to the Philosophy of Cognitive Science.* Oxford: Oxford University Press, 2001.
Cotterill, Rodney. *Enchanted Looms: Conscious Networks in Brains and Computers.* Cambridge: Cambridge University Press, 1998.
Culpin, Daniel. "This Algorithm Can Create an Imitation Van Gogh in 60 Minutes." *Wired.* Accessed 29 May 2016, http://www.wired.co.uk/article/art-algorithm-recreates-paintings.
Damasio, Antonio. *Descartes Error: Emotion, Reason, and the Human Brain.* New York: HarperCollins, 1994.
Deacon, Terrence. *The Symbolic Species: The Coevolution of Language and the Brain.* New York: W. W. Norton, 1998.
Deleuze, Gilles. *Difference and Repetition.* Translated by Paul Patton. New York: Columbia University Press, 1994.
Deleuze, Gilles, and Félix Guattari. *A Thousand Plateaus: Capitalism and Schizophrenia*, Volume 2, translated by Brian Massumi. Minneapolis: University of Minnesota Press, 1983.
Deleuze, Gilles, and Félix Guattari. *What is Philosophy?* translated by Hugh Tomlinson and Graham Burchell. New York: Columbia University Press, 1996.
Edelman, Gerald, and Giulio Tononi. *A Universe of Consciousness: How Matter Becomes Imagination.* New York: Basic Books, 2000.
Habermas, Jürgen. *The Philosophical Discourse of Modernity.* Cambridge: MIT Press, 2004.
Haraway, Donna J. "A Cyborg Manifesto: Science, Technology, and Socialist-Feminism in the Late Twentieth Century." In *Simians, Cyborgs, and Women: The Reinvention of Nature*, 183–202. London: Routledge, 1991.
Hatfield, Gary. "Descartes' Physiology and Its Relation to the Body," in *The Cambridge Companion to Descartes*, edited by John Cottingham, 335–370. Cambridge: Cambridge University Press, 1992.
Haugeland, John. *Artificial Intelligence: The Very Idea.* Cambridge: MIT Press, 1985.
Holland, John. *Complexity: A Very Short Introduction.* Oxford: Oxford University Press, 2014.
Jang, J.-S.R., Chuen-Tsai Sun, and Eiji Mizutani. *Neuro-Fuzzy and Soft-Computing: A Computational Approach to Leaning and Machine Intelligence.* New York: Prentice Hall, 1997.
Johnson, Steven. *Emergence: The Connected Lives of Ants, Brains, Cities, and Software.* New York: Touchstone, 2011.
Jones, Rhett. "Elon Musk-backed AI Company Claims It Made a Text Generator That's Too Dangerous to Release." *Gizmodo*, 15 February 2019. Accessed 2019, https://gizmodo.com/elon-musk-backed-ai-company-claims-it-made-a-text-gener-1832650914.
Koch, Christof. *The Quest for Consciousness: A Neurobiological Approach.* Englewood: Roberts and Company, 2004.
Lázsló-Barbási, Albert. *Linked: The New Science of Networks.* New York: Perseus, 2002.
Le, Quoc V. et al. "Building High Level Features Using Large-Scale Unsupervised Learning." *Proceedings of the 29th International Conference on Machine Learning*, edited by Quoc V. Le, et al. Edinburgh, Scotland, UK, 2012.
LeDoux, Joseph. *Synpatic Self: How Our Brains Become Who We Are.* New York: Bradford Books, 2003.
Lister, Martin, et al. *New Media: A Critical Introduction*, 2nd edition. London: Routledge, 2009.
Llinás, Rodolfo. *The I of the Vortex: From Neurons to Self.* Cambridge: MIT Press, 2001.
MacMillan, Robert. "Siri Will Soon Understand You a Whole Lot Better." *Wired*, 30 September 2014. Accessed 12 February 2016, http://www.wired.com/2014/06/siri_ai/.
Malabou, Catherine. *What Should We Do with Our Brain?* translated by Sebastian Rand. New York: Fordham University Press, 2008.

Markoff, John. "Scientists See Promise in Deep-Learning Programs." *New York Times*, 23 November 2012.
Markie, Peter. "The Cogito and Its Importance." In *The Cambridge Companion to Descartes*, edited by John Cottingham. Cambridge: Cambridge University Press, 1992.
Martin, Elizabeth, and Robert Hine. *The Oxford Dictionary of Biology*, 6th ed. Oxford: Oxford University Press, 2008.
Mitchell, Melanie. *Complexity: A Guided Tour*. Oxford: Oxford University Press, 2009.
Mordvinstev, Alexander, Christopher Olah, and Mike Tyka. "Inceptionism: Going Deeper into Neural Networks." *Google AI Blog*, 17 June 2015. Accessed 8 January 2016, https://ai.googleblog.com/2015/06/inceptionism-going-deeper-into-neural.html.
Newman, Mark. *Networks*, 2nd ed. Oxford: Oxford University Press, 2018.
Osbourne, Catherine. *Dumb Beasts and Dead Philosophers: Humanity and the Humane in Ancient Philosophy and Literature*. Oxford: Oxford University Press, 2007.
Pasquinelli, Matteo. "The Eye of the Algorithm: On the Topology of Data and the Growth of Pattern Police," presentation at the Pratt Institute Aesthetics and Politics Lecture Series, Brooklyn, NY, 3 March 2016.
Spitzer, Manfred. *The Mind within the Net: Models of Learning, Thinking, and Acting*. New York: Bradford, 2000.
Stiegler, Bernard. *Technics and Time, Vol. 1, The Fault of Epimetheus*, translated by Richard Beardsworth and George Collins. Palo Alto, CA: Stanford, 1998.
Taigman, Yaniv, Ming Yang, Marc-Aurelio Ranzato, and Lior Wolf. "Deep Face: Closing the Gap to Human-Level Performance in Face Verification." *The IEEE Conference on Computer Vision and Pattern Recognition (CVPR)*, 2014.
Taylor, Diane. "UK Couple Have Dead Dog Cloned in South Korea," *The Guardian UK*, Accessed 30 May 2016, https://www.theguardian.com/science/2015/dec/23/uk-couple-await-birth-of-two-clones-of-dead-dog.
Turing, Alan M. "Computing Machinery and Intelligence," *Mind LIX* no. 236 (October 1, 1950): 433–460.
Wagner, Andreas. *Robustness and Evolvability in Living Systems*. Princeton, NJ: Princeton University Press, 2007.
Waldrop, M. Mitchell. *Complexity: The Emerging Science at the Edge of Order and Chaos*. New York: Simon and Schuster, 1993.
Vitale, Christopher. *Networkologies: A Philosophy of Networks for a Hyperconnected Age—A Manifesto*. London: Zero Books, 2014.
Vlatsis, Anna. "Tech Metaphors Are Holding Back Brain Research." *Wired*, 22 June 2017. Accessed 1 January 2018, https://www.wired.com/story/tech-metaphors-are-holding-back-brain-research/.

NOTES

1. Joseph L. Bower and Clayton Christensen, "Disruptive Technologies: Catching the Wave," *Harvard Business Review* (January–February 1995), 43–53.
2. Manfred Spitzer, *The Mind within the Net: Models of Learning, Thinking, and Acting* (New York: Bradford, 2000), 59, 122–34.
3. Andy Clark, *Mindware: An Introduction to the Philosophy of Cognitive Science* (Oxford: Oxford University Press, 2000), 103–39.
4. Spitzer, *The Mind within the Net*, 171–73.
5. Spitzer, *The Mind within the Net*, 224–26.
6. Spitzer, *The Mind within the Net*, 176–87.
7. Spitzer, *The Mind within the Net*, 89–121.
8. Rodney Cotterill, *Enchanted Looms: Conscious Networks in Brains and Computers* (Cambridge: Cambridge University Press, 1998), 98–210; Spitzer, *The Mind within the Net*, 91–95.
9. Gilles Deleuze, *Difference and Repetition*, trans. Paul Patton (New York: Columbia University Press), 1994.

10. Philip Ball, *Critical Mass: How One Thing Leads to Another* (London: Farrar, Strauss, and Giroux, 2004), 386.
11. Cotterill, *Enchanted Looms*, 388–96.
12. Gerald Edelman and Giulio Tononi, *A Universe of Consciousness: How Matter Becomes Imagination* (New York: Basic Books, 2000), 136–58.
13. Edelman and Tononi, *A Universe of Conciousness*, 42, 96, 176–90.
14. Damasio, 1994, 100–13; Edelman and Tononi, *A Universe of Conciousness*, 93–101.
15. Cotterill, *Enchanted Looms*, 61–75.
16. Cotterill, *Enchanted Looms*, 227–38; Edelman and Tononi, *A Universe of Conciousness*, 85–91.
17. Ball, *Critical Mass*, 163–328; Steven Johnson, *Emergence: The Connected Lives of Ants, Brains, Cities, and Software* (New York: Touchstone, 2011).

Chapter Twelve

Actual Fantasy, Modulation Chains, and Swarms of Thought-Controlled Babel Drones

Art and Digital Ontology in the Posthuman Era

Adam Nash

What is the posthuman? A very human concept, it is both the contraction and expansion of anthropocentrism. How did this happen, and what is its relationship with the concept of the anthropocene? The key is the *digital*. If, as Rosi Braidotti has it, bodies are reduced to their informational substrate,[1] then this move can be understood via a conception of the digital as *chains of modulation*. Drawing heavily on the work of Gilbert Simondon,[2] this concept allows an ontogenetic understanding of digital processes. Consequently, seemingly disparate fields like *artificial intelligence* and *evolution*, or *robotics* and *live performance*, or *virtual reality* and *love*, can be resolved and modulated into a new individuating entity, without abandoning the ongoing individuation of each field. When this modulation process is not allowed to happen, individuals are artificially reified, and the only possible product is anxiety.

In this chapter, I draw on my practice as a digital virtual artist to explore the concept of the posthuman. From live performances in virtual space, through robots jamming with artificial intelligence (AI)–driven virtual environments, to sentences that mindlessly reenact the building of Babel over and over in response to the utterances of strangers in a multiuser game world, my artwork attempts to enact a speculative ontology of the digital. By using practice-based research to work with the theories of posthuman thinkers like Simondon (2005, 2009, 2012, 2017), Braidotti (2013), Donna Haraway

(1991), Anna Munster (2006, 2013) and Bernard Stiegler (2013), I show how all concepts of live performance, music, visuals, text, voice, dance, and so on have merged into a postconvergent generic continuum. This can be used to facilitate a posthuman understanding of global digital networks in the anthropocene as a *metastable* environment in which individuating entities can participate in a *transindividual* rather than be subjectivised as digital slaves in a global anxiety factory.

THE POSTHUMAN

What is the posthuman? In one way of looking at it, it is simply the extreme realization of Marshall McLuhan's (1964) simultaneously naïve and prescient assertion of media as extensions of the human. Other ways of looking at the posthuman, like Jane Bennett's (2010) nuanced political economy of objects, situate the human as generically equal in the network of the world, its history and its future. In a related, but perhaps inverted, and less consciously positive frame, the concept of the *anthropocene*, apparently in use by Soviet scientists since the 1960s, and popularized by atmospheric chemist Paul J. Crutzen (Steffen et al. 2007), puts the very geological history of the planet in the hands of the human, *anthropos* being old Greek for *human* and *kainos* for *recent*. In McLuhan's sense, this is the *human* era because we have created tools that extend our being across the planet; in Bennett's, and in the somewhat related object-oriented ontologists' sense, this is the *post* human era, because we have created things and networks that transcend our being on the planet; for Crutzen, it is quite literally *the human era*, because we have become the determining force of the planet.

Of course, all of these definitions rely on an assumption that the concept of *the human* is well defined and well understood. We humans consider it common sense: we are all humans, we are all of the same species, a species so well defined and easily recognizable that we can talk of human rights, rights that are ascribed, by humans, only to humans. And yet, human rights are often aspirational rather than realized. They revolve around freedom and safety, conditions that many humans are denied. Related are legal concepts of statehood, again a condition that many humans are denied. Still other conceptions of humans and our rights rely on legal concepts of agency and participation, again often denied to many of us. So perhaps a commonsense definition appeals to the equally fraught and contested concept of *nature*, since there most definitely were humans before there were codified human rights. But common sense falters almost immediately in this appeal, since one of the great historical foundations of humanity is that we are an anomaly in nature, a species capable of *reason*, that great and brutish stick with which, along with our opposable thumbs, we humans are able to transcend nature, to bend it to our will, to subjectivise that to which all other species are subject. Certainly, human rights are a forthright expression of this super-natural attitude, since it is up to us to redress the crude lack in nature of such definitively human and superior concepts as *fairness* and *justice*. While this triumph over nature allows us to define ourselves as human, and of course provides the basis on which is built the Enlightenment philosophy of the human subject that brings forth the very idea of human rights, it also prevents us from calling on nature to support our claims to specieshood. Like so many so-called commonsense ideas, it ends up that we know what the human is until we start to think about it.

Of course, the death of this particular human subject has been discussed in philosophical terms at least since Nietzsche in the West, and non–European-based philosophies have debated whether it ever attained a status substantial enough to require much effort to kill it anyway. It is perhaps more realistically a product of the relentless campaign of subjectivisation waged upon humans by global free-market ideology in the last thirty or so years. As Laurie Penny (2016) has written, "[t]here is no structural imbalance, according to this view—there is only individual maladaption, requiring an individual response," and "[w]e are supposed to believe that we can only work to improve our lives on that same individual level."[3]

Braidotti (2013) points out that part of the invitation, or challenge, of the posthuman era is to reconsider the status and condition of the human. For Braidotti, this requires dispensing with dichotomous binaries, especially the one that opposes culture and nature, or what she calls the "constructed and the given,"[4] instead perceiving a continuum based on the autopoietic force of living matter. This is clearly a progressive and promising approach, but it is not without a couple of problems that are well countenanced from a Simondonian perspective, of which more detail is given a little later.

The problem with the continuum approach is twofold. First, a "continuum" still implies a duality that the continuum runs between: *from* nature *to* culture. Perhaps I am doing unjust violence by reducing this monistic philosophy to a continuum between two poles that ultimately reinforces a dualism that it was expressly intended to avoid, but this continuum-based view is concerned with salvaging the human subject within the posthuman, albeit by gaining a new understanding of that subject. This seems to lead to a subjectivised individuality that, by establishing a boundary of itself, even a porous boundary, guarantees a dualism. The very concept of *autopoeisis* produces such a dyad. As Eve Kosofsky Sedgwick says, "it's far easier to deprecate the confounding, tendentious effects of binary modes of thinking . . . than it is to articulate or model other structures of thought. Even to invoke nondualism, as plenty of Buddhist sutras point out, is to tumble right into a dualistic trap."[5]

Secondly, in dealing with the concept of the continuum, while aspiring to a smooth or undifferentiated genericism, one has to be very careful to prevent the quality of linear movement, inherent in a continuum between poles, from sacrificing the quality of reticulation. Should this sacrifice not be assiduously avoided, things and concepts are then only ever *carried forward*. In other words, it is not necessarily that reticulation is not possible in an ostensible continuum, rather that a tendency towards considering history as an arrow can prevail.

Nonetheless, it *is* clear that the posthuman problematizes the difference between the human and its other. Julian Savulescu and Ingmar Persson, of the Oxford Uehiro Centre for Practical Ethics, give the example of the human-pig chimera. In their words,

> [S]cientists take a skin cell from a human and from this make stem cells capable of producing any cell or tissue in the body, known as "induced pluripotent stem cells." They then inject these into a pig embryo to make a human-pig chimera. In order to create the desired organ, they use gene editing, or CRISPR, to knock out the embryo's pig's genes that produce, for example, the pancreas. The human stem cells for the pancreas then make an almost entirely human pancreas in the resulting human-pig chimera, with just the blood vessels remaining porcine. Using this controversial technology, a human skin cell, pre-treated and injected into a genetically edited pig embryo, could grow a new liver, heart, pancreas or lung as required.[6]

It is important to note that this process has never actually been done, and it is not known whether it will actually work, but scientists are working on it. The question, for these ethicists, is whether the human-pig chimera should have human rights or not. Of course, if it does, then it would not be possible to take out its organs to put into "real," nonchimeric, humans. On the other hand, if the human-pig chimera is not ascribed human rights, then it is pretty much impossible to claim a continuum, since there is a clear demarcation between human and other. Indeed, looked at this way, the very concept of human rights betrays a noncontinuous taxonomy of life. This is a difficult problem for ethics, and one that is of course repeated for the humanities: must it become the posthumanities, regarding the endeavours of all life as within its purview, or does the humanities simply go away in the posthuman era?

A problem that is somewhat less terrifying, or at least less meaty and easier to understand because it relies on the kind of digital operations we are used to in our contemporary daily lives, but is certainly no less consequential, can be found in the example of the swarm of thought-controlled drones built by Panagiotis Artemiadis and team at Arizona State University's *Human-Oriented Robotics and Control Lab* earlier this year (Dormehl 2016). Self-consciously using sci-fi–tinged military terms like "human commander"

(I would have gone with "The Thinker"), Artemiadis describes a process whereby a human's specifically rehearsed thought patterns are recorded and then used to mold variables for drone control software. The thinker can then control the flight and navigation of what Artemiadis calls "swarms of,"[7] but in the video is actually three, drones. This is a classic modulation and display process, of which more later, and is comparatively simple to do. Originally used in research to controlling prosthetic limbs, the problem displays itself via the scientist's vocabulary choice, highlighted earlier, which betrays an alarmingly lax philosophical attitude to the problem of the nature–culture divide. To wit, Artemiadis sets up the explanation of the work by saying, "The brain is wired to control artifacts that resemble human limbs."[8] There is much that is contestable in this phrase, but let's concentrate on the choice of the word "wired." This is one we are all used to hearing in relation to definitions of the human. "Our brains are hardwired for this and that" is a common phrase in documentaries and science for the layperson publications, despite there being very little evidence to support such claims. Two sentences later, Artemiadis says "the brain can adapt to output control actions for a swarm of . . . robots."[9] Now, adapting to something is the qualitative opposite of being wired to do something. Being wired to do something implies that nature has done it to us, whereas adaptation implies we are doing it to nature. This would be a crucial problem for the posthumanities to consider: the symbiotic relationship between language and technodeterminism, where existing vocabulary is repurposed on the run, or neologisms and linguistic chimeras are hastily constructed in response to some new technology. Certainly, there is currently a crushing conformity emerging from Silicon Valley, linguistically and otherwise, a kind of fascism of the unreflexively "cool," that needs to be rigorously examined and challenged.

Silicon Valley is of course the de facto home of the digital, and the digital is the key to all of the concepts underlying the posthuman, the medium and enabler of all these posthuman endeavours, regardless of their place on the continuum. The digital has so completely and so quickly infiltrated every layer and aspect of the contemporary condition to become so foundational that it is often forgotten as a subject of study. And yet any attempt to understand contemporary moves is really impossible without a rigorous understanding of the digital. In the rush to keep up with the latest cool thing, social media, robotics, Pokémon Go, or the return of virtual reality, there is a tendency for critical theory to devolve into a reactionary, superficially phenomenological descriptivism that misses the forest of the digital for the trees of individual trends or devices. The digital is the generic foundation enabling all of this, and yet it is not well understood. It is important not to mistake the naming of a thing for the understanding of a thing. It is not that the posthuman era, for example, is a result of the digital, it is that the posthuman era *is* the digital era. Therefore, an ontology of the digital is required and one of the primary tasks of the posthumanities should be to ontologize the digital. Towards that end, I would like to briefly lay out such an ontology, before discussing some examples of my own artwork that enact various aspects of this ontology.

DIGITAL ONTOLOGY

Ontology has traditionally been unable to think being and media together, based as it is on the Aristotlean dichotomy of form and matter. German media scholar Friedrich Kittler (2009) points out that even Heidegger's (1996) update of Aristotle to address this problem was resistant to the relationship between ontology, technical media, and mathematics. Yet digital media seems to merge form and matter through the use of mathematical logic, somehow dissolving a binary using binary. At the same time, contemporary media studies either ignore ontology in favour of phenomenology, or undermine attempts at ontology by privileging historicism or nonanthropocentrism (Clemens and Nash 2015). In the philosophy of Gilbert Simondon (2009), the old dichotomy of form and matter is replaced with an operational theory of ontogenesis which he calls "transduction."[10] Rather than ontology, there is ontogenesis, a process of individuation that, without relying on vitalism at all, dispenses with the auto–allo poeisis binary. The profoundly nonanthropocentric nature of Simondon's thought can be seen in his insistence that the "organic" and the "inorganic" are but modes of being, orders of gradation within a continuum. Echoed in contemporary times by the thought of Jane Bennett (2010), this nonanthropocentrism can equally attend to human concerns as it can to chemistry, climate, and technology, since they are all related in an emergent continuum.

Rather than individuals, for Simondon (2009), there are only individuations in process. These individuating processes operate within and through what he calls, borrowing from chemistry, a "metastable"[11] environment, a milieu which the individuating process both emerges from and carries within itself. The idea of "the individual" is replaced in this ontogenetic system of thought by a multiplicity of individuations, a continual process of reciprocal relations (Combes 2013). The structure and operations of digital data and networks is a working display of this ontogenetic model that we are able, to a certain extent, to manipulate at will. Digital data can only be said to exist as a series of modulatory operations that bear no indexical relation to any putative source (Kittler 1999; Nash 2012). The only way that digital data can appear in the world is through an individuating process of modulation into a display state of some sensible mode (visual, audible, olfactory, etc.). This process requires a set of protocols encoded throughout all elements participating in the process (e.g., hardware, software, electricity, networks, and people), facilitating constant reciprocal processes of differentiation. Digital data in its undifferentiated state (i.e., when it is not participating in a modulatory individuating process, when it is indistinguishable, contra object-oriented ontology, from any other digital data) might be seen as a parallel of Simondon's preindividual metastable environment. While protocols ensure predictable modulation, they can only work precisely because the data carry within themselves this digital preindividual. Only thus can they modulate (i.e., individuate) into sensible digital entities. Therefore, the digital is a stark illustration of Simondon's thought that no individual can really be said to exist except in the most contingent and processual way.

We can see how Simondon's ontogenetic system describes and uncovers digital networks and other large networks of operations like human society and climate, but how could it be applied to individual human subjects, since Simondon is apparently disavowing their existence? Simondon's system of thought is extremely nuanced and complex, but we do not do it too much violence if we consider human individual subjects as participants in a reciprocal process of becoming in relation to an "outside" that is not surrounding an already given subject, rather an environment that participates constantly in the subject's constitution in an ongoing cycle of reciprocal, mutual affectivity. With this we see the world not as a collection of predetermined individuals with a clearly demarcated inside and outside; rather it is affectivity that describes and becomes the relations of an "individual" to itself and to the world. This affective relation is interior and exterior to the individual at the same time, so that we are never separate from the world.

So, for Simondon,[12] a subject is more than simply an individual, and indeed is defined by an incompatibility with itself. This tension between a subject and itself has to be resolved through a giving over to transindividual being. In the contemporary world of Western liberal values that privilege individuality and competition, most of us human subjects do the opposite: we turn inwards, trying to find a system of discrete interior relations in order to reinforce a static individual identity that is separate from our environment. For Simondon, this is an impossible attempt, since the subject will always be affected by the preindividual milieu in which it participates. By turning inward in an attempt to close off from its milieu which is already within the subject anyway, the subject feels invaded by the preindividual's capacity to exceed the individual, and it is this sense of invasion that Simondon classifies as anxiety. I have written elsewhere (Nash 2016) how this anxiety is precisely the commodity of digital social networks like Facebook, Instagram, and so on, a commodified anxiety that is endlessly produced and consumed by individuals, the constitution of whom, as anxious individuals, is constantly reinforced in a perverse global distortion of the concept of the transindividual.

One of the instruments that helps facilitate this is the conflation of the concepts of *data* and *information*. Simondon[13] considers perception to be always a resolution of conflict. This is because perception individuates, and individuation is always the resolution of two disparate fields. Perception resolves the conflict into something new, as it retains the traces of the preindividuated fields within itself. Rather than thinking in hylomorphic terms of "individuals" and "reality," Simondon acknowledges only individuation within a metastable environment. This is a useful way of thinking about digital data networks, because it takes the concept of information seriously, as "two different orders that are in a state of disparation."[14] Information is not thereby conflated—as it is in our contemporary digital era—with the concept of data, but as the orienting partner of perception. This enables us to reconsider networks as always in the process of formation, insofar as they are constantly orienting or in-form-ing perception.

Recently, the phenomenon known as *Big Data* has cast the global network of digital data in the role of the information that today must not only orient, but dominate and direct the perception of humans in society. Many adherents of Big Data as an ideological practice, such as Christian Rudder who started the dating site OK Cupid (Rudder 2014) and Eric Schmidt who used to run Google (Schmidt and Cohen 2013), even cleave to an extreme version of this. As a result, Big Data is seen as providing the only true picture of everything, especially we humans in society. "Big" in this sense is neither pejorative regarding size as a function of ethical practice (as in "Big Pharma"), nor paranoid of a vicariously exerted political program (as in "Big Brother"), but rather crowds out all other methods and epistemologies by the ordering of a collection so vast that it simply must constitute the best possible picture of reality. "Knowledge" becomes a mere derivative of data. Moreover, the results generated by unprecedentedly massive data sets, and the technical operations that produce them, can and must be applied without hesitation to all aspects of human (and nonhuman) existence as a matter of urgency. Whether we are dealing with possible terrorist threats, epidemiological risk, or literary history, Big Data provides all the answers. The Austrian-English philosopher Ludwig Wittgenstein once remarked that "the limits of my language mean the limits of my world."[15] Our new proselytizers for Big Data maintain that those limits are established quantitatively.

They are not entirely wrong to do so. As Justin Clemens and I have argued, one of the crucial consequences of digitization is that "numbers are themselves essentially ideological in a digital framework. . . . What is peculiar about this ideology is that it is also essentially true: numbers (in the form of statistics, the modelling of rates of change on a mass scale, the correlation of data from an enormous range of different sources, etc.) are the only way to ensure a minimally rational comparability and consistency of data sets."[16] Yet such an ideology ignores the individuating and processual nature of all interactions, where any subject is actually an ensemble or assemblage that contains within itself the preindividual, a remnant of the metastable environment from which its individuation emerged. This remnant forms, within the subject, the ground for new individuations to occur in any interaction with its environment, including with other subjects, which also carry such enduring preindividual remnants within them. This phenomenon of the remnant is what Simondon calls the "transindividual."[17] According to Simondon, the psychosocial is the transindividual.[18]

A global digital network of data, in which everyone can participate, creating ever more data in which to participate, may seem the perfect milieu in which subjects may *en masse* resolve what Simondon saw as the problem of subjectivity: that the subject is incompatible with itself. According to Simondon, anxiety is produced when the individual cannot resolve, within itself, the disparity between its subjectively constituted individuality and its preindividual part. Therefore, the only answer is for the individual to participate in the transindividual, and what better stage on which to enact the transindividual than the global data network? And yet, it is the individual that is the subject of Big Data or, more precisely, the collection of individuals who are defined as such, as they are captured, within Big Data. In other words, to ensure the existential guarantee of Big Data, that money can be made from it, the data must be data about individuals. Therefore, the architecture of the engines of Big Data—social networks and personalised digital services—must facilitate and exacerbate only what Simondon called "interindividual relations."[19] Such interactions do not "penetrate the individuals" and are incapable of resolving the problem of "incorporated immanence,"[20] and therefore can only create anxiety. Because Simondon saw every interaction as an amplifying relation, we are compelled to see the global data network as an anxiety amplifier on a planetary scale.

ART IN THE POSTHUMAN ERA

How and what can art do in the digital? To rephrase, what is art in the posthuman era? Digital environments are postconvergent, that is, in McLuhan's sense,[21] containing all prior media as content (Nash 2012). A postconvergent medium is the dynamic whole that is created by the convergence of all prior media, plus the excess that is both created by, and is required to create, such convergence. I have written elsewhere (Nash 2017) about how contemporary art is now both subject to, and yet strangely ignorant of, the historical genericising move that the digital has brought on. Such postconvergent moves can perhaps be identified throughout the history of media, but the digital is distinguished by converging all previously differentiable media into an undifferentiable continuum, that of digital data.[22] Consequently, for media to be differentiated in the digital era, digital data must be modulated into some kind of sensible display state via protocols that virtually reassemble the required medium, be it a visible, audible, or some other kind of sensible medium. This is why there is no meaningful distinction between art forms in the digital—sound, music, visuals, motion, words—every previously discrete form is converged into an undifferentiated generic form. The digitization process contributes its own operations to this process, creating an excess that cannot be rationalized exclusively in terms of a meta-media, because the concept of a meta-media is itself one of the media that is, or can be, explicitly virtualized as content within itself, just as the process confers a retroactive virtuality on all prior media being digitized as virtual content, creating both the prior media and the excess of their own virtuality. But, is it even possible to talk of art in a posthuman context? Isn't art purely a human construct? How can it possibly survive a migration to a posthuman state?

It is simple to *re-create* art forms in the digital, and this happens all the time. Music now is always digital, for example. But for music to exist as music, as understood in the predigital era as a discrete form, in the digital era requires eliding the fact that the distribution medium of the music is identical to the production medium. This is easily done, and is the method of the vast majority of artworks in the digital era (i.e., a virtual reconstruction of a predigital form). This is unlikely to contribute to any new understanding of either the art form itself, or the practitioner or perceiver of the work, or the society in which it exists. For a digital art to contribute original thought, it must not be a virtual reassembly; it must somehow work with the intrinsic qualities of the digital. It must somehow be posthuman.

For Simondon (2017), *aesthetic thought* is more fundamental (or primal) than scientific or ethical thought because it occurs before the division of the religious and technical phases of human culture into practical and theoretical modes. As Simondon (2017) outlines:

> This is precisely the goal to be attained: the mission of reflexive thought is to lift upright and perfect the successive waves of genesis through which the primitive unity of man's [sic] relation with the world splits in two and comes to sustain both science and ethics through technics and religion, between which aesthetic thought develops.[23]

This can, and should, be applied to aesthetics, to art, and to practice. It is modulation that allows aesthetics to theorize the relationship between thought and the sensible. It allows enacting the reality that art, or practice, is not a kind of language, or a discursive ordering of sense. Modulation also highlights the dangerous reductiveness of the idea of the tool, as in the colloquial "Photoshop is just a tool," or Heidegger's tool-being. It also avoids recourse to dialectics, with its negative power, and instead affirms difference.

We have seen that individuation occurs through disparation in a milieu that does not preexist the individual, but, on the contrary, is constituted by a transduction, or modulation. In other words, modulation is the process of individuation and its milieu in relation, in communication, in emergent resolution. This is a *metastable* relation between two orders of different realities that enter into resonance. Artists are very aware of this process, even if they have not articulated it to themselves as such. This process is a mode of individuation that is precisely not confused with that of a thing or a subject. This is important for art because the subject–object dichotomy is basically incapable of thinking art without casting it into some kind of dialectic that prevents it from existing as an individuating process in communication with its milieu. In other words, it is incapable of explaining how Beethoven's music still exists without getting caught up in all sorts of unproductive discourse around the subject.

This fundamental deficiency especially reveals itself in the arena of networked interactions, as in digital social networks or multiuser games or even telephone conversations. The solution to avoiding this centuries-old trap is to think only in terms of agency. Guided by Simondon's (2017) concepts of modulation, this can extend to all art, to all practice. Further, the concept of *agency* is then recognised as that of *affect*. Where there is affect, there is individuation. These moves allow a nonanthropocentrism to be thought by people, and for art and its works to have their own individuation, in communication with their milieu which includes but is not limited to people, including the artist, without forming an indissoluble identity. We might say "what you do is not you," even if we encourage people by saying "you are what you do." It is the disparate (i.e., difference itself) which causes sensibility and thought to emerge as a resolution of disparate fields.

This is how we can account for the affect and effect of art, the material effect and the affective power upon the recipient, the interactor, the listener, the player, as well as the artist. Unlike hermeneutics, which attaches the work to the subject, and unlike structuralist or sociological interpretations, which locates the affectivity of objective structures in the work, the process of modulation retains the heterogeneity of disparate forces, and synthesizes from them a new force. It eliminates the need for struggles about figurative resemblance or structural identity and leaves only modulation of disparity that constitutes the work, its public, the artist, and the artist's milieu. The apparently disparate fields—at least they have been treated as such by aesthetics since Kant—of art and technics are resolved in this way as well, so that it is not possible to speak of the conceptual aspect of the work as separate from the technical aspect of the work, whether in the technical manipulation of matter or the technical manipulation of form distinctions that previously prevented aesthetics from falling into a dualistic trap, which then required it to be "saved" by dialectics by "overcoming" the trap through brute negative force rather than procedural resolution.

Simon Mills[24] reminds us that crucial in this attempt is an understanding of media as environmental, rather than simply a transmission method, and this applies to the concept of the tool discussed earlier just as much as it does to paint, words, video, multiuser virtual environments, and music. We as artists are a part of this environment. Just as much as it is a part of us, it is our milieu, and it is not only cultural, it is also natural, technological, psychological, and social. It is a vast complex of transductive operations occurring on all sorts of reticulated stages and phases. The digital era is the era of media as environment. The digital is the exemplar par excellence of the Simondonian modulation process. We all of us as artists interact with the digital constantly, crucially, and completely, regardless of whether, like myself, we explicitly do this or, like others, consider it but part of the work. The same modulation process, the same allagmatic epistemology of Simondon, is at play whether programming a virtual environment or trying to understand the affective power of music.

There is a fairly strong connection here between Simondon and Spinoza—obviously there are some significant differences as well, but both outline a kind of monism and both are very much concerned with affect. The famous postulate 1 of Spinoza's (1994) *Third Part of the Ethics: Of the Origin and Nature of the Affects* reads, "The human body can be affected in many ways in which its power of acting is increased or diminished, and also in others which render its power of acting neither greater nor less."[25] Simondon assumes that this extends to all things, *all* things physical, vital, conceptual, extant or not. There is no reason to think that Spinoza himself doesn't in fact also do this, but in Simondon it is very explicit. For Spinoza, there is the power of thinking and the power of acting, but they are not two different things, rather degrees of the same thing. So too with Simondon we can see the individuation of becoming and the individuation of thought required to think the individuation of becoming. This is really the crux of the application of Simondonian thought to art: in order to think individuating becoming, thought itself needs to modulate. As Simondon says, "Beings can be known by knowledge of the subject but the individuation of beings can be seized only by individuation of the knowledge of the subject."[26]

As I have hopefully made clear, the distinction between data and display, via modulation, is constitutive of the digital. Therefore, my works try to explicitly modulate data into display. The digital also potentially allows equal participation in a work, since the distinction between creator and player is also an explicit act of modulation. As an artist first and foremost, I am compelled to conclude by briefly enunciating the ways in which some of my works enact the thoughts contained in this chapter.

ARTWORKS AS/AND DIGITAL ONTOLOGY

In this section, I briefly describe some works I have made or collaborated on. Each of them enacts, or attempts to enact, some of the aspects of digital ontology that I have discussed in this chapter, by trying to affectively engage with the principles of modulation, or transduction, of digital data.

Neuron Conductor (2017–2019) is a hybrid biological–machine generative artwork. It is a collaboration between myself, artist John McCormick, and neuro-euro-engineer Asim Bhatti. It uses an artificial neural network to interact with a biological neural network in order to learn new creative musical procedures. A biological neural network, consisting of real mosquito neurons, is cultured on a multielectrode array, where signature neural spiking patterns are produced from the introduction of various viruses. These patterns are filtered through the artificial neural network to create the movement of the robot, which in turn generates the music in real time. Viruses such as dengue and zika become the source material for the striking compositions conducted by the biological machine. This biorobot is a study of a system that incorporates biological, digital, and hardware components into itself for its own purpose of creation, and is a good example of modulations of data from and between disparate registers: electrical signals from neurons, hardware robot joint movements, digital virtual environments, musical scales, and realtime visual images.

Child in the Wild (2016–2018) is an interactive installation that enables human participants and a child-sized humanoid robot to co-create an immersive audiovisual artwork through the use of the robot's artificial neural networks that do object and image recognition. It is a collaboration between myself and artist John McCormick. Visitors show the robot pictures and objects, which the robot "recognizes" using artificially intelligent image recognition routines. The robot uses text-to-speech to speak out loud what it "thinks" the image or object is. It then searches on the internet for images and information related to the recognized image or object. As well as speaking out loud the information found in the search results, it also causes the returned image results to be displayed via projector. These displayed images are then "decomposed" and animated according to pixel values. These pixel values are simultaneously used to generate a musical score in real time. All of these things happen more or less simultaneously, creating an immersive environment of generative sound, colour, speech, images, and animation, all "conducted" by a child-sized humanoid robot sitting in a pram. This work is an assemblage of hardware robot, peoples' phones, AI image and object recognition, web search results, projected animations and music, all engaging in an ongoing transductive network of individuating relationships in realtime.

Out of Space (2015–2016) is a playable abstract audiovisual virtual environment, using a custom hardware system developed by Stefan Greuter and myself before such a system became commercially available. This custom system was a low-cost experimental platform that enables participants to experience full-body interaction with virtual-reality scenes. The platform combines a commodity head-mounted display (Oculus Rift), with a depth-based camera (Kinect) capturing movement of body and limbs within the physical and virtual space. The work itself, the virtual reality scene that the player enters via the head-mounted display and interacts with by moving his or her body in physical space, is an abstract audiovisual construction based on a minimal algorithm that governs size, shape, colour, and position of the geometry and tone, pitch, timbre, and rhythm of the sounds that are generated in response to the player moving through the geometry. If the role of art is to question everything, then when artworks are composed of digital data, art must question digital data. Data is not information. Information is not knowledge. Knowledge is not wisdom. Data is not necessarily digital, but this work is digital. It creates digital data that is, in some ways, aware of itself as data. Is this unique to digital art? Perhaps. In the predigital, is oil paint, in some ways, aware of its own status as part of an artwork? Perhaps not, but certainly it uses chemical affordances to behave as paint in a painting. Not only does this work create and use data, it is, in fact, constituted by, and as, digital data. Everything about digital data is hard to define once you start to question it, and this work is no exception. Using data, this work creates itself as data in *real time*, displaying itself as an immersive audiovisual environment. Perhaps "datascape" is the best word for it. Then it takes data as input. This time, it is tracking data from a person walking around in the gallery space and digitizes it. It sorts, filters, and labels this data and then incorporates it into its own limited knowledge system. From that point on, the relationship that this data shares with its source (i.e., a person walking around) is purely arbitrary and requires constant reinforcement to ensure the relationship is ostensibly maintained. The work uses the affordance of the data source (i.e., the walking person) being physically present to maintain the visual illusion that the walking around is the same thing as the data captured by the walking around. But it is not the same thing, and the art, such as it is, is in riding a balance between legible relationships and the void opened up when this process is recognized.

Reproduction (2010–2012) is an ongoing collaboration between myself and John McCormick. The work involves experimentation in audiovisual, performative, evolving, virtual entities spawning and reproducing in virtual environments, capable of intercommunication with the material world via various systems of motion and data capture. Loosely based on principles of artificial evolution, the parameters that we as the artists initially selected are, rather than the standard artificial evolution parameters like strength and fitness, all audiovisual performative parameters like red, green, blue, opacity, rhythm, timbre, tempo, tone (pitch), and so on. The entities "evolve," "reproduce," "live," and "die" over thousands of generations according to a constantly emergent evolution of these crude parameters that is informed, but not determined, by both their interaction with humans in the material world and with their interactions with each other. In other words, the original parameter set becomes, after the first generation, virtualized content for the next emergent generation. All the while, the entities are organizing (or perhaps socializing) and improvising movements and "songs" amongst themselves, whilst observing and improvising with any human visitors to their "space." The space in this case means both their digital virtual environment (accessible by humans via an online multiuser environment) as well as the physical space of wherever the work happens to be being exhibited. In the latter case, motion and data capture are used by the entities to perceive humans, while a modulated audiovisual display allows humans to perceive the entities. Our desire, as artists, is to engage—using sound, music, movement and dance—in what we might call a "genuine" improvisation with these digital entities, by which we mean the human and digital performers share equal responsibility and value in the emergence of the improvised performance, dynamically building a shared performative vocabulary by learning from each other's nuances, gestures, and performative suggestions.

Autoscopia (2009–2016) is a virtual artwork by Justin Clemens, Christopher Dodds, and Adam Nash, commissioned by the National Portrait Gallery of Australia. Autoscopia allows users to enter names to create virtual portraits based on Internet searches. These searches manifest as web portraits dynamically generated by search results, and audiovisual animated sculptures dynamically generated in the multiuser virtual environment called *Second Life*. The *Second Life* component closed at the end of 2010, but the web portraits continue to grow, all the while tweeting their existence, recursively feeding themselves back into the results of future searches. Autoscopia's *Second Life* portraits are built using data from Internet-based vanity searches conducted within the *Second Life* installation. Each name creates a unique outcome composed of twenty-seven "limbs." Each limb is fed data from websites such as Google, Facebook, Twitter (and other more invasive, though publicly available, sources), with colours, geometry and audio, affected by variations in search volume. Data is then republished via discrete web pages automatically composed through text and images collected during the search. The identity created will thereafter be reincorporated into future search results. Each portrait also "tweets" its existence on Twitter, with both the web pages and tweets looping back into future portraits, creating a kind of time-based network meta-animation.

Babelswarm (2007) was a collaboration between myself, Christopher Dodds, and Justin Clemens. It was the result of the inaugural Australia Council Multi-User Virtual Environment Artist-in-Residence program in 2007. It was staged physically in the Lismore Regional Gallery, NSW, Australia, and in the realtime 3D multiuser virtual environment *Second Life*. Activated by the voices of visitors in the real-world gallery and chat messaging from virtual visitors in *Second Life*, a swarm of letter cubes—programmed to seek out their original word position—slowly builds a morphing, virtual Tower of Babel. This tower is constructed from the utterances of visitors to it, constantly reconfiguring itself according to the "artificial stupidity" of the individual letter forms. As Justin Clemens (2007) wrote in his introduction to the work:

> What sorts of conceptual figures are available to think such a thing? The very old: the Tower of Babel from the Book of Genesis, which melds the frightening possibilities of technology, language, and power in a single startling image. And the very new: swarm intelligence as an ideal that expresses how innumerable different individuals can nonetheless come to produce radical innovations in excess of the powers of any one of them—and in the midst of apparent disorder. Babelswarm is a project that draws on the most traditional elements of religion, art, and literature, as it engages with the challenges of a scientific and technological age.[27]

All of these works attempt in some way to explore the invitation that is opened to art by the concept of the posthuman, which I have identified here as analogous to the digital, when understood as a modulating, transductive process of reciprocal relations within and between ongoing individuating processes and their milieu. This is the practice of an ontogenetic understanding of digital processes, where disparate fields can be resolved and modulated into a new individuating entity, without abandoning the ongoing individuation of each field. When this modulation process is allowed to happen, we abandon the artificial reification of the individual, which is the hallmark of global capitalism and its automated production of anxiety. We are well advised by Rosi Braidotti to resist these forces that would—indeed do—use the advent of the posthuman as an opportunity to negatively erase, rather than connect across, difference in the exploitative pursuit of resources and growth. Perhaps only art is capable of individuating, from the generic levelling that the digital inaugurates, new concepts of affective relations that operate beyond the human.

BIBLIOGRAPHY

Bennett, Jane. *Vibrant Matter*. Durham: Duke University Press, 2010.
Braidotti, Rosi. *The Posthuman*. Cambridge: Polity Press, 2013.
Clemens, Justin, and Adam Nash. "Being and Media: digital ontology after the event of the end of media." *The Fibreculture Journal* 24 (2015).
Clemens, Justin, Dodd, and Adam Nash. 2007.
Combes, Muriel. *Gilbert Simondon and the Philosophy of the Transindividual*. Cambridge: MIT Press, 2013.

Dormehl, Luke. "This Scientist Can Control a Swarm of Drones with His Thoughts." *Digital Trends*, 15 July 2016. https://www.digitaltrends.com/cool-tech/drone-swarm/.
Haraway, Donna. *Simians, Cyborgs and Women: The Reinvention of Nature*. New York: Routledge, 1991.
Heidegger, Martin. *Being and Time*. Translated by J. Stambaugh. Albany: SUNY Press, 1996.
Kittler, Friedrich. "Towards an Ontology of Media." *Theory Culture Society* 26, no. 2–3 (2009): 23–31.
Krtolica, Igor. "The Question of Anxiety in Gilbert Simondon." In *Gilbert Simondon: Technology and Being*, edited by A. de Boever, A. Murray, J. Roffe, and A. Woodward, 73–91. Edinburgh: Edinburgh University Press, 2012.
Lacan, Jacques. *Anxiety: The Seminar of Jacques Lacan, Book 10*. Translated by A. R. Price. Cambridge: Polity Press, 2014.
McLuhan, Marshall. *Understanding Media*. London: Routledge, 1964.
Mills, Simon. *Gilbert Simondon: Information, Technology and Media*. London: Rowman & Littlefield International, 2016.
Munster, Anna. *Materializing New Media: Embodiment in Information Aesthetics*. Hanover: Dartmouth College Press, 2006.
Munster, Anna. *An Asthenia of Networks: Conjunctive Experience in Art and Technology*. Cambridge: MIT Press, 2013.
Nash, Adam. 2012. "Affect and the Medium of Digital Data." *Fibreculture Journal* 21.
Nash, Adam. 2016. "Affect, People and Digital Social Networks." In *Emotions, Technology, and Social Media*, edited by Sharon Y. Tettegah, 3–24. London: Academic Press.
Nash, Adam. "Art Imitates the Digital." *Lumina* 11, no. 2 (2017): 110–25.
Penny, Laurie. "Life-Hacks of the Poor and Aimless." *The Baffler*, 8 July 2016. http://thebaffler.com/blog/laurie-penny-self-care.
Sauvagnargues, Anne. *Artmachines*. Edinburgh: Edinburgh University Press, 2016.
Savulescu, Julian, and Ingmar Perrson. "Should a human-pig chimera be treated as a person?" *Aeon*, 14 July 2016. https://aeon.co/ideas/should-a-human-pig-chimera-be-treated-as-a-person.
Scott, David. *Gilbert Simondon's Psychic and Collective Individuation: A Critical Introduction and Guide*. Edinburgh: Edinburgh University Press, 2014.
Sedgwick, Eve Kofosky. *Touching Feeling: Affect, Pedagogy, Performativity*. Durham, NC: Duke University Press, 2003.
Simondon, Gilbert. 2003.
Simondon, Gilbert. 2013.
Simondon, Gilbert. "The Genesis of the Individual." In *Incorporations*, edited by Jonathan Crary and Sanford Kwinter, 297–319. New York: Zone Books, 1993.
Simondon, Gilbert. *L'individuation à la lumière des notions de forme et d'information*. Grenoble: Éditions Jérôme Millon, 2005.
Simondon, Gilbert. *On the Mode of Existence of Technical Objects*. Translated by C. Malaspina and John Rogove. Minneapolis: Univocal Publishing, 2017.
Simondon, Gilbert. "The Position of the Problem of Ontogenesis." *Parrhesia* 7 (2009): 4–16.
Simondon, Gilbert. "Technical Mentality." In *Gilbert Simondon: Technology and Being*, edited by Anne De Boever, Alex Murray, Jon Roffe, and Ashley Murray, 1–18. Edinburgh: Edinburgh University Press, 2012.
Spinoza, Benedict de. *Ethics*. Translated and edited by Edwin Curley. London: Penguin Books, 1994.
Steffen, Will, Paul J. Crutzen, and John R. McNeill. "The Anthropocene: Are Humans Now Overwhelming the Great Forces of Nature?" In *Ambio* 36, no. 8 (December 2007): 614–21.
Stiegler, Bernard. *What Makes Life Worth Living: On Pharmacology*. Cambridge: Polity Press, 2013.
Wittgenstein, Ludwig. *Tractatus Logico-Philosophicus*. Translated by D. F. Pears and B. F. McGuinness. London: Routledge, 2014.
Wolfe, Cary. *What Is Posthumanism?* Minneapolis: University of Minnesota Press, 2010.

NOTES

1. Rosi Braidotti, *The Posthuman* (Cambridge: Polity Press), 12.
2. Gilbert Simondon, "The Position of the Problem of Ontogenesis," *Parrhesia* 7 (2009), 7.
3. Laurie Penny, "Life-Hacks of the Poor and Aimless," *The Baffler*, 8 July 2016, http://thebaffler.com/blog/laurie-penny-self-care.
4. Braidotti, *The Posthuman*, 2.
5. Eve Kofosky Sedgwick, *Touching Feeling: Affect, Pedagogy, Performativity* (Durham, NC: Duke University Press, 2003), 2.
6. Julian Savulescu and Ingmar Perrson, "Should a Human-Pig chimera Be Treated as a Person?" *Aeon*, 14 July 2016, https://aeon.co/ideas/should-a-human-pig-chimera-be-treated-as-a-person.
7. Luke Dormehl, "This Scientist Can Control a Swarm of Drones with His Thoughts," *Digital Trends*, 15 July 2016, https://www.digitaltrends.com/cool-tech/drone-swarm/.
8. Dormehl, "This Scientist."
9. Dormehl, "This Scientist."
10. Simondon, "The Position of the Problem," 11.
11. Simondon, "The Position of the Problem," 6.
12. Simondon, "The Position of the Problem," 5.
13. Simondon, "The Position of the Problem," 6.
14. Simondon, "The Position of the Problem," 9.
15. Ludwig Wittgenstein, *Tractatus Logico-Philosophicus*, trans. D. F. Pears and B. F. McCuinness (London: Routledge, 2014), 68.
16. Justin Clemens and Adam Nash, "Being and Media: Digital Ontology after the Event of the end of Media," *The Fibreculture Journal* 24 (2015), 19.
17. Gilbert Simondon, "The Genesis of the Individual," in *Incorporations*, edited by Jonathan Crary and Sanford Kwinter (New York: Zone Books, 1993), 307.
18. Simondon, 2003, 8.
19. Muriel Combes, *Gilbert Simondon and the Philosophy of the Transindividual* (Cambridge: MIT Press, 2013), 37.
20. David Scott, *Gilbert Simondon's Psychic and Collective Individuation: A Critical Introduction and Guide* (Edinburgh: Edinburgh University Press, 2014), 138.
21. Marshall McLuhan, *Understanding Media* (London: Routledge, 1964), 10.
22. Friedrich Kittler, "Towards and Ontology of Media," *Theory Culture Society* 26, no. 2–3 (2009), 2.
23. Gilbert Simondon, *On the Mode of Existence of Technical Objects*, trans. C. Malaspina and John Rogove (Minneapolis: Univocal, 2017), 175.
24. Simon Mills, *Gilbert Simondon: Information, Technology and Media* (London: Rowman & Littlefield International, 2016), 174.
25. Benedict de Spinoza, *Ethics*, trans. and ed. Edwin Curley (London: Penguin, 1994), 70.
26. Gilbert Simondon, 2013, 36.
27. Justin Clemens, Dodd, and Adam Nash, 2007, n.p.

Index

Abella, Irving, 82n37
The Abolition of Man (Lewis), 11
Abraham, Nicolas, 93
academics, 24
adaptive systems, 198. *See also* artificial neural networks (ANNs)
Adorno, Theodor, 78
affectivity, 211, 215
Agamben, Giorgio, 89–90
agency, 104, 113, 123, 215
aging, 153, 155, 156. *See also* death; immortality
Agricultural Adjustment Act (1933), 34
agriculture, 3, 32–36, 45, 174
Aiko, 156
Aktion Suhnezeichen, 75
Alarms and Discursions (Chesterton), 118
Alcor Life Extension Foundation, 155
Algae Opera (Burton Nitta), 174–175
Algae Opera House (Burton Nitta), 175
algae, 174–175
algorithms, 191, 218. *See also* artificial neural networks (ANNs)
Alliance for Bhikkhunis, 53–54, 56–57
Amerianization, 85–86. *See also* grief commodification
American Association for the Advancement of Science (AAAS), 31, 35
American flag, 87, 88

American Widow (Torres), 83, 84, 87–89, 90
amnesia, 92, 93, 94. *See also* remembrance
analogue, 195–196
Anders, William (Bill), 15–18, 25
animals, 167, 168, 172, 173, 188, 191
anonymity, 25
anthropocene, 206. *See also* nonanthropocentrism
anticompetition practices, 41
anti-Semitism, 74, 75, 76, 77, 78, 104. *See also* Holocaust
anxiety, 151, 205, 206, 211, 213
anxiety commodification, 211
apocalypse, 121–123, 123, 124–126, 126–127, 128–129
apocalyptic fiction, 121–130
Apollo 8 mission, 15–19, 25
Apostles, 73
Apple, 42, 187
An Architect's Journey (Freed), 69
Aristotle, 210
art: artificial neural networks (ANNs), 190; and audiences, 171; and cyborgs, 165, 167; as digital ontology, 217–220; and Holocaust, 101–102. *See also* Rachel (survivor artist); and memory, 91–92, 94; and posthumanism, 4, 213–216; and technics, 215–216; *specific artists*
Artemiadis, Panagiotis, 208–209
artificial evolution, 218–219

Index

artificial intelligence (AI), 5, 156–157, 181–182, 187, 188, 217
artificial neural networks (ANNs): abstraction, 190–191; artworks, 190, 217; challenging binarism, 194, 194–195; drone strikes, 190; and emergence, 200; evolution, 190; facial recognition, 189–190; and humans, 199; overview, 187–189; shifting society, 191–192; studying, 191, 198–199
The Art of Therapy (unreleased film), 114n2
art therapy, 102, 106–108, 112, 112–114
Ashcroft, Louise, 174, 175
Asian Values (AV) debates, 52–53
Asia-Pacific region, 50–53, 58. *See also* Buddhism
Asimov, Isaac, 147, 181
Association of Southeast Asian Nations (ASEAN), 51, 52, 58, 61n18
astronauts. *See* Apollo 8 mission
Atkey, Ron, 82n37
atonement, 74–75, 137
Auschwitz-Birkenau, 70, 71
Auschwitz-Birkenau State Museum, 70, 72–78
Auslander, Shalom, 83–84, 90–95
Australian Transport Accident Commission, 172
autopoeisis, 207
Autoscopia (Clemens, Dodds and Nash), 219

Babelswarm (Nash, Dodds and Clemens), 219–220
babies, 124–125
Babi Yar, 70
back-propagation, 188, 190
Badiou, Alain, 1
Bakhtin, 135
Bakhtin, Mikhail, 94
Barrett, Frank J., 135
Bauman, Zygmunt, 78; *On the Beach* (Chute), 127
Beattie, Steven W., 135–136
Becker, Ernest, 151–152, 160
Bennett, Jane, 3, 92–93, 205, 210

Bert Molson (character), 138–140, 144n26, 145n53
Bhatti, Asim, 217
Bicentennial Man (film), 181
Big Data, 184, 212–213. *See also* digital data
Big Dog, 189
big history, 20–21, 24
Big History and the Future of Humanity (Spier), 19, 21
Billy Constable (character), 140–141
binarism, 167, 194–195, 207, 210, 215. *See also* dualism
bindis, 167–168, 169, 176
biomedical system, 11. *See also* healthcare; hospitals; medicine, modern
biosphere, 23–24
"In the Black Chamber" (Kingsnorth), 129–130
Blake, William, 154
Bloodlands (Synder), 70
Blue Frog, 156
Boat People crisis (Vietnamese refugees), 82n37
Bollywood, 167
Bolus-Reichert, Christine, 121–131, 131n1–131n20
book overview, 2–8, 12–13, 66–67, 117–119, 147–149, 182–183
Borman, Frank, 16, 17–18
Botai, Stella, 168–169
Böttcher, Frits, 20
Bower, Joseph L., 187
Braidott, Rosi: on art, 4; and binaries, 207; on bodies reduced, 205; on capitalism and posthumanism, 220; on common references, 2; influencing Vitale, 182, 183; on living, 1; on new wars, 4; on posthuman as multidimensional, 84
brains, 191–194, 196–198. *See also* artificial neural networks (ANNs); mind
Brett's, E. A., 102
Brown Girl in the Ring (Hopkinson), 121, 122, 128–129
Buddha, 11
Buddhism, 49–50, 52, 55–58, 61n16, 62n29, 62n41
Burton, Michael, 174–176

Burton Nitta, 174–176
Bush, George W., 87, 89
Butler, Judith, 84–85, 87–88, 89, 95
"Cages" (Vanderhaeghe), 138, 144n26

calavera, 126
candle light, 110–112
Čapek, Karel, 157
capitalism: abusing posthumanism, 220; abusing technology, 182; disaster capitalism, 121–122; and humanity, 207; vs. individuals, 43–44; as a network, 200; vs. social investment, 52. *See also* shock doctrine
car accidents, 172, 175
carbon footprint, 36
Carmelite convent, 78
Cartesianism, 148, 154, 173, 194, 195. *See also* binarism; Descartes, René; dualism
Catholicism, 74–76. *See also* Christianity; religion
Cat's Cradle (Vonnegut), 127
cell phones, 22
centralization, 200
Chaisson, Eric, 21
Charley Brewster (character), 135–138
Chesterton, G. K., 118, 119
child abuse, 103–104
Child in the Wild (Nash and McCormick), 217
children, 124–125, 172–173
The Children of Men (James), 121–122, 124, 127, 128–129, 130
China, 62n41. *See also* Asia-Pacific region
chivalry, 135, 135–136, 138, 141–142
Christensen, Clayton, 187
Christian, David, 20
Christianity: and Crespo, 170; and Judaism, 74–78; role in Holocaust, 74–76, 76. *See also* Holocaust memorial sites; religion; witnessing
Chute, Nevil, 127
Citizen Jane: Battle for the City (film), 129
civilization problems, 38–39, 43–45
class, 135, 136, 139, 141
Clemens, Justin, 212, 219–220
climate change, 44–45, 127, 130
climate change conferences, 44–45
Cloud, Preston, 21–22

Club of Rome, 19–20
code, 188
Cold War, 21, 122
collective memory, 91
collective shock, 121. *See also* shock doctrine
commodification: anxiety, 72, 211; economic, 88; grief, 84–94; Holocaust memorial sites, 72; reproductive, 167, 176, 178n5
communication, 22–23
community, need for, 106
Companion Robot Buddy, 156
complex systems science, 198, 200. *See also* artificial neural networks (ANNs)
computation, 194
computer industry, 39–43, 42
computers, 155–156, 188, 189, 193, 194, 198. *See also* cyborgs; robots
Connell, R. W., 133–135, 138
consciousness, 196, 197. *See also* mind; *res cogitans*
Consumer Price Index (CPI), 33
consumption, 89, 92
continuums, 207–208, 210
Cook, Sarah, 62n29
cool, 209
corn production, 36
corpses, 155–156
Cosmos (television show), 21
Cosmos, Earth, and Man: A Short History of the Universe (Cloud), 21–22
"Counsellor Sally Brings Me to the Tunnel" (Vanderhaeghe), 138–140, 144n26, 145n53
CPR (cardiopulmonary resuscitation), 158
creative writing, 190. *See also* novels
Crespo, Andrea, 168–171, 176
crisis. *See* apocalyptic fiction
"A Crisis of Bigness" (Kingsnorth), 129
CRISPR, 208
critics, 122
"Crosses in Auschwitz: Crisis and Turning" (Neusner), 76
Crutzen, Paul J., 206
CT (computed tomography), 155
Cuba, 40
culture: art and viewers, 171; and cyborgs, 165; and posthumanism, 207; and

women's rights, 54–56, 58. *See also* art; religion
"The Cyborg Manifesto" (Haraway), 165, 171
cyborgs: and academics, 165; in Burton Nitta art, 174–175; and consciousness transfer, 159; in Crespo art, 168–169, 169–171, 176; as future, 176; Jernigan and VHP, 156; in Kher art, 167, 168, 176; in McKay art, 170–171, 176; and ontology, 159–160, 172; in Piccinini art, 172–175; and popular culture, 165, 173; and tools, 192. *See also* hybridity; robots
"Cyborgs: Humanity's Future and Interdisciplinary Contemporary Art" (panel), 166

Daddy Lenin and Other Stories (Vanderhaeghe), 133, 135–142
dairy industry, 35
Damasio, Antonio, 196
Dark Matter MM (Kher), 167–168
Dark Mountain Project, 129, 130
Dark Tourism (Lennon and Foley), 72
data. *See* Big Data; digital data; fuzzy data
datascape, 218
The Day of the Triffids (Wyndham), 123, 126, 127
D'Costa, Gavin, 74
Deacon, Terrence, 192
death, 126, 139–140, 151–152, 158–159, 161. *See also* apocalypse; apocalyptic fiction; dying process; immortality
death studies, 152
death tourism, 85, 86, 90, 92. *See also* Holocaust memorial sites; trauma
decentralized relationships, 84
Deep Dream, 187
Deep Face, 187
defamiliarization, 92, 93–94
de Grey, Aubrey, 153
Deleuze, Gilles, 192
Dellamonica, A. M., 128–129
democracy, 53
The Denial of Death (Becker), 152
Descartes, René, 154, 159, 194. *See also* Cartesianism

Descartes' Error: Emotion, Reason, and the Human Brain (Damasio), 196
development, 52, 57. *See also* United Nations Sustainable Development Goals (SDGs)
diet, 36, 45
Di Giovine, Michael A., 71, 72, 77
digital, 209–210, 213–214, 216. *See also* cyborgs; technology
digital data, 210–216, 218. *See also* Big Data
digital doppelganger, 156
digital ontology, 205–206, 209–210, 217–220
digitization, 212, 214
diminishing returns: agriculture in 1920s, 35; and costs, 35, 36; defining, 30; longevity, 38; software, 39–40, 43
disaster capitalism, 121–122. *See also* capitalism; shock doctrine
disease, 38
diversity, 88, 89
DNA, 153, 153–154, 155, 156
Dodds, Christopher, 219–220
Doss, Erica, 85–86
double-voicing, 135, 137, 138, 140, 141–142, 142–143
drones, 190, 208–209
dualism, 194–196, 198, 199–200, 207, 215–216. *See also* binarism
dying process, 151–152, 157–158
dystopia, 117, 119. *See also* apocalyptic fiction

Eagleton, Terry, 118
Earth. *See* big history, 16–25
Earth Day, 19
Earthrise, 16–19, 21–22
Earthrise (photo), 19, 21
Earthrise: How Man First Saw the Earth (Poole), 19
"Eat Light: Dawn of the Plantimals" (Mackenzie and Lepage), 175
ecological sensibility, 3–4, 93
economic commodification, 88
education of big history, 24
"Elderly Bearded Man" (Rachel), 106–108, 107, 108
"Elderly Man with Hat" (Rachel), 108, 109

emergence, 160, 198–200, 210, 219
empathy, 94–95
employment, 43–44, 44
empowerment, 50–54, 57–58, 60n4
The End, 122. *See also* apocalypse; apocalyptic fiction; death
environmental issues, 19–20, 36, 44–45, 127, 130
Erasing Death (Parnia), 158–159
Essay on Population (Malthus), 32
ethanol, 36
ethics, 94–95, 102, 181, 208
Evans, Sarah, 166, 167, 176
executed criminals, 155

Facebook, 22, 187, 190, 191
facial recognition, 189–191
farms. *See* agriculture
fascism, 78, 118
Faust, 39
feedback, 188–191, 198
feeling, 197–198, 199
Feinberg, Kenneth, 88
Feinberg Compensation Fund/House Resolution 2926, 88
Felman, Shohana, 90
femininity, 141, 142
feminism, 135, 171
First Nations, 125
fMRI. *See* MRI (magnetic resonance imaging)
Foley, Malcolm, 72
food production, 3, 32–36, 45, 174
food security, 32
food waste, 35
foreknowledge, 123–124
forgetting/amnesia, 92, 93, 94. *See also* remembrance
form, 210, 214–216
"The Foundation and Manifesto of Futurism" (Marinetti), 117–118
Francis (pope), 76. *See also* Catholicism
Frank, Anne, 93–94
Freed, James Ingo, 69, 73
Freud, Sigmund, 193
Friedman, Milton, 122
fruit flies, 153
future: Chesterton's musing, 119; choice for, 23; discussions about, 23–25; and ethics, 181; as grim, 117; and past-oriented people, 12; views of, 31. *See also* apocalypse; apocalyptic fiction; dystopia; *On the Future: Prospects of Humanity* (Rees), 181
futurism, 117–118
fuzzy data, 188–190. *See also* digital data

Galbraith, John Kenneth, 29, 32
Geer, Dan, 43
gender: anxiety, 133; and empowerment, 50–54, 60n4; norms, 135, 144n26; post-gender of cyborgs, 166, 167, 169–170; and poverty, 61n16; and religion; (*see* gender equality); transgender people, 170. *See also* masculinity
Gender Development Index (GDI), 51
gender equality, 49–58
gender indexes, 51
genes, 153–156
germ theory, 36–38, 40
Gilbert, Ruth, 90–91, 93–94
Global Gender Gap Index (GGGI), 51
Global Gender Gap Report, 60n4
GOFAI, 188, 193. *See also* artificial intelligence (AI)
Goldfarb, Michael, 72
Goldman, Marlene, 126
Google, 187, 189–190
Goudsblom, Johan, 20
Gourevitch, Philip, 86
Graham, Elaine, 155, 159
graphic novels. *See American Widow* (Torres)
Great Depression, 32–34. *See also* stock market crash of 1929
Greenberg, Irving, 69, 74
Greuter, Stefan, 217–218
grief commodification, 84–91, 93–94. *See also* trauma
Guattari, Felix, 184
Gupta, Joyeeta, 53, 55, 62n29

Habermas, Jürgen, 194–195
habits, change in, 31
hairy-nosed wombats, 173–174
HanSaRam, 156
happiness, 11
Harari, Yuval Noah, 11–12, 13

228 Index

Haraway, Donna: blurring boundaries, 168; on changing the story, 2, 7; on cybernetic convergence, 157; on gender, 167, 169–170; hybridity, 168; on light, 169; making kin vs. working on, 1–2, 7; overview, 165–166; on *Still Life with Stem Cells*, 172–173; on tools, 192. *See also* cyborgs
Hartman, Geoffrey, 86–87, 91, 92
Hastings, David A., 51
Hayles, N. Katherine, 154, 160
healthcare, 37, 38, 41, 171. *See also* biomedical system; medicine, modern
hegemonic masculinity, 133–142. *See also* masculinity
Heidegger, Martin, 210
Heim, Albert, 158
Heller, Dana, 87, 89
heroism, 135, 137, 138, 144n38
heteronormativity, 167
Heuner, Jonathan, 75
Hine, Douglas, 129
Hirsch, Marianne, 84–85, 88, 92
history of humans, 32
Hockfield, Susan, 31, 35
Holocaust: Americanization of, 85; and art, 101–102. *See also* Rachel (survivor artist); and Canadian government, 75, 97n37; emotions surrounding, 101; hiding during, 103, 114; in *Hope: A Tragedy*, 84, 91–93, 93–94; and Islam, 77; and 9/11 attacks, 94; and religion, 69; and storytelling, 65–66, 101; and true witnesses, 89
Holocaust memorial sites: atonement, 74–75; Auschwitz-Birkenau State Museum, 70, 72–78; Babi Yar, 70; as commodified, 72; reconciliation, 75–77; and religion, 70–72; and remembrance, 91; rituals, 76–77; and souvenirs, 92; United States Holocaust Memorial Museum, 69, 73; witnessing, 73–74
home movies, 16
Homo Deus: A Brief History of Tomorrow (Harari), 11–12
honour, 135
Hope: A Tragedy (Auslander), 83–84, 90–95

Hopkinson, Nalo, 128–129. *See also Brown Girl in the Ring* (Hopkinson)
hospitals, 151
House Resolution 2926/Feinberg Compensation Fund, 88
human body, 5, 155–156, 157, 182, 216. *See also* cyborgs; hybridity
Human Genome Project (HGP), 153, 154, 155
humanism, 181, 199
humanities, 11, 12, 208
humanity, 1, 3, 206–207
humanity, defined, 184
humanization, 92–93
Human-Oriented Robotics and Control Lab, 208–209
human-pig chimera, 208
human rights, 52–53, 206–208
hunger, 34, 35–36, 43
hunter-gatherers, 39
hybridity, 168–174. *See also* cyborgs

identity, 154, 156, 159, 167
images of thought, 192–193, 200, 217
immortality, 152, 153, 155, 160. *See also* posthumanism
improvisation, 219
inclusion, 62n29
India, 166–167, 178n5
Indigenous Peoples, 125
individuals/individuality, 210–211, 213
individuating processes, 210–213, 215, 216, 220
industrial food production, 3, 32–36, 45, 174
inequality, 22, 50, 51, 53, 61n16, 62n29. *See also* Buddhism; poverty
infertility. *See The Children of Men* (James)
information, 212, 218
Inglehart, Ronald, 51–52
Internet, 22–23, 25, 193, 217, 219
Iraqi war, 88
Islam, 77

Jacobs, Jane, 129
James, P. D., 128–129. *See also The Children of Men* (James)
jellyfish, 153

Jenkins, Catherine, 151–163, 163n1–164n62
Jernigan, Joseph Paul, 155, 156
Jesus Christ, 73
John Paul II (pope), 75–76, 76. *See also* Catholicism
Judaism: and Christianity, 74–78; and Islam, 77; and Rachel, 108. *See also* Rachel (survivor artist)

Kahn, Jack, 168–169
Keil, Chris, 72
Kennedy, Robert E., 76
Kermode, Frank, 122, 126
Kertzer, David I., 74
Kher, Bharti, 166–168, 167–168, 176
Kim, Eun Mee, 55, 58
Kim, Jong-Hwan, 156, 157
Kinect camera, 218
Kingsnorth, Paul, 129–130
Kittler, Friedrich, 210
Klein, Naomi, 121, 122, 125
Knezic, Sophie, 172
knowledge, 212, 218
Kohr, Leopold, 129
Koller, Daphne, 5
Kosmos (von Humboldt), 24
Kriss, Eric, 41–43
Kruk, Laurie, 65–68, 147–149, 235
Kubota, Shin, 153

language, 192, 195–196, 209, 212
language translation, 181–182
LaTour, Bruno, 184
law of diminishing returns. *See* diminishing returns
Lawrence, D. H., 141
Leder, Drew, 159
Lee Kuan Yew, 53
Lemler, Jerry, 155
Lennon, John, 72
Lepage, Michael, 174–175
Le Trung, 156
Levy, Daniel, 85, 92
Levy, David, 157
Lewis, Bernard, 74
Lewis, C. S., 11, 12, 13
LGBTQ people, 166–167, 170
liability, 43

liberalism, 128
Life After Life (Moody), 158
life expectancy, 147, 152–153, 161
life extension, 152–155, 157–159, 161
life support, 157–158
The Limits to Growth: A Report for the Club of Rome... (report), 19–20
linear movement, 208
Litalien, Manuel, 49–60, 60n1–63n47
"Live Large" (Vanderhaeghe), 140–141
living wires, 196–197
longevity, 38–39, 45
Lovell, Jim, 16–18

Mac computers, 42
Macfarlane, Robert, 71
machines, 3, 193, 198. *See also* artificial intelligence (AI); artificial neural networks (ANNs); computers; cyborgs; technology
Mackenzie, Debora, 174–175
MacLeish, Archibald, 15
madness, 65–66
Malthus, Thomas, 32
Mandel, Emily St. John, 123–126
Man Descending (Vanderhaeghe), 138
maps, 191, 193, 196
marginalized people, 53, 133–135
Marinetti, Filippo Tommaso, 117–119
Marjikian, Mary, 127
The Masculinities Reader (Whitehead and Barrett), 135
masculinity, 119, 133–142, 172
mathematics, 210, 218
matter, 194–198, 199–200, 207–210, 215–216. *See also* Cartesianism
McCann, Gillian, 69–80, 80n1–82n49
McCormick, John, 217–219
McKay, Sally, 166, 171, 176
McLuhan, Marshall, 205, 213
Meadows, Dennis, 19–20
meat consumption, 36, 45
mechanization/automation, 43, 44. *See also* machines
media, 213–214, 216
media studies, 210
mediation, 92, 93, 113
medicine, modern, 36–39, 37, 45. *See also* healthcare; hospitals

Meet Graham (Piccinini), 172, 173, 175
Meier, Diane, 157
memento mori, 126
memorialization, 83–91. *See also* Holocaust memorial sites; 9/11 memorials
memory, 91–92, 94–95, 126, 196. *See also* artificial neural networks (ANNs); forgetting/amnesia; Holocaust memorial sites; memorialization; 9/11 memorials; remembrance; trauma
memory, fractured, 91, 113
mental health issues, 105
Mephistopheles, 39
metafeeling, 198
metamaps, 196. *See also* maps
metastable environment, 210–213, 215
Microsoft, 39–43, 42
Mills, Simon, 215–216
mind, 194, 196, 198–200. *See also* brains; Cartesianism; dualism; *res cogitans*; thought
mobile phones, 22
mobots, 189
Modernism, 32
modernity, 72
modulation, 205, 210, 214–216, 219
Moody, Raymond, 158
moon landing. *See* Apollo 8
Moore, Lisa, 135
mortality. *See* death; immortality
"Mother and Son" (Rachel), 110–112
MRI (magnetic resonance imaging), 5, 155, 171
murder, 190
music, 214, 217

Nash, Adam, 205–222, 222n1–222n27
nationalism, 4, 73, 86–89, 91, 94
National Library of Medicine (NLM), 155, 156
nature, 129–130, 198, 206–207. *See also* climate change
Nature's Little Helper (Piccinini), 173
Nazi Germany. *See* Holocaust; Holocaust memorial sites, 118
near-death experiences (NDEs), 139–140, 158–159
nerve cells, 196, 197

networking feeling, 197–199
networks, 205, 212, 213, 215. *See also* artificial neural networks (ANNs); social media
networks, study of, 198. *See also* artificial neural networks (ANNs)
Neuron Conductor (Nash, McCormick and Bhatti), 217
neurons. *See* artificial neural networks (ANNs)
Neusner, Jacob, 76
"Never Forget" souvenirs, 85
Night (Wiesel), 65–66, 73
nihilism, 127
9/11 attacks, 83, 88–90, 94
9/11 memorials, 83, 85–89
"A 9/11 Widow's Advice..." (Torres), 95
Nitta, Michiko, 174–176
nonanthropocentrism, 210, 215. *See also* anthropocene
None Is Too Many (Abella and Troper), 82n37
The Nonhuman Turn (Lewis), 1
Norris, Pippa, 51–52
novels, 130. *See also* creative writing; *various novels*
nuclear holocaust, 21
numbers, 212–213. *See also* Big Data; digital data; fuzzy data; mathematics
nuns. *See* Buddhism

objectivity, 215
Oculus Rift, 218
ontogenesis, 210–211
ontology: and artificial intelligence, 187; and cyborgs, 159–160, 172; digital, 205–206, 209–210, 217–220; and information, 182; and media, 210; tools, 206
open source, 40, 43
operas, 174–175
operating systems, 39–43, 42
organs, 208
The Origin of Artificial Species: Genetic Robot (Kim), 156
Out of Space (Nash), 217–218

Parabiosis: Neurolibidinal Induction Complex (video), 168–171

Parnia, Sam, 158–159
Parpart, Jane, 49–50
past, views of, 31
The Patient as Person: Explorations in Medical Ethics (Ramsey), 152
patriarchy, 55–56, 133, 141
patriotism. *See* nationalism
patterns, 188–191, 197, 209, 217
Pendleton, Mark, 86
Penny, Laurie, 206–207
perception, 212
performative contradiction, 195
Persson, Ingmar, 208
photography, 16–22, 25
Piccinini, Patricia, 172–174, 175
pilgrimages, 70–72, 77–78, 86
pinches in feedback, 190–191
Planck, Max, 36
Plato, 158
poetry, 126
policy measures, 31, 34–36, 43–45
polio vaccine, 36, 37
Poole, Robert, 19
The Popes Against the Judaism, 74
population, 31, 34
Porter, Roy, 154
post-apocalypse. *See* apocalypse; apocalyptic fiction
posthumanism: and anthropocentrism, 205; and art, 213–220; and art therapy, 4; and Auslander, 94; and Bennett, 206; and consciousness transfer, 159; and continuum approach, 207; defining, 147, 154, 159; as digital, 209–210; emergence, 160; humanity as, 184; and human rights, 208; and Kugel, 93; and McLuhan, 206; and scanners, 171. *See also* cyborgs; immortality
postmemory, 84–85, 87, 90, 94, 95. *See also* death tourism; trauma
posttraumatic stress disorder (PTSD), 102, 104. *See also* trauma
poverty, 22–23, 50–51, 61n16, 62n29
power, 67, 127–128, 216
preindividual, 211, 213
Probst, Christopher J., 74
productivity, 34–39, 39
progress, 31–32, 39
proof of concept, 195

Prosono, Marvin, 78
Protestant, 74–75. *See also* Christianity; religion
Public Documents, 41–43

Quaedackers, Esther, 20
Quakers, 73–74
quality vs. quantity, 152, 161

Rabbis, 106–108
Rachel (survivor artist): about, 103–105; art overview, 101–102; drawing story and style, 105–112; family reception of art, 112–113
racism, 89
Radia, Pavlina, 2–8, 8n1–9n16, 83–96, 96n1–99n102, 235
Ramsey, Paul, 152
rational science, 29
reconciliation, 75–77
Rees, Martin, 3, 181
refugees, 75, 82n37
regenerative medicine, 153
reinforcement learning, 188
religion: and aesthetic thought, 214; Asia-Pacific region concentration, 50–51, 61n8; *Babelswarm* (Nash, Dodds and Clemens), 220; and gender equality, 49–58, 60n4, 62n41; and the Holocaust, 69, 70–71; role in Holocaust, 74–76; and United Nations 2030 Agenda, 51
remembrance. *See* Holocaust memorial sites, 83, 86, 91, 93. *See also* amnesia; memorialization; 9/11 memorials
Remnants of Auschwitz (Agamben), 89
Reproduction (Nash and McCormick), 218–219
reproductive commodification, 167, 176, 178n5
The Republic (Plato), 158
res cogitans, 148, 154, 156, 157, 159. *See also* consciousness; mind
resources, exploitation of, 22
resuscitation, 158
reticulation, 208
Reynolds, Kimberly, 117
rituals, 76–77
"Rituals at Auschwitz-Birkenau" (Kennedy), 76

Rity, 156
robots, 147, 156–157, 189, 217. *See also* cyborgs; drones
Rose, Nikolas, 153–154, 159, 160
Rosling, Hans, 152
Rothberg, Michael, 71
R.U.R. (Rossum's Universal Robots) (Čapek), 157

safe spaces, 102–103, 112
Sagan, Carl, 21
Sakyadhita, 53–54, 56–57
Sama Resource Group for Women and Health, 166–167, 178n5
Sangha Act (1928), 55
satire, 92, 93, 135, 140
Savulescu, Julian, 208
scale of dreams, 129
scanners, 168–171. *See also* Visible Human Project (VHP)
Schnabel, Landon, 51
schools, 43
science: vs. aesthetics, 214; biochemical treatments of mood, 11; changing humanity, 5, 160; critiquing, 29–30; and death, 151–155; and future-oriented people, 11; growing organs, 208; laws in, 30; limits of technology research; (*see* diminishing returns); as religion, 29–30; single vision, 154–155; Visible Human Project (VHP), 155–156. *See also* complex systems science; DNA; technology
SDGs (United Nations Sustainable Development Goals), 49–50, 52, 53, 54–55, 57–58
Second Life (Clemens, Dodds and Nash), 219–220
Sedgwick, Eve Kosofsky, 207
self-assorting feature maps, 191
self-employment, 104–105
Selling 9/11 (Heller), 88
Semmelweis, Ignaz, 36–39
The Sense of an Ending (Kermode), 122
sexual assault, 104
Shaming, Mark, 89–90
Shannon, Claude, 193
Shklovsky, Victor, 92, 93
shock doctrine, 121, 123, 127, 130

The Shock Doctrine: The Rise of Disaster Capitalism (Klein), 121
"Sightseeing in the Mansions of Death" (Keil), 72
Simondon, Gilbert, 205, 210–216
"Singing to the Forest" (Kingsnorth), 130
Sion, Brigitte, 83, 86
Siri, 187, 190
Snyder, Timothy D., 70
social media, 22, 211, 215, 219
Sodaro, Amy, 85, 86, 89
software, 39–43, 42
souvenirs, 85, 92
Sozialistische Jugend, 75
species extinction, 172–174
speculative fiction. *See* dystopia
Spier, Fred, 15–25
Spinoza, Benedict de, 216
spirulina, 174
Star of David, 108, 112
"The State of Our Home Planet" (academic proposal), 24–25
Station Eleven (Mandel), 123–124, 126, 127
stem cells, 208
Stiegler, Bernard, 192, 195
Still Life with Stem Cells (Piccinini), 172–173
stock market crash of 1929, 32–33, 33. *See also* Great Depression
storytelling: altering future, 129, 130; through art, 67, 113; ethics of, 102; motivation for telling, 65–66, 117; paradox of, 101; styles, 135. *See also various books*
Strategies for Engineered Negligible Senescence (SENS), 153
The Structure of Big History (Spier), 21
subjectivity, 1, 211, 213, 215
suicide, 127, 128
superoxide dismutase, 153
surrogacy, 166, 176, 178n5
Surrogate, 173
swarm intelligence, 220
Sznaider, Natan, 85, 92

Tainter, Joseph, 35
Taylor, Affrica, 173, 174
technics and art, 215–216

technology: as always improving, 29–30; capitalism's abuse of, 182; as challenge, 3; fertility, 166–167; as forming humans/humans forming, 192, 193; and imperfections, 129–130; investment in, 31, 34–35. *See also* diminishing returns); and language, 209; artificial neural networks (ANNs); cyborgs; digital; Internet; posthumanism; science
television, of Apollo 8 mission, 16–17
testimony, 86–87, 89–90. *See also* witnessing
Thailand, 55. *See also* Asia-Pacific region
thalamus, 196
thanatology, 152
thematics of focalization, 135
The Theory of the Subject (Badiou), 1
Third Part of the Ethics: Of the Origin and Nature of the Affects (Spinoza), 216
"This Way and Never Another…" (Kher), 166
thought: aesthetic vs. scientific, 214; and drones, 209; images of thought, 192–193, 200, 217; as networking, 194–196, 196–198, 199; thinking with, 7; traditional notions of, 187, 191–192, 194. *See also* artificial neural networks (ANNs)
"Tick Tock" (Vanderhaeghe), 135–138
Time magazine, 15, 19
Tomalin, Emma, 36
Tomorrowland (film), 126–127
tools, 192, 214–216
Torok, Maria, 93
Torres, Alissa, 83, 84, 87–89, 90, 94, 95
tourism, 71, 72, 83. *See also* death tourism; pilgrimages
Tower, John, 153, 155
Tower of Babel, 220
Toyota, 156
transgender people, 170
transindividuality, 211, 213
trauma: and art therapy, 102–103, 106–108, 112–114; closure, 88, 90, 94; fact and fiction, 83–84, 91–92; family, 103–104, 110, 138, 139; and mediation, 92, 93, 113; and nationalism, 84, 86–89, 91; public and private spheres, 83–84, 86, 88, 89. *See also* grief commodification; rape, 104; transgenerational, 113; grief commodification; Holocaust; Holocaust memorial sites; memorialization; 9/11 attacks; 9/11 memorials
traumascapes, 86
Troper, Harold, 82n37
The Trouble with Heroes (Vanderhaeghe), 135
The Truman Show (film), 181
Turing, Alan, 194
Turner, Edith, 72
Turner, Victor, 72
turritopsis dohrnii, 153

Ukraine, 70
Undivided (Piccinini), 173
United Nations 2030 Agenda, 50, 51, 53, 58. *See also* SDGs
United Nations Sustainable Development Goals (SDGs). *See* SDGs (United Nations Sustainable Development Goals)
United States Holocaust Memorial Museum, 69, 73, 85, 86
utopia, 129–130, 160

Vanderhaeghe, Guy, 135, 137, 138, 142–143, 144n38. *See also Daddy Lenin and Other Stories* (Vanderhaeghe)
Vass, Zolton, 102
Vegelin, Courtney, 53, 55, 62n29
Venter, Craig, 153–154, 155, 157
video games, 190
Vietnamese refugees, 82n37
Vint, Sherryl, 154, 159
violence: drone strikes, 190; futurism, 118; gender, 54; and progress, 4; rape, 104; in Vanderhaeghe stories, 135–139, 142. *See also* apocalyptic fiction; Holocaust; 9/11 attacks
virtual environments, 181, 189, 195, 217–220
virtuality, 214
Visible Human Project (VHP), 155–156
Vitale, Christopher, 187–202, 202n1–203n17

von Humboldt, Alexander, 24
Vonnegut, Kurt, 127

Waldby, Catherine, 155
Walford, Roy, 152–153
War on Terrorism, 122
Weichel, Eric, 165–178, 178n1–180n43
Weiss, Aaron, 101–114, 114n1–115n21
Weyler, Rex, 74
wheat, 33–34, 34
Whitehead, Stephen, 135
Wiesel, Elie, 65–66, 73
Wiesenthal, Simon, 101
Williams, Simon, 148, 157
Wilson, Woodrow, 34
Windows computers, 39–43, 42
Winters, Sarah, 117–120, 120, 235

wiring, 208
wisdom, 218
witnessing, 73–74, 83–85, 89–91, 92
Wittgenstein, Ludwig, 212
Witzling, David, 29–47, 47n1
wombats, 173–174
World Values Survey (WVS), 51–52
World War I, 32–34
World War II, 101–102, 103. *See also* Holocaust; Holocaust memorial sites
"Wrath of a Terror Widow" (Torres), 83, 89
Wyndham, John, 123. *See also The Day of the Triffids* (Wyndham)

ZOLL AutoPulse, 158

About the Editors

Laurie Kruk is Professor of English Studies at Nipissing University. She has published *The Voice Is the Story: Conversations with Canadian Writers of Short Fiction* (2003) and *Double-Voicing the Canadian Short Story* (2016). She has also published three collections of poetry: *Theories of the World* (1992), *Loving the Alien* (2006), and *My Mother Did Not Tell Stories* (2012).

Pavlina Radia is Dean of the Faculty of Arts and Science and Professor in English Studies at Nipissing University. She is also Director of the Centre for Interdisciplinary Collaboration in the Arts and Sciences at Nipissing University. She is the author of *Nomadic Modernisms and Diasporic Journeys of Djuna Barnes and Jane Bowles: "Two Very Serious Ladies"* (2016) and *Ecstatic Consumption: The Spectacle of Global Dystopia in Contemporary American Literature* (2016). She is also a co-editor of *Food and Appetites: The Hunger Artist and the Arts with Ann McCulloch* (2012).

Sarah Fiona Winters is Associate Professor in English Studies at Nipissing University. Her research focuses on the representations of evil in postwar children's fantasy and on the relationship of fandom studies to digital pedagogies. She has published articles on C. S. Lewis, Philip Pullman, J. K. Rowling, Suzanne Collins, and Margaret Mahy.

About the Contributors

Christine Bolus-Reichert is Associate Professor of English at the University of Toronto and author of *The Age of Ecl ecticism: Literature and Culture in Britain, 1815-1885* (2009). Her articles have appeared in *Romanticism, Nineteenth Century Prose, Studies in the Novel,* and *ELT: English Literature in Transition, 1880-1920*. In 2014, she published her first short story, "What Happened at the Pond," in *Luna Station Quarterly*; it was subsequently reprinted in *The Best of Luna Station Quarterly: The First Five Years* (2015). Her first scholarly work on science fiction, "Sky Sailing: Steampunk's Reenchantment of Flight," was published in *Children's Literature and Imaginative Geography* in 2018.

Catherine Jenkins completed her PhD in the joint graduate program for Communication and Culture at Ryerson-York Universities in Toronto, Canada, with the dissertation *Older Patient-Physician Communication: An Examination of the Tensions of the Patient-Centred Model within a Biotechnological Context*. This research drew on her experience teaching communication skills to healthcare students and professionals at the University of Toronto. In addition to her literary career, she has published papers in peer-reviewed journals and academic collections, including *Medicine and What it Means to be Human* (Routledge, 2018); *postmedieval: Medievalism and the Medical Humanities* (summer 2017); *Finding McLuhan* (University of Regina Press, 2015); and *The Power of Death* (Berghahn Books, 2014). Her current research includes the medicalization of comic book superheroes. Catherine holds an MA in Cultural Studies from Trent University in Peterborough, Canada, and she teaches Professional Communication at Ryerson University.

Laurie Kruk is Professor of English Studies at Nipissing University. She has published *The Voice is the Story: Conversations with Canadian Writers of Short Fiction* (2003) and *Double-Voicing the Canadian Short Story* (2016). She has also published three collections of poetry: *Theories of the World* (1992), *Loving the Alien* (2006), and *My Mother Did Not Tell Stories* (2012).

Manuel Litalien is Associate Professor at Nipissing University, Department of Social Welfare and Social Development. He is a co-investigator for PhiLab (2018), a funded research group focusing on Philanthropy (https://philab.uqam.ca). He has published a monograph, *La philanthropie religieuse en tant que nouveau capital démocratique* (Presses de l'Université Laval), and book chapters in *Wild Geese: Buddhism in Canada* (McGill-Queen's); *Secular States and Religious Diversity* (UBC Press); *Ethnic Claims and Moral Economies* (UBC Press). He has also published in the *Journal of Buddhist Ethics* (2018). His areas of interest include Southeast Asia, development, welfare regimes, philanthropy, governance, social policy, religion, ethnicity, identity politics, diasporic studies, nationalism, and violence. He also currently holds an adjunct position at Mahidol University in Thailand.

Gillian McCann, is Associate Professor in the Religions and Cultures Department at Nipissing University, North Bay, Ontario. Her book *Vanguard of the New Age. The Toronto Theosophical Society 1891-1945* was published in 2012 and *The Sacred in Exile: What It Really Means to Lose Our Religion,* co-written with Gitte Bechsgaard, was published in 2017.

Adam Nash is widely recognized as one of the most innovative artists working in virtual environments, RealTime 3D and mixed-reality technology. Based in Melbourne, Australia, he is a digital virtual artist, composer, programmer, performer, and writer. His work has been presented in galleries, festivals and online in Australia, Europe, Asia, and The Americas

He is Director of the Playable Media Lab in the Centre for Game Design Research, and Program Manager of the Bachelor of Design (Digital Media), both in the School of Media and Communication at RMIT University, Melbourne, Australia. His academic writing explores the ontology and the aesthetics of the digital, and the connection between the digital and philosophical notions of the virtual. As a PhD supervisor, he specializes in practice-based research of playable digital art.

Pavlina Radia is Dean of the Faculty of Arts and Science and Professor of English Studies at Nipissing University. She is also Director of the Centre for Interdisciplinary Collaboration in the Arts and Sciences at Nipissing University. She is the author of *Nomadic Modernisms and Diasporic Journeys of*

Djuna Barnes and Jane Bowles: "Two Very Serious Ladies" (2016) and *Ecstatic Consumption: The Spectacle of Global Dystopia in Contemporary American Literature* (2016). She is also a co-editor of *Food and Appetites: The Hunger Artist and the Arts with Ann McCulloch* (2012).

Fred Spier is Senior Lecturer, Big History Emeritus at the University of Amsterdam. He studied biochemistry at the University of Leyden (1970-1978), and cultural anthropology at the Free University Amsterdam (1981-1987). His Ph.D. cum laude at the University of Amsterdam dealt with the history of religion, politics and ecology in Peru, where he did extensive fieldwork in the Andean village of Zurite between 1985 and 1996. As of 1993, he became the driving force of big history at the University of Amsterdam. He is now writing a book about his fresh theory of the history of the biosphere, of life, and of humanity.

Christopher Vitale is Associate Professor of Media Studies at Pratt Institute, in Brooklyn, NY, where helped found the graduate program in Media Studies, coordinates the Cinema Studies minor, and teaches courses on artificial intelligence, networks, philosophy, media theory, film, and film theory. He is the author of *Networkologies: A Philosophy of Networks for a Hyperconnected Age – A Manifesto* (Zer0 Books, 2014), the forthcoming *Post-Selfing: A Networked Philosophy of the Post-Self* (Zer0 Books, 2020) and *Networks and Temporality: A Relational Philosophy of Time from Clocks to Quantum* (Punctum Books, 2020), as well as several other works in progress. More information, as well as additional writing on a variety of topics, can found at his website, https://networkologies.wordpress.com.

Eric Weichel received his PhD in Art History from Queen's University in 2013. His research areas include the role of palace women in facilitating visual and literary cross-cultural exchanges in the courtly sphere: broader interests include sexuality and nationhood in the academic tradition, the interconnectivity of gardens and grieving in poetry and art, and the commemorative expression of performative ephemera—such as dance, ritual, and festival—in visual art.

Aaron A. Weiss worked in the media industry since the age of 13. His 2009 documentary, "Our School" addressed the issue of equity in education policy, focusing on Canada's first publicly funded Africentric school. He has been actively involved in community engagement, bringing arts-based programming and sports activities to schools and NGOs in underserved communities. Aaron completed a Bachelor of Arts in Radio and Television from Ryerson University in 2001, an MA in Cinema & Media Studies at York University in 2014, and he is currently completing his PhD in Humanities at

York University. His dissertation research focuses on comics as propaganda during wartime. Other areas of research are art therapy; epigenetic inheritance and trauma; and comics as a pedagogical tool for learning and social justice discourse. He currently teaches Introduction to Sociology, Sociology of the Marriage and Family, and Sociology of Mass Media at Tyndale University College in Toronto.

Sarah Fiona Winters is Associate Professor in English Studies at Nipissing University. Her research focuses on the representations of evil in children's fantasy and on the relationship of fandom studies to digital pedagogies. She has published articles on C. S. Lewis, Philip Pullman, J. K. Rowling, Suzanne Collins, and Margaret Mahy.

David Witzling is an inter-disciplinarian moving between the worlds of filmmaking, teaching, poetry, scholarship, independent publishing, permaculture, and coding. His current interests include intellectual property and media appropriation, open source software, diminishing returns on societal investments in complexity, and the deep history of western science. His motion pictures have screened internationally at venues such as the Festival de Cannes, Montreal Underground Film Festival, Winnipeg Underground Film Festival, Oakland Underground FilmFestival, and the Wisconsin Film Festival. He has also been published in journals like *Science* and *The Journal of Short Film*.

www.ingramcontent.com/pod-product-compliance
Lightning Source LLC
Chambersburg PA
CBHW032038300426
44117CB00009B/1106